Integrated Marketing Communications in Football

This book takes an important step forward in showing how Integrated Marketing Communications (IMC) have been applied within the English Premier League (EPL) – arguably the most commercialised and watched sport league in the world – and how it can and should be utilised in the context of other sports properties.

Drawing on cutting-edge empirical research, the book offers a detailed view into the marketing communications practices of EPL clubs (such as brand management and communications alignment), the football clubs' practitioners' perspectives of IMC and the integration processes taking place within the clubs. It examines the key marketing communications practices that strategic IMC entails, including marketing strategies and goals, cross-functional communication, external communication management and brand management, and helps researchers and practitioners to understand how IMC can have the maximum positive impact on the brand of an organisation, by managing their content, channels, stakeholders and results.

This book is fascinating reading for any researcher, advanced student or practitioner with an interest in sport management, the business of football, sport marketing or innovative approaches to marketing and business communications in other commercial spheres.

Argyro Elisavet Manoli is an Associate Professor (Senior Lecturer) of Sport Marketing and Communications at Loughborough University, UK, following a career in the professional sport industry. Her research focuses on two main strands: marketing communications management and integrity in sport. Dr Manoli was involved in the European Commission Expert Group for Sport Integrity, while being invited to author a mapping report for the European Union. Her research on the English Premier League was awarded the 2018 Highly Commended Award by Emerald Publishing. Dr Manoli is also the Scientific Chair of Sport Media and Communications in the European Association of Sport Management, while sitting on a number of Editorial Boards of prestigious journals.

Critical Research in Football
Series Editors:
Pete Millward, Liverpool John Moores University, UK
Jamie Cleland, University of Southern Australia
Dan Parnell, University of Liverpool, UK
Stacey Pope, Durham University, UK
Paul Widdop, Manchester Metropolitan University, UK

The *Critical Research in Football* book series was launched in 2017 to showcase the inter- and multi-disciplinary breadth of debate relating to 'football'. The series defines 'football' as broader than association football, with research on rugby, Gaelic and gridiron codes also featured. Including monographs, edited collections, short books and textbooks, books in the series are written and/or edited by leading experts in the field whilst consciously also affording space to emerging voices in the area, and are designed to appeal to students, postgraduate students and scholars who are interested in the range of disciplines in which critical research in football connects. The series is published in association with the *Football Collective*, @FB_Collective.

Available in this series:

Football, Politics and Identity
James Carr, Daniel Parnell, Paul Widdop, Martin J. Power and Stephen R. Millar

Football, Family, Gender and Identity
The Football Self
Hanya Pielichaty

Sport Mega-Events, Security and COVID-19
Securing the Football World
Jan Andre Lee Ludvigsen

Integrated Marketing Communications in Football
Argyro Elisavet Manoli

For more information about this series, please visit: https://www.routledge.com/Critical-Research-in-Football/book-series/CFSFC

Integrated Marketing Communications in Football

Argyro Elisavet Manoli

LONDON AND NEW YORK

First published 2022
by Routledge
4 Park Square, Milton Park, Abingdon, Oxon OX14 4RN

and by Routledge
605 Third Avenue, New York, NY 10158

Routledge is an imprint of the Taylor & Francis Group, an informa business

© 2022 Argyro Elisavet Manoli

The right of Argyro Elisavet Manoli to be identified as author of this work has been asserted in accordance with sections 77 and 78 of the Copyright, Designs and Patents Act 1988.

All rights reserved. No part of this book may be reprinted or reproduced or utilised in any form or by any electronic, mechanical, or other means, now known or hereafter invented, including photocopying and recording, or in any information storage or retrieval system, without permission in writing from the publishers.

Trademark notice: Product or corporate names may be trademarks or registered trademarks, and are used only for identification and explanation without intent to infringe.

British Library Cataloguing-in-Publication Data
A catalogue record for this book is available from the British Library

Library of Congress Cataloging-in-Publication Data
A catalog record has been requested for this book

ISBN: 978-0-367-69057-1 (hbk)
ISBN: 978-0-367-69064-9 (pbk)
ISBN: 978-1-003-14023-8 (ebk)

DOI: 10.4324/9781003140238

Typeset in Goudy
by codeMantra

Contents

1	Introduction	1
2	Integrated Marketing Communications	17
3	Integrated Marketing Communications Perceptions and Implementation	36
4	Marketing Strategy, Marketing Goals and Internal Communication	61
5	Communications Alignment and Brand Management	78
6	Football Practitioners' Perceptions of Integrated Marketing Communications	95
7	Integration Scenarios	113
8	Conclusion	129
	Index	145

Chapter 1

Introduction

Introduction

This chapter provides an overview of the research, while situating the topic within the pertinent literature, presenting the rationale for this book and relating it to the original contributions to knowledge that are addressed by the research. Following this section, the English Premier League (hereafter EPL), the sector examined in this book is presented, which can facilitate the appreciation of the overall research.

Research Aim

The purpose of this book is to gain understanding of Integrated Marketing Communications' (hereafter IMC) appreciation and implementation in EPL clubs. Since this book intends to deepen our understanding of IMC by gaining a more holistic view of IMC's appreciation and implementation, its aim is two-fold; first, to investigate practitioners' perceptions of IMC, and second, to examine whether and to what extent IMC is implemented in the football clubs studied. Through this examination, a new theoretical framework can be developed that can illustrate IMC's appreciation and application in the EPL. This book will investigate IMC's appreciation and implementation through a qualitative research design which allows for rich information to be collected, enabling the author to gain deep insight to both the practices encountered and the views expressed. The framework and rationale for this book will be presented in the following sections in more detail.

Framework

Since this book aims at examining the appreciation and implementation of IMC in a spectrum of organisations within a particular industry, a case study approach is selected. In more detail, the EPL, the sector selected, comprises of multiple case studies that represent the companies – football clubs that operate within it. In this book the focus is drawn on the EPL, which consists of the multiple case studies / football clubs that participated in the league in any of the following five consecutive seasons: 2010/2011, 2011/2012, 2012/2013, 2013/2014 and 2014/2015.

DOI: 10.4324/9781003140238-1

This method chosen aligns with the author's critical realist perspective and the epistemological approach selected (retroduction), while allowing for rich and valuable information to be acquired, bearing in mind the complexity involved in examining phenomena related with organisations and relationships within them (Creswell, 2013). Taking into consideration the author's effort to conduct engaged scholarship (Van de Ven, 2007) and study practitioners' perceptions and implementation of theory, this collective case study approach that allows for multiple case studies of EPL clubs to be examined would permit for a more holistic view of IMC's appreciation and implementation to be acquired.

Based on the complexity of the industry and on the disparities that exist both globally and within each country on aspects such as structure, finance and customer base and reach (Szymanski & Smith, 1997; Noll, 2002; McNamara et al., 2013), the focus of the research was limited to the clubs in the top level of English professional football, the EPL. Additionally, due to the promotion–relegation phenomenon, and in order for this research to be accurate in representing the industry sector, the EPL clubs of the following five consecutive seasons (2010/2011, 2011/2012, 2012/2013, 2013/2014 and 2014/2015) were chosen, 30 in total. Based on the fact that the clubs included in this research represent 66.66% of the total number of clubs that have participated in the league since it was created in 1992, while the majority of them have participated in the EPL for the greater part of its existence, it could be argued that increasing the number of seasons, and therefore increasing the number of clubs, would not have affected the findings of the research significantly (Belk, 2007).

In more detail, the clubs included in this research are: Arsenal, Aston Villa, Birmingham City, Blackburn Rovers, Blackpool, Bolton Wanderers, Burnley, Cardiff City, Chelsea, Crystal Palace, Everton, Fulham, Hull City, Leicester City, Liverpool, Manchester City, Manchester United, Newcastle United, Norwich, Queens Park Rangers, Reading, Southampton, Stoke City, Sunderland, Swansea, Tottenham Hotspur, West Bromwich Albion, West Ham United, Wigan Athletic and Wolverhampton Wanderers.

In more detail, in-depth, semi-structured interviews were conducted with the key individuals responsible for marketing and marketing communications activities in the 30 football clubs comprising the census of this research. The interviews took place between August 2014 and March 2015 and were conducted in-person in either the office or the training ground of each club, while following a coherent interview protocol.

Rationale for This Book

Jobber and Ellis-Chadwick (2012) argue that marketing is led by three forces: customer orientation, goals orientation and integrated efforts. These forces have in fact changed the traditionally perceived one-way communication process of an organisation to a two-way dialogue between an organisation and its stakeholders (Kotler, 2000) where value is co-created (De Chernatony, 2001), which has, in turn, changed the way in which marketing communications are defined. According to Shimp (2007, p. 651),

> *marketing communications is the collection of all elements in an organisation's marketing mix that facilitates exchanges by establishing shared meaning with the organisation's customers or clients.*

The significant changes in the marketplace mentioned above, paired with the shifting views in the way in which marketing is perceived and applied, made Webster (2002, p. 23) argue that '*it's patently clear that marketing management needs a new paradigm*'. According to Kitchen and Schultz (1999, p. 21) the answer to this call was found in IMC, as the following quote demonstrates:

> *IMC is undoubtedly the major communications development of the last decade of the 20th century*' which can lead to '*a key competitive advantage associated with marketing.*

A number of definitions have been presented for IMC as it will be discussed in the following chapter, in an attempt to shed light on what it captures and the role it can play within modern corporations. These definitions also demonstrate the different perceptions of IMC, what it is and how it fits within marketing. From the early definitions that present IMC as a concept of alignment of communication messages in order for the advertising function to be facilitated (Keegan et al., 1992; Schultz, 1992, 1993a, 1993b), to the views that argue that IMC derives from relationship marketing (Schultz & Schultz, 1998, 2004; Duncan, 2002) or that it is synonymous with brand management (Kliatchko, 2005, 2008), IMC and the way in which it is located within marketing has been discussed extensively over the last 25 years. Porcu et al. (2012, p. 326) propose the latest definition of IMC, which presents it as:

> *The interactive and systemic process of cross-functional planning and optimization of messages to stakeholders with the aim of communicating with coherence and transparency to achieve synergies and encourage profitable relationships in the short, medium and long-term.*

As it is argued through their work and the recent work of academics focusing on IMC such as Kliatchko (2008), Schultz and Patti (2009), Moriarty and Schultz (2012), Kliatchko and Schultz (2014), Gambetti and Schultz (2015) and Vernuccio and Ceccotti (2015), IMC is not a mere marketing communications concept or tool, but a strategic cross-functional process that exceeds the '*boundaries*' of marketing and communications and '*runs throughout an organisation*', while having:

> *the potential to lead to global restructuring of the marketing and communication roles, through the elimination of boundaries between the main areas of marketing communication and between the business units.*
>
> Porcu et al. (2012, p. 325)

Academics such as Baker and Hart (2008), Thorson and Moore (2013) and Armstrong et al. (2014) see IMC as an amalgam of relationship marketing, brand management and communications systems, with elements of strategy and planning. According to Thorson and Moore (2013) and Keller (2016), IMC is a strategic planning process that allows for marketing and communications programmes to have the maximum effects possible on the brand of an organisation, by managing their content, channels, stakeholders and results. In more detail, IMC includes the management of the exchange of meaningful messages (content), through the most relevant and preferred contact points of the stakeholders (channels), in order for a purposeful dialogue and potential relationship with the most profitable and relevant target aggregates (stakeholders) to be achieved, while analysing the return of investment (results) of the appropriate resources allocated on marketing communications (Schultz & Schultz, 1998; Duncan, 2002; Kliatchko, 2005, 2008; Kitchen, 2016).

Taking all the above into consideration, the author agrees with what is suggested through Kitchen's (2016) and Schultz et al.'s (2014, p. 455) work that *'IMC can be recast as the base for rethinking and replacing traditional marketing theory'*, while emphasising elements of strategic planning, holistic approaches, message synergy and brand and relationship management. As a result, the significance of studying, understanding and implementing IMC can be underlined. IMC's importance and benefits have been researched and supported extensively by academics such as Ewing et al. (2001), Naik and Raman (2003), du Plessis (2005), Tsai (2005), Reinold and Tropp (2012) and Luxton et al. (2015). These benefits include a stronger behavioural and consumer impact, better control over marketing and communications budget, higher campaign effectiveness, and better market and financial performance of a brand.

A question can then be raised regarding the recent decline in academic publications on the topic and the overall scarcity of sources examining practitioners' appreciation and implementation of IMC (Manoli & Davies, 2014). This scarcity influenced the decision of the author to examine practitioners' perceptions and implementation of the theory, as it will be discussed below, and informed her choice to focus on the EPL, an industry sector that has yet to be fully explored (Boyle & Haynes, 2014; Chadwick, 2015) and could benefit greatly from IMC's application.

It could be argued that the lack of research on IMC's appreciation and application is in line with a broader lack of efforts to link theory with practice and address this knowledge translation and transfer problem, by practising what Van de Ven (2007, p. 17) calls *'engaged scholarship'*. As it is argued in his work:

> *Social science today suffers from elaborating theories that are often based on insufficient grounding in concrete particulars. It also suffers from a lack of relevance as perceived by the intended audiences or users of the research. As a consequence, theories tend to be grounded in myths and superstitions.*

As Van de Ven (2007) suggests, in order for a theory to be relevant and grounded on facts, its appreciation and implementation needs to be studied. Engaged scholarship, or the study of theory and practice, is *a form of research for obtaining the perspectives and advice of key stakeholders, to understand a complex social problem…that produces knowledge that is more penetrating and insightful.*

(Van de Ven, 2007, p. 109)

By conducting engaged scholarship, the current knowledge translation and transfer problem often documented in management studies (King & Learmonth, 2014; Tucker & Lowe, 2014) can be addressed, the relevance of research for practice can be enhanced and the research knowledge in a discipline can be advanced (Van de Ven & Johnson, 2006; Lukka, 2014). In other words, the knowledge produced within academia can be translated into knowledge understood by practitioners, which can then be transferred into practice. As it has been argued repeatedly, studies on areas such as marketing and management cannot exist in isolation, since what is in fact being studied in them is the empirically based knowledge about human-made objects and phenomena, which reflect the inherent influence of history and context, and function as dynamic and adaptive systems (Rynes et al., 2001, 2007; Hodgkinson & Rousseau, 2009). As a result, distancing a management study from the practical management itself would not only harm the future of management practices, but it would also decrease the relevance of the research, making its findings outdated and potentially invalid (Gelade, 2006; Latham, 2007). On the contrary, research informed by practice and well-grounded in organisational contexts can provide more informed theory building, where competing theories and diverse underlying mechanisms can be investigated, and decisions made about explanatory power as well as practical effects are brought into light (Pearce, 2006; Rousseau et al., 2008). This effort to bridge the gap between theory and practice can assist scholars to better appreciate the conditions under which theory can be implemented, while adding depth to their existing understanding of phenomena within organisations, and overall scientific constructs and theory. Interestingly, when engaged scholarship or research informed by practice has been conducted, it has been widely celebrated by academia[1] (e.g. Lawler, 1994; Locke & Latham, 2002; Mohrman & Lawler, 2011).

In order for this to be achieved, and for the gulf between theory and practice to be bridged, practitioners, their understanding and practices have to become the focal point of research. As Pettigrew (2001) argued,

the dichotomy of theory and practice cannot be answered with the mere dissemination of information, since dissemination is too late if the wrong questions have been asked.

What Pettigrew (2001) suggests through his analysis of this 'dichotomy', and what Van de Ven and Johnson (2006) and Van de Ven (2007) have argued, is that any research on theory implementation would inevitably lead to a study more or less comparing theory with practice, or academics versus practitioners. Additionally, in his work (Pettigrew, 2001), it is supported that management research has yet to succeed in being truly engaged with users and other stakeholders, while suggesting that more studies should be conducted on the perception and implementation of management research, in order for the existent knowledge transfer problem to be overcome. In other words, it could be argued that in order for knowledge on IMC to progress, there is a need to study practitioners' perception and implementation of IMC, which might, in turn, include or lead to examining theory versus practice.

Perception

According to Barnes (2015, p. 89) perception can be defined as '*a way of regarding or understanding or interpreting something, or an intuitive understanding and insight*' and is a multidimensional concept that has received extensive academic interest. Studies from numerous fields, such as neuroscience, psychology and sociology, have questioned the origins of perceptions and its aspects (George, 1992; Andereck et al., 2011). Hochberg (1956) argues that "*"perception" frequently carries with it the various connotations of "awareness", of a "discrimination" between stimuli and of a conviction of the "real" environmental presence of the perceived object / person /situation etc*', and as a result, it is a complex and ill-defined concept overall. According to Brunswik[2] (1948) and Bruner et al. (1951) perceptions are determined by each individual, their age, sex, personality, experiences, memories, knowledge and education. The socio-cultural influences and the environment in which they are in, as well as the characteristics of the era in which they were raised, are also considered key aspects of how perceptions are formed. As a result, an individual's perception is a subjective view, which defines the way in which they respond and behave towards a situation, idea, object or person. George (1992) separates the origins of perception in management studies into extrinsic and intrinsic, while arguing that the way in which management theory is perceived is directly linked with the way in which it is applied. According to McGregor (1960), Burns (1978) and Dean and Bowen (1994), theory appreciation can affect the overall quality of a number of key aspects within the organisation such as quality management, leadership, strategic planning, human resource management, interpersonal relations and interdepartmental communication, and as a result, it could also affect the future of an organisation and its potential success. Interestingly, a number of these key aspects affected by theory appreciation, such as strategic planning, interpersonal relations and interdepartmental communication, are closely linked with the implementation of IMC. Perception is believed to be a key issue in management studies, since, as Henry and Walker (1991) and Henry (1999, 2001) argue, the importance of soft data in managerial thought is often overlooked, while the critical role of unconscious learning, tacit knowledge and intuitive judgement in business decisions is also undermined. What is underlined through Henry's (2001, p. 3) study is that individuals' perceptions within an organisation dictate their behaviour and choices, and as a result influence the overall organisation's course of actions, which might in fact '*counter the traditional management focus on rationalism, predictability, planning and control*'. In other words, it is argued that theory perception in management can shape theory implementation and influence not only an individual's actions but also the overall course of actions of an organisation.

Implementation

Implementation is according to Hill (2014, p. 213) *'the translation of theory into action'*. This simple and short definition is used to encapsulate a long, challenging and complex process that involves a number of internal and external factors that lead to implementing theory in practice. Psychology, sociology, organisational and operational studies have discussed implementation from various viewpoints, with particular areas such as change management, governance and policy, developing extensive literature on the topic (Jauch & Glueck, 1988; Davis et al., 1997; Mischen & Jackson, 2008). In management research, implementation is believed to be based upon individuals' psychological attributes and organisations' situational characteristics. According to Steers and Porter (1991), Steers and Black (1994) and Davis et al. (1997), the former include the extrinsic and intrinsic motivation of individuals, their identification with their role and with the overall organisation's mission, vision and objectives, the social comparison made between individuals, and the use of power as a user or a receiver. The latter comprises the management philosophy of an organisation, its overall culture and cultural differences within it and its risk orientation, time frame and overall objectives. As it is argued by Hogwood and Gunn (cited in Hill, 2014, p. 217), an individual's perception and understanding of a theory is directly and strongly linked with the way and the extent to which this theory can be implemented, since *'the circumstances external to the implementing agency do not impose crippling constraints'*. The barriers and challenges that originate from the environment and are outside the control of the individuals can make the process of implementation more demanding and time and resource consuming; however, translating theory into practice originates and is led by the individual and their knowledge, appreciation and will (May et al., 2009). As a result, implementation is guided by subjective views, which lack a strict and well-defined approach. According to Hogwood and Gunn (cited in Hill, 2014, p. 217), since no universal prescriptive model of implementation exists, any attempts to translate theory into practice will be guided by subjectivity and could involve potential flaws, making *'perfect implementation unattainable'*. What Mischen and Jackson (2008, p. 314) argue in their work is that implementation can be viewed as the process of *'connecting the dots in knowledge management'*, where theory perception can lead to theory implementation. It is underlined, however, that implementation uncertainty or the extent to which management theory will be successfully implemented (Rosenberg & Brault, 1993) is a factor that has to be taken into consideration when examining theory implementation in management. According to Rosenberg and Brault (1993) and Butterworth and Punt (1999) implementation uncertainty has been largely ignored by management procedures and their evaluation processes that tend to overlook the possibility of a concept not being fully and successfully implemented. On the contrary, traditional management processes expect for perfect implementation to materialise, despite the above-mentioned argument that full and successful implementation is in fact unachievable (Hill, 2014). This rather myopic view of the potential and practicalities of theory implementation could be linked with the overall lack of understanding of how theory is perceived and implemented, which can once again lead to the argument that management studies would benefit greatly from additional engaged scholarship studies (Pettigrew, 2001).

Taking the above into consideration, in order for practitioners' implementation of IMC to be studied, their perceptions of IMC have also to be examined. Analysing both aspects could then deepen the existing understanding of IMC, while making the knowledge produced more relevant, as engaged scholarship suggests.

IMC has been a platform for research for almost three decades (Kitchen & Tourky, 2015), with numerous academics expressing their appreciation of IMC and its potential, as the above quotes from Kitchen and Schultz (1999) and Porcu et al. (2012) have demonstrated. However, IMC's implementation that could examine this potential in practice is still unclear and rarely reported. In fact, IMC's implementation can be considered under-researched, with the majority of the available literature so far focusing on the theoretical and definitional aspects of the term (Kliatchko, 2005, 2008; Kitchen, 2016). Even though the term '*integration*' was first introduced by Schultz in 1992 (p. 100) to refer to the practice of implementing IMC, it could be argued that today, more than two decades later, it still remains a rather under explored area.

In the few studies that research IMC's implementation, practitioners' perceptions are studied before the practice of IMC is examined (Dmitrijeva & Batraga, 2012; Kliatchko & Schultz, 2014; Schultz et al., 2016). The focus of these studies, however, appears to be misplaced on agencies, rather than client organisations, despite the widely accepted argument that clients drive integration (Caywood & Ewing, 1991; Eagle et al., 2007). The few studies that examine client marketers are centred around a narrow sample of successful and large organisations operating in a number of sectors, while neglecting less successful and smaller companies (Ewing et al., 2000; Han et al., 2004; Vantamay, 2011). This rather myopic and often methodologically questionable choice of IMC academics so far has created a significant research gap in the IMC and the overall marketing literature. This lack of research on IMC's implementation has led to a shortage of information regarding practitioners' knowledge and appreciation of IMC and their respective marketing communications practices.

Taking all the above into consideration and in an effort to address the literature gaps discussed above and deepen the understanding of IMC, the focus of this book was drawn on practitioners' perceptions and implementation of IMC. Since a holistic view of IMC's appreciation and application was intended, the focus was drawn on a wider spectrum of client organisations operating within the selected sector, the EPL. In other words, in this research, the EPL is the platform – sector that includes the instrumental case studies[3] on which IMC's implementation is examined, in order for a detailed view to be offered on practitioners' perceptions and whether and to what extent IMC is applied. The reasons behind the selection of EPL as the focus of this research will be presented below.

Being a rapidly developing industry that has been experiencing significant growth even through troubling financial times (Szymanski & Smith, 1997; Szymanski, 2010), the EPL is currently considered one of the fastest growing industry sectors in the UK, with a remarkable growth rate difference when compared to any other UK sports leagues (e.g. Football League, Rugby League, – Deloitte, 2016). The EPL is currently considered the most commercially advanced football league in Europe, collecting almost double the revenue of the second (in 2014/2015, EPL's revenue was 4,400 million € compared to the Italian's Serie A revenue of 2,392 million €), and being often referred to as the *'world's highest earning sports league'* (Deloitte, 2016, pp. 10, 14).

Aside from the financial success of the league, the EPL is considered to be one of the most popular sports leagues globally, attracting the interest of more than 60% of the global population (more than any other sports league – Sportfive, 2012). According to the same study, the EPL is also believed to be the *'most-watched'* sport league in the world. The Premier League (2016) reports that its matches are broadcasted in 212 territories around the world, reaching 643 million homes and achieving a TV audience of 4.7 billion people for its games. This global appeal of the league is also enhanced by the multinational nature of clubs' playing squads, managers, owners, sponsors and investors. Deloitte (2016) and UEFA (2015) argue that the EPL is the most competitively balanced sports league, which combined with the recently introduced financial fair play regulations could also make it the most financially balanced league in Europe. Fetchko et al. (2013) underline that, compared with other North American and Asian sports leagues, the EPL has minimum state intervention and limited dependence to the governing bodies of the sport, which allows the league to function like an independent industry sector.

In terms of its marketing and communications functions, academics such as McCarthy et al. (2014), Manoli (2016, 2020), Manoli and Kenyon (2018) and Manoli and Hodgkinson (2017, 2019, 2021) suggest that EPL clubs have invested extra effort, time and resources on developing them over time, possibly due to the need created by an increasing 'hunger' for news on behalf of the fans, the media and other stakeholders. This emphasis placed on marketing and communications can be seen through the early and widespread adoption of new and social media by football clubs, which has even led academics to argue that brand management and *'fandom shaping'* is currently conducted predominantly through them (Nash, 2000; McCarthy et al., 2014). Boyle and Haynes (2014, p. 135) suggest that despite this emphasis on marketing and communications, the EPL's brand *'is not managed as successfully as it could, when compared to other established sports markets'*, and as a result it is suggested that additional attention should be drawn on understanding the targeted audience and aiming for a more coherent brand management overall. Relationship marketing and management are also no strangers to EPL clubs, with researchers arguing that both areas have progressed significantly over the past years, while leaving nevertheless ample room for improvement (Bee & Kahle, 2006; Buhler & Nufer, 2012; Manoli, 2018). In fact, it is suggested that the use of social media can prove particularly useful in this relationship building in football (Abeza et al., 2013), which further underlines the need for additional focus on the topic.

A supplementary factor that is added when discussing marketing communications in football or sports in general is the importance sponsorship can have not only in terms of financial benefits but also regarding a sports organisation's brand. Even though academics such as Chadwick (2004) suggest that sponsorship can be a powerful tool for sports marketing communications, it is argued that the potential of sponsorship as a long-term strategic marketing communications instrument in the EPL has yet to be reached (Chadwick & Thwaites, 2005). As a result, IMC that calls for strategic planning of coherent marketing communications (Porcu et al., 2012) could have considerable effects on EPL's future development on the topic.

All the above-mentioned factors (financial and commercial success, marketing communications emphasis and importance) were considered in order for the EPL to be selected as a platform on which this IMC's appreciation and implementation study would take place. Additionally, even though increasing scholarly interest has been attracted to football, it could still be considered a rather under-researched territory (Chadwick, 2015; Manoli & Hodgkinson, 2017), with a number of areas, such as marketing communications practices, still in need for further study. This suggests that any research conducted on the topic can have a contribution to the future of the industry, regarding both the potential academic interest on the area and the managerial practices employed.

Finally, due to the author's affiliation with the industry, valuable and unique insights could be obtained, which could have been difficult to be acquired otherwise. As Roderick (2006) argues in his work, gaining access and acquiring information from all 30 EPL clubs would not have been possible, had the author not been trusted and considered an 'insider' to the industry. Indeed, the author's choice to use the EPL as a platform for this IMC study was also directed by her personal and academic interest, as well as by her professional career so far.

Conclusion

Having presented the guiding research question of this study, its aims and rationale, as well as details on the EPL that represents the case study, comprising of multiple case studies that this research will focus upon in this introductory chapter, the following chapters will focus on the theoretical appreciation of IMC before progressing to the discussion of its implementation and appreciation in EPL clubs.

Notes

1 Both Ed Lawler and Gary Latham have been awarded the Academy of Management Scholar Practitioner Award in 2006 and 2007 respectively, for their work on bridging the gap between academia and practice (Hodgkinson & Rousseau, 2009).

2 The author will follow Brunswik's (1948) suggestion and treat the terms *appreciation* and *perception* as synonymous, while using them interchangeably in this study.
3 The EPL football clubs in this research are what Stake (2005, p. 445) calls instrumental case studies, where '*a particular case or cases are examined mainly to provide insight into an issue… The case is of secondary interest, it plays a supportive role, and it facilitates our understanding of something else*'.

References

Abeza, G., O'Reilly, N. & Reid, I. (2013) 'Relationship marketing and social media in sport', *International Journal of Sport Communication*, 6 (2) 120–142.

Andereck, K., Gayan, L. & Nyaupane, P. (2011) 'Exploring the nature of tourism and quality of life perceptions among residents', *Journal of Travel Research*, 50 (3) 248–260.

Armstrong, G., Adam, S., Denize, S. & Kotler, P. (2014) *Principles of marketing*, Sydney: Pearson.

Baker, M. & Hart, S. (2008) *The marketing book*, London: Routledge.

Barnes, J. (2015) 'Perception in tourism & hospitality: A meta analysis', *AU-GSB*, 8 (2) 89–107.

Bee, C. C. & Kahle, L. R. (2006) 'Relationship marketing in sports: A functional approach', *Sport Marketing Quarterly*, 15 (2) 101–119.

Belk, R. W. (2007) *Handbook of qualitative research methods in marketing*, New York: Edward Elgar Publishing.

Boyle, R. & Haynes, R. (2014) Sport, public relations and social media. In A. C. Billings & M. Hardin (Eds.) *Routledge handbook of sport and new media* (pp. 133–142), London: Routledge.

Bruner, J. S., Postman, L. & Rodrigues, J. (1951) 'Expectation and the perception of color', *American Journal of Psychology*, 64 (2) 216–227.

Brunswik, E. (1948) 'Statistical separation of perception, thinking, and attitudes', *American Psychologist*, 3 (3) 342–358.

Buhler, A. & Nufer, G. (2012) *Relationship marketing in sports*, New York: Routledge.

Burns, J. M. (1978) *Leadership*, New York: Harper & Row.

Butterworth, D. S. & Punt, A. E. (1999) 'Experiences in the evaluation and implementation of management procedures', *ICES Journal of Marine Science: Journal du Conseil*, 56 (6) 985–998.

Caywood, C. & Ewing, R. (1991) 'Integrated marketing communications: A new master's degree concept', *Public Relations Review*, 17 (3) 237–244.

Chadwick, S. (2004) *Determinants of commitment in the professional football club/shirt sponsorship dyad*. Unpublished PhD Thesis, Leeds University Business School.

Chadwick, S. (2015) 'English football's premier league TV rights auctions reveals opportunities for academic researchers', *Sport, Business and Management: An International Journal*, 5 (2). available at https://www.emerald.com/insight/content/doi/10.1108/SBM-03-2015-0007/full/html?casa_token=WfQDH0mYN00AAAAA:4xlFQwrvD-3WovPaDufG26qugWyPCRYPcHIS6o47L5o4mWjmOubk98Q_lICi903_kIxYobxlW-BoFB2X5pWiHk4hJHv3S8JKHudLKTp2KcTnCK6LRRbY65aw (accessed March 3, 2022).

Chadwick, S. & Thwaites, D. (2005) 'Managing sport sponsorship programs: Lessons from a critical assessment of English soccer', *Journal of Advertising Research*, 45 (3) 328–338.

Creswell, J. W. (2013) *Qualitative inquiry and research design: Choosing among five approaches* (3rd ed.), London: Sage Publications.

Davis, J. H., Schoorman, F. D. & Donaldson, L. (1997) 'Toward a stewardship theory of management', *Academy of Management Review*, 22 (1) 20–47.

De Chernatony, L. (2001) 'A model for strategically building brands', *The Journal of Brand Management*, 9 (1) 32–44.

Dean, J. W. & Bowen, D. E. (1994) 'Management theory and total quality: Improving research and practice through theory development', *Academy of Management Review*, 19 (3) 392–418.

Deloitte. (2016) *Annual Review of Football Finance*, Manchester: Deloitte.

Dmitrijeva, K. & Batraga, A. (2012) 'Barriers to integrated marketing communications: The case of Latvia (small markets)', *8th International Strategic Management Conference*, 21–23 June 2012, Barcelona, Spain.

du Plessis, E. (2005) *The advertised mind: Ground-breaking insights into how our brains respond to advertising*, London: Kogan Page.

Duncan, T. R. (2002) *IMC: Using advertising and promotion to build brands* (International Edition), New York: The McGraw-Hill.

Eagle, L., Kitchen, P. J. & Bulmer, S. (2007) 'Insights into interpreting integrated marketing communications: A two-nation qualitative comparison', *European Journal of Marketing*, 41 (7/8) 956–970.

Ewing, M. T., de Bussy, N. M. & Caruana, A. (2000) 'Perceived agency politics and conflicts of interest as potential barriers to IMC orientation', *Journal of Marketing Communications*, 6 (1) 107–119.

Ewing, M. T., Du Pleiss, E. & Foster, C. (2001) 'Cinema advertising re-considered', *Journal of Advertising Research*, 41 (1) 78–85.

Fetchko, M., Roy, D. & Clow, K. E. (2012) *Sports marketing*, Boston, MA: Pearson.

Gambetti, R. C. & Schultz, D. E. (2015) 'Reshaping the boundaries of marketing communication to bond with consumers', *Journal of Marketing Communications*, 21 (1) 1–4.

Gelade, G. A. (2006) 'But what does it mean in practice? The Journal of Occupational and Organizational Psychology from a practitioner perspective', *Journal of Occupational and Organizational Psychology*, 79 (1) 153–160.

George, J. M. (1992) 'Extrinsic and intrinsic origins of perceived social loafing in organizations', *Academy of Management Journal*, 35 (1) 191–202.

Han, D., Kim, I. & Schultz, D. E. (2004) 'Understanding the diffusion of integrated marketing communications', *Journal of Advertising Research*, 44 (1) 31–45.

Henry, J. (1999) 'Changing conscious experience—Comparing clinical approaches, practice and outcomes', *British Journal of Psychology*, 90 (4) 587–609.

Henry, J. (2001) *Creativity and perception in management*, London: Sage.

Henry, J. & Walker, D. (1991) *Managing innovation*, London: Sage.

Hill, M. (2014) *Policy process: A reader* (4th ed.), London: Routledge.

Hochberg, J. (1956) 'Perception: Toward the recovery of a definition', *Psychological Review*, 63 (6) 400–423.

Hodgkinson, G. P. & Rousseau, D. M. (2009) 'Bridging the rigour–relevance gap in management research: It's already happening!', *Journal of Management Studies*, 46(3) 534–546.

Jauch, L. R. & Glueck, W. F. (1988) *Business policy and strategic management*, New York: McGraw-Hill.

Jobber, D. & Ellis-Chadwick, F. (2012) *Principles and practice of marketing* (7th ed.), New York: McGraw-Hill.

Keegan, W., Moriarty, S. E. & Duncan, T. R. (1992) *Marketing, branding*, Hoboken, NJ: Prentice Hall.

Keller, K. L. (2016) 'Unlocking the power of integrated marketing communications: How integrated is your IMC program?', *Journal of Advertising*, 45 (3) 286–301.
King, D. & Learmonth, M. (2014) 'Doing management critically: An experiment in critically engaged scholarship', *Academy of Management Proceedings*, 14 (1) 101–137.
Kitchen, P. J. (2016) Is IMC "Marketing Oriented"? In L. Petruzzellis and R. S. Winer (Eds.) *Rediscovering the essentiality of marketing* (pp. 441–442), New York: Springer International Publishing.
Kitchen, P. J. & Schultz, D. E. (1999) 'A multi-country comparison of the drive for IMC', *Journal of Advertising Research*, 39 (1) 21–38.
Kitchen, P. J. & Tourky, M. (2015) *Integrated communications in the postmodern era*, Hampshire: Palgrave Macmillan.
Kliatchko, J. (2005) 'Towards a new definition of integrated marketing communications (IMC)', *International Journal of Advertising*, 24 (1) 7–34.
Kliatchko, J. (2008) 'Revisiting the IMC construct: A revised definition and four pillars', *International Journal of Advertising*, 27 (1) 133–160.
Kliatchko, J. G. & Schultz, D. E. (2014) 'Twenty years of IMC: A study of CEO and CMO perspectives in the Asia-Pacific region', *International Journal of Advertising*, 33 (2) 373–390.
Kotler, P. (2000) *Marketing management* (10th ed.), London: Prentice Hall International.
Latham, G. P. (2007) 'A speculative perspective on the transfer of behavioral science findings to the workplace: "The times they are a-changing"', *Academy of Management Journal*, 50 (8) 1027–1032.
Lawler, E. E. (1994) 'Total quality management and employee involvement: Are they compatible?', *The Academy of Management Executive*, 8 (1) 68–76.
Locke, E. A. & Latham, G. P. (2002) 'Building a practically useful theory of goal setting and task motivation: A 35-year odyssey', *American Psychologist*, 57 (9) 705.
Lukka, K. (2014) 'Engaged scholarship requires close collaboration', *Controlling & Management Review*, 58 (4) 57–72.
Luxton, S., Reid, M. & Mavondo, F. (2015) 'Integrated marketing communication capability and brand performance', *Journal of Advertising*, 44 (1) 37–46.
Manoli, A. E. (2017) Media relations in English football clubs. In J. J. Zhang & B. G. Pitts (Eds.) *Contemporary sport marketing: Global perspectives*, (pp. 120–138), London: Routledge.
Manoli, A. E. (2018) 'Sport marketing's past, present and future', *Journal of Strategic Marketing*, 26 (1) 6–18.
Manoli, A. E. (2020) 'Brand capabilities in English premier league clubs', *European Sport Management Quarterly* 20 (1) 30–46.
Manoli, A. E. & Davies, M. (2014) 'IMC and the practitioners' strategy paradox', *Paper presented at the International Conference on Research in Advertising (ICORIA)*, 26–28 June, Amsterdam.
Manoli, A. E. & Hodgkinson, I. R. (2017) 'Marketing outsourcing in the English premier league: The right holder/agency interface', *European Sport Management Quarterly*, 17(4) 436–456.
Manoli, A. E. & Hodgkinson, I. R. (2019) 'The implementation of integrated marketing communication (IMC): Evidence from professional football clubs in England', *Journal of Strategic Marketing*, 28 (6) 542–563.
Manoli, A. E. & Hodgkinson, I. R. (2021) 'Exploring internal organisational communication dynamics in the professional football industry', *European Journal of Marketing*, 55 (11) 2894–2916.

Manoli, A. E. & Kenyon, J. A. (2018) Football and marketing. In S. M. Chadwick, P. Widdop, D. Parnell, & C. Anagnostopoulos (Eds.) *Routledge handbook of football business and management*, (pp. 88–100), Oxon: Routledge.

May, C. R., Mair, F., Finch, T., MacFarlane, A., Dowrick, C., Treweek, S. & Murray, E. (2009) 'Development of a theory of implementation and integration: Normalization Process Theory', *Implementation Science*, 4 (1) 1.

McCarthy, J., Rowley, J., Jane Ashworth, C. & Pioch, E. (2014) 'Managing brand presence through social media: The case of UK football clubs', *Internet Research*, 24 (2) 181–204.

McGregor, D. (1960) *The human side of enterprise*, New York: McGraw-Hill.

McNamara, P., Peck, S. I. & Sasson, A. (2013) 'Competing business models, value creation and appropriation in English football', *Long Range Planning*, 46 (6) 475–487.

Mischen, P. A. & Jackson, S. K. (2008) 'Connecting the dots: Applying complexity theory, knowledge management and social network analysis to policy implementation', *Public Administration Quarterly*, 32 (3) 314–338.

Mohrman, S. A. & Lawler, E. (2011) *Useful research: Advancing theory and practice*, London: Berrett-Koehler Publishers.

Moriarty, S. & Schultz, D. E. (2012) Four theories of how IMC works. In S. Rodgers & E. Thorson (Eds.) *Advertising theory* (pp. 491–505), New York: Routledge.

Naik, P. A. & Raman, K. (2003) 'Understanding the impact of synergy in multimedia communications', *Journal of Marketing Research*, 40 (4) 375–388.

Nash, R. (2000) 'Globalised football fandom: Scandinavian Liverpool FC supporters', *Football Studies*, 3 (2) 5–23.

Noll, R. G. (2002) 'The economics of promotion and relegation in sports leagues the case of English football', *Journal of Sports Economics*, 3 (2) 169–203.

Pearce, J. L. (2006) *Organizational behavior: Real research for real managers*, Irvine, CA: Melvin & Leigh.

Pettigrew, A. M. (2001) 'Management research after modernism', *British Journal of Management*, 12 (1) 61–S70.

Porcu, L., del Barrio-García, S. & Kitchen, P. J. (2012) 'How integrated marketing communications (IMC) works? A theoretical review and an analysis of its main drivers and effects/¿ Cómo funciona la Comunicación Integrada de Marketing (CIM)? Una revisión teórica y un análisis de sus antecedentes y efectos', *Comunicación y sociedad*, 25 (1) 313–348.

Premier League. (2016) *The world's most watched league*, available at: http://www.premierleague.com/en-gb/about/the-worlds-most-watched-league.html [accessed 3 Apr. 2016].

Reinold, T. & Tropp, J. (2012) 'Integrated marketing communications: How can we measure its effectiveness?', *Journal of Marketing Communications*, 18 (2) 113–132.

Roderick, M. (2006) *The work of professional football: A labour of love?*, London: Routledge.

Rosenberg, A. A. & Brault, S. (1993) Choosing a management strategy for stock rebuilding when control is uncertain. In S. J. Smith, J. J. Hunt & D. Rivard (Eds.) *Risk evaluation and biological reference points for fisheries management* (pp. 243–249), Ottawa: Fisheries and Aquatic Sciences.

Rousseau, D. M., Manning, J. & Denyer, D. (2008) 'Evidence in management and organizational science: Assembling the field's full weight of scientific knowledge through syntheses', *Academy of Management Annals*, 2 (4) 475–515.

Rynes, S. L., Bartunek, J. M. & Daft, R. L. (2001) 'Across the great divide: Knowledge creation and transfer between practitioners and academics', *Academy of Management Journal*, 44 (3) 340–355.

Rynes, S. L., Giluk, T. L. & Brown, K. G. (2007) 'The very separate worlds of academic and practitioner periodicals in human resource management: Implications for evidence-based management', *Academy of Management Journal*, 50 (8) 987–1008.

Schultz, D. E. (1992) 'Integrated marketing communications: The status of integrated marketing communications programs the US today', *Journal of Promotion Management*, 1 (1) 99–104.

Schultz, D. E. (1993a) 'Integrated marketing communications: Maybe definition is in the point of view', *Marketing News*, 18 January.

Schultz, D. E. (1993b) 'We simply can't afford to go back to mass marketing', *Marketing News*, February 15.

Schultz, D. E., Chu, G. & Zhao, B. (2016) 'IMC in an emerging economy: The Chinese perspective', *International Journal of Advertising*, 35 (2) 200–215.

Schultz, D. E., Kim, I. & Kang, K. (2014) Integrated marketing communication research. In H. Cheng (Ed.) *The handbook of international advertising research* (pp. 455–483), London: Wiley Blackwell.

Schultz, D. E. & Patti, C. H. (2009) 'The evolution of IMC: IMC in a customer driven marketplace', *Journal of Marketing Communications*, 15 (2–3) 75–84.

Schultz, D. E. & Schultz, H. F. (1998) 'Transitioning marketing communication into the twenty-first century', *Journal of Marketing Communications*, 4 (1) 9–26.

Schultz, D. E. & Schultz, H. F. (2004) *IMC: The next generation*, New York: McGraw-Hill.

Shimp, T. A. (2007) *Integrated marketing communications in advertising and promotion* (7th ed.), Mason: Thomson Higher Education.

Sportfive. (2012) *European football*, Hamburg: Sportfive.

Stake, R. E. (2005) Qualitative case studies. In N. K. Denzin & Y. S. Lincoln (Eds.) *The Sage handbook of qualitative research* (3rd ed., pp. 443–466), London: Sage.

Steers, R. M. & Black, J. S. (1994) *Organizational behavior*, New York: Harper Collins.

Steers, R. M. & Porter, L. W. (1991) *Motivation & work behaviour* (5th ed.), New York: McGraw-Hill.

Szymanski, S. (2010) 'The financial crisis and English football: The dog that will not bark', *International Journal of Sport Finance*, 5 (1) 28–40.

Szymanski, S. & Smith, R. (1997) 'The English football industry, profit, performance and industrial structure', *International Review of Applied Economics*, 11 (1) 135–153.

Thorson, E. & Moore, J. (2013) *Integrated communication: Synergy of persuasive voices*, New York: Psychology Press.

Tsai, S. P. (2005) 'Integrated marketing as management of holistic consumer experience', *Business Horizons*, 48 (5) 431–441.

Tucker, B. P. & Lowe, A. D. (2014) 'Practitioners are from Mars; academics are from Venus? An investigation of the research-practice gap in management accounting', *Accounting, Auditing & Accountability Journal*, 27 (3) 394–425.

UEFA. (2015) *The European club footballing landscape*, Nyon: UEFA.

Van de Ven, A. H. (2007) *Engaged scholarship: A guide for organizational and social research*, Oxford: Oxford University Press.

Van de Ven, A. H. & Johnson, P. E. (2006) 'Knowledge for theory and practice', *Academy of MANAGEMENT REVIEW*, 31 (4) 802–821.

Vantamay, S. (2011) 'Performances and measurement of integrated marketing communications (IMC) of advertisers in Tailand', *Journal of Global Management*, 1 (1) 1–12.

Vernuccio, M. & Ceccotti, F. (2015) 'Strategic and organisational challenges in the integrated marketing communication paradigm shift: A holistic vision', *European Management Journal*, 33 (6) 438–449.

Webster, F. E. (2002) 'Marketing management in changing times', *Marketing Management*, 11 (1) 18–23.

Chapter 2

Integrated Marketing Communications

Introduction

This research's focus is to examine IMC's implementation in the EPL through the investigation of practitioners' appreciation and application of the theory. This chapter aims at critically examining the literature on IMC and the way in which it is perceived, in order to understand the nuances and various aspects of IMC and to formulate the basis on which the research that follows will be constructed.

State of IMC Literature

The synthesis of the relevant literature suggests that IMC has attracted considerable interest among both academics and practitioners over the last three decades (Kliatchko & Schultz, 2014; Kitchen, 2016). As it is suggested, IMC did not emerge unexpectedly as a modern business trend, but progressed gradually after careful consideration, research and evaluation of the changing business environment (Kitchen & Tourky, 2015). Nowadays, it is widely accepted as a continuously developing subject and *'one of the most influential marketing management frameworks of our time'* (Schultz et al., 2013, p. 75). However, regardless of the scholarly interest the topic has attracted, it can be argued that IMC, as an idea and mainly as a practical process, is still not clear or well defined as to its characteristics, implementation, implications and outcomes (Kliatchko, 2008; Keller, 2016). Academics who have studied the subject since the late 1980s have not always been able to agree on several of its dimensions, its outcomes or even its definition (Laurie & Mortimer, 2011). More than two decades later, and it is still argued that

> *Integrated Marketing Communications (IMC) continues to stir debate, discussion and, in some cases, confusion.*
> (Kliatchko & Schultz, 2014, p. 373)

This extended discussion and occasional confusion is indeed reflected on the IMC-focused literature so far. In more detail, the majority of the IMC literature is conceptual research that examines IMC's definition, key issues and debates

DOI: 10.4324/9781003140238-2

(Schultz, 1992, 1993a; Kliatchko, 2005, 2008; Porcu et al., 2012). This research includes the examination of IMC's outcomes (Kallmeyer & Abratt, 2001; Schultz et al., 2013), benefits (Reinold & Tropp, 2012; Seric et al., 2014; Batra & Keller, 2016), barriers (Awad, 2009; Schultz & Patti, 2009) and reasons that led to its emergence (Duncan, 2002; Barger & Labrecque, 2013; Keller, 2016), as well as debates on its originality (Cornelissen, 2001, 2003; Porcu et al., 2012; Schultz et al., 2014), organisational structure (Low & Mohr,1999, Low, 2000; Vernuccio & Ceccotti, 2015), leadership implications (Cornelissen, 2003; Gambetti & Schultz, 2015), measurement (Reinold & Tropp, 2012; Luxton et al., 2015; Munoz-Leiva et al., 2015) and control (Swain, 2004; Homburg et al., 2015). As it will be discussed in this chapter even within this extensive literature, the key debates of IMC have yet to find a unanimously accepted answer. The same applies for IMC's and its role's appreciation within the literature, which is also explored below.

The majority of the existing studies examine IMC from a conceptual point of view, with no effort made to link their arguments with IMC's implementation in practice or to conduct engaged scholarship. Even when the topic under discussion is IMC's application and its outcomes (e.g. in Barnes, 2001; Schultz, & Patti, 2009) the study's discussion occurs disconnectedly from any empirical data or practitioners' participation in the study. These theoretically driven pieces have attracted the lion's share of the scholarly interest available since the 1990s[1]; however, a decline can be noted in the last six years.[2] This decline could be linked to Pettigrew's (2001) and Van de Ven's (2007) argument that scholars often opt to move to the '*next big thing*' rather than engage with the application and outcomes of a current rather challenging issue.

A substantially smaller proportion of the IMC literature focuses on the application of the theory, by examining practitioners and their perceptions and implementation of IMC.[3] Methodologically, this examination takes place through the collection of primary data either with the use of standardised questionnaires[4] (e.g. Phelps et al., 1994; Beard, 1997; Reid et al., 2001; Reid, 2002; Gabrielli & Balboni, 2010) or structured and semi-structured interviews[5] (e.g. Kitchen et al., 2008; Awad, 2009; Kliatchko & Schultz, 2014; Schultz et al., 2016). While the standardised questionnaires aim at uncovering the practices of the organisations, the interviews focus more on practitioners' perceptions and the implementation of IMC. According to the review, the latter has been studied primarily using limited multiple case studies (from 3 to 25 cases per study) that are selected through an often vague criterion sampling (e.g. companies that operate within the Asia-Pacific region – Kliatchko & Schultz, 2014). An equally vague criterion sampling is often used in studies that collected data through survey questionnaires,[6] while some opt for a convenience sampling approach (e.g. Swain, 2004). The criterion used is often the country or the geographic region in which a company operates, with each study concentrating on a specific number of countries, varying from one to five, and differing in a number of factors such as language used (e.g. Latvian in Dmitrijeva & Batraga, 2012; Chinese in Schultz et al., 2016), cultural idiosyncrasies (e.g. China in Kitchen & Tao, 2005 and Schultz et. al., 2016, USA in Phelps et al., 1996, Schultz & Kitchen, 1997 and Atkinson, 2003), marketplace maturity (e.g. South Korea vs. UK vs. USA in Kitchen et al., 2008) and development stage (e.g. New Zealand vs UK in Eagle et al., 2007). Often a mixture of client and agency marketers is included in the sample, who are employed in various levels of seniority within their respective organisations (e.g. both middle and top level managers in Han et al., 2004 and Schultz et. al., 2016), which might also vary in terms of size (e.g. both medium and large client organisations operating in Thailand in Vantamay, 2011), discipline focus (e.g. both advertising and PR agencies in Kitchen et al., 2004a) and market-share (e.g. both state-owned and privately owned local and international advertising agencies in China in Schultz et al., 2016).

An overview of the state of the IMC literature suggests that a considerable literature gap exists in IMC's implementation research and practitioners' perceptions and practices. In more detail, non-English speaking developing countries, smaller client organisations and the full spectrum of an industry sector are in need for further attention. Interestingly, this lack of research on IMC's implementation is underlined in all 34 studies that include practitioners' participation, as well as in numerous other conceptual IMC-focused studies (e.g. Percy, 2014; Kerr & Patti, 2015; Kitchen & Tourky, 2015; Madhavaram et al., 2016).

As the discussion in this chapter will further demonstrate, a number of deficiencies can be found in IMC's literature. First, it could be argued that the extensive focus on definitional and theoretical issues has obstructed scholars from researching IMC in practice, which, in turn, has resulted in the current limited literature on the topic (Kliatchko, 2005, 2008; Gambetti & Schultz, 2015). As a result, IMC's appreciation and implementation remains an understudied area, with academic research on the matter still focusing on a rather limited sample, offering incomplete indications on the current integration landscape. A clear manifestation of this deficiency is the frequent use of the stages of IMC's development framework (developed by Kitchen & Schultz, 1999) in the studies that examine IMC's implementation. This framework is used to indicate only the extent to which IMC is implemented, while neglecting to examine whether integration actually occurs. In response to this deficiency, as it will be presented later on in this chapter, this study suggests the addition of an extra IMC level, level 0, to the framework, in order for the research on more diverse samples of organisations (such as a full industry sector) to be facilitated, as Manoli and Hodgkinson (2019) have also suggested in their work.

Additionally, this chapter suggests that IMC literature has been regarding integration through a rather optimistic lens, focusing mainly on full strategic integration. Consequently, other potential integration states or scenarios remain understudied, even though indications of their existence have been noted (Kitchen et al., 2004a; Eagle et al., 2007; Dmitrijeva & Batraga, 2012). This book aims to answer this need and follow on from the work conducted by Manoli and Hodgkinson (2019) in order to investigate for any additional integration scenarios, the first of which, the *practitioners' strategy paradox*, is introduced and defined in this chapter. Since both scenarios (full strategic integration and *practitioners' strategy paradox*) have emerged based on the limited studies available, it could be argued that further research (e.g. on a full industry sector) could lead to the study of additional scenarios that are yet to be examined.

In regards with the focus of this book, the review of the IMC literature suggests that IMC in sports in general and football in particular can be considered an unchartered territory, which further underlines the importance of this and further study. The five themes identified within the IMC literature will be examined in more detail in this and the following chapter.

IMC's Theoretical Appreciation

IMC has received remarkable attention within the academic community, with numerous attempts made to define the term since it was first presented in 1989 (Schultz, 1993a). However, as it will be discussed below, not all attempts have been successful in receiving a consensus from the academic community. In fact, it is only a small number of definitions that have been used repeatedly in the IMC literature. Investigating these definitions can help the reader understand the evolution of comprehending IMC through time. Following this, IMC's key issues and debates will be examined in an attempt to further explore the theoretical appreciation IMC has received. Presenting the IMC-focused literature will also allow for the notable decline in recent studies on the topic to be underlined, while pinpointing the different viewpoints available.

Defining IMC

IMC was first introduced in 1989 as a concept that can assist in achieving clarity, consistency and maximum communication impact (AAAA in Schultz, 1993a), while calling for various key marketing tools to be used in a coherent manner. Such tools according to Schultz include advertising, sales promotion and public relations. In 1992, the connection between IMC and customer loyalty was also added to the definition, with more focus being put on the behavioural change that any information on a product or a service provided could trigger (Schultz, 1992, 1993b). Schultz in his article in 1993 was also the first one to mention the difference between the '*important customers*' and the '*transients*' and underline the significance of differentiating these two groups. In other words, emphasis was placed on buying behaviour and taken away from the collection and analysis of general attitudinal and awareness data. It was shortly after when IMC started being discussed as a strategic process of coordination and integration of all messages and communication channels (Keegan et al., 1992; Kotler, 2000). Keegan and colleagues and Kotler also clarified in their work that IMC aims at achieving a clear, consistent, coherent and persuasive message or a collective influence. These scholars (Keegan et al., 1992; Kotler, 2000) also underlined the strategic importance of the concept, rather than the operational value of it that had been previously presented. According to their studies, IMC as a concept exceeds the mere coordination of marketing communications tools, extending to a more strategic and long-term process. Brand value was also mentioned by Keegan et al. (1992) for the first time in IMC's definition. Schultz and Schultz (1998) are the first scholars to present IMC as a business process that is driven by customer data and points towards a clear evaluation methodology. Their study is also the first one to introduce the Four Levels of IMC (p.18) that will later be established as the Stages in IMC Development (Kitchen & Schultz, 1999, p. 34). These stages, as it will be discussed later on in this chapter, present the reader with the steps a company should follow in order to implement IMC to its full potential.

Duncan (2002) drew additional attention to IMC's relation not only with customers but also with other stakeholders, and highlighted the idea of a purposeful dialogue between the organisation and all stakeholder groups. His IMC Process Model presents the circular nature of this dialogue process instead of the traditional linear one. In his definition, brand value is recognised by a company as sales, profits and brand equity, introducing the idea of evaluating profitable customer relationships. Schultz (2004, p. 9) presented a similar definition and even named these stakeholders as: '*consumers, customers, prospects, employees, associates and other targeted, relevant external and internal audiences*'. Schultz and Schultz (2004) reintroduced their earlier definition and highlighted measurability as well, while emphasising duration and widening the relevant internal and external audiences. Widening the general timeframe in which IMC can function as well as introducing return on investment (ROI) measurement techniques to evaluate IMC was featured in their definition, developing further the idea behind IMC.

In 2005, Kliatchko (p. 23) summarised IMC as:

> *the concept and process of strategically managing audience-focused, channel centred and results-driven brand communication programmes over time.*

His study introduced the Three Pillars of IMC that he re-examined and presented in 2008 as the Four Pillars of IMC, which include the Stakeholders, the Content, the Channels and the Results. Kliatchko also revised his definition of IMC in 2008 (p. 140) to:

> *an audience-driven business process of strategically managing stakeholders, content, channels, and results of brand communication programs.*

This last definition appears to be used in the majority of recent studies (Reinold & Tropp, 2012; Schultz et al., 2013, 2014; Kliatchko & Schultz, 2014). His work also presented an interplay between the IMC levels or stages and the IMC pillars, which will be examined in detail later on in this chapter.

In line with the overall decline in the number of IMC-focused studies produced, there has only been one other attempt to define IMC since 2008, by Porcu et al. (2012, p. 325), as:

The interactive and systemic process of cross-functional planning and optimization of messages to stakeholders with the aim of communicating with coherence and transparency to achieve synergies and encourage profitable relationships in the short, medium and long-term.

This definition, however, is not often used in recent studies that still reference Kliatchko's work when examining IMC (Kliatchko & Schultz, 2014; Schultz et al., 2014; Gambetti & Schultz, 2015).

The overview of the IMC's definitions allows us to better understand the process through which IMC has been defined, understood and appreciated within the literature. At first, IMC is seen as the concept behind the 'one-voice' idea that all promotional efforts from a company or organisation should share the same 'look, sound and feel' (Ouwersloot & Duncan, 2008, p. 193), which indicates that integration should exist, but mainly at the executional level. The idea behind strategic integration is presented later on, along with the studies that associate IMC not only with branding but also with customer service, behaviour and loyalty (Moriarty, 1994; Hutton, 1996; Duncan & Moriarty, 1998). Soon after that, the two-way communication process between the company and the customer is introduced, while the concept of IMC is widened to include not only customers but also other stakeholder groups, with special attention drawn on the organisation's employees (Ahmed & Rafiq, 1995; Rafiq & Ahmed, 2000). Finally, the idea of IMC as a company-wide concept and process is proposed as a result of the growing appreciation of this developing idea. Moriarty (1994, 1997) and Duncan and Moriarty (1998) analyse further the importance of IMC being appreciated and actively applied throughout each part of the company, taking into consideration the significance each stakeholder group has, with particular attention placed on the employees.

From the above-mentioned definitions' analysis, the reader is also introduced to the continuous change in IMC's appreciation as a concept, a process or both. When examining IMC's appreciation over time, the reader can see the transition between the early stages of IMC's definition, where it is regarded only as a concept, followed by a few years when some scholars begin to present IMC as a process while some insist on its previous classification as a concept. This confusion in appreciating IMC as either a concept or a process has hindered, according to Duncan and Everett (1993), the establishment of a unanimously accepted definition. Schultz and Schultz (1998) and Smith and Taylor (2004) present IMC as a cross-functional process that extends beyond the operational level. For the following years IMC is recognised merely as process, until Kliatchko's definition (2005) describes its dual nature, both a concept and a process. Finally, Kliatchko's (2008) and Porcu et al. (2012) definitions present IMC as a wider business process, instead of merely a marketing communication process. This study's author's opinion is that viewing IMC only as a process and not as a concept and a process deprives us from understanding that in order to truly apply IMC as a process, its concept needs to be acknowledged and appreciated at all times. As Duncan and Everett (1993, p. 31) put it, 'IMC *is both a concept and a process and the degree of integration within each dimension can greatly vary*'. Additionally, since the process of IMC has a continuous and long-term nature and involves many people in an organisation, it is imperative for the concept of IMC to be kept in mind throughout the process of integration in order to succeed in its implementation.

Finally, through the analysis of IMC's definition over time an additional pattern can be observed. IMC's definitions appear to be developing in a coherent fashion and thus in a way that complements the previous definitions, rather than contradicting or challenging them. As a result, if we were to present the progress of the definitions in a figure, we could illustrate that they have been developing as nested circles over the original definition of IMC, and have gradually grown bigger in order for new elements to be added to the previous versions.

This practice of repeatedly redefining IMC in order to incorporate the wide spectrum of ideas it represents is, according to some, evidence that the notion behind IMC has yet to be fully understood (Gambetti & Schultz, 2015; Kerr & Patti, 2015). While for some, this lack of a clear and precise unanimous definition is an indication that the topic has not been researched enough (Kitchen & Burgmann, 2010; Kitchen, 2016). Nevertheless, the evolution of IMC's definition, as presented above, could be compared with the evolution of the marketing term, as well as with the evolution of marketing itself (Laurie & Mortimer, 2011). As expected and argued by Laurie and Mortimer, from a macro-economic viewpoint the environment in which companies operate changes and accordingly do the companies within it. Since new matters arise, such as technological advancements, and new academics appear, introducing new theories or their perspective on existing ones, the definition and implementation of concepts such as IMC or marketing in general are expected to evolve over time (Luck & Moffatt, 2009; Kitchen & Tourky, 2015). Additional attention is expected to be drawn on IMC in relation to the Internet and its applications such as on-line marketing, new interactive media and the rapid increase in social media use which is attracting growing scholarly interest (Hoffman et al., 1995; Geissler, 2001; Peltier et al., 2003; Gurau, 2008; Wang, 2008; Naik & Peters, 2009; Owen & Humphrey, 2009; Valos et al., 2010; Ivanov, 2012). Future challenges, such as the recent COVID-19 pandemic, are also expected to affect IMC and marketing in general, transforming them possibly into something different from what they are perceived as today.

Key Issues and Debates of IMC

As discussed above, IMC has been defined repeatedly and has evolved over time. However, presenting the definition cannot provide enough information for the reader to fully understand the emergence of IMC or the debate it has created in the academic community. In order for these to be comprehended, the key issues and debates of IMC will be discussed below.

Key Issues

First, the reasons that led to IMC's emergence have been researched extensively within the literature available. The shift from a company-driven brand creation to a consumer – company dialogue that leads to the co-creation of a company's brand meaning has been argued repeatedly (De Chernatony, 2001; Duncan, 2002; Burmann & Zeplin, 2005). This phenomenon is increasing the demand for better coordinated marketing communications that need to be coherent, clear and consistent regarding a brand's identity and meaning (Cova, 1997; Holt, 2002). Since the importance of customer loyalty is widely accepted, academics seem to agree on the significance of such dialogue between a company and its customers that can lead to brand value and profitable customer relationships (sales, profits and brand equity[7]). This change in customer behaviour is one of the main reasons that led to IMC's emergence. Additional reasons include marketplace changes (Schultz et al.,1993; Schultz & Patti, 2009; Kitchen & Tourky, 2015), audience segmentation (Kitchen et al., 2004b; Dmitrijeva & Batraga, 2012), increase of available products and services (Kallmeyer & Abratt, 2001; Schultz et al., 2013), media multiplication (Naik & Peters, 2009; Owen & Humphrey, 2009), and technological advances (Valos et al., 2010; Ivanov, 2012). In regards with the latter, emphasis has been placed on Internet and mobile Internet, arguing that this might even lead to a new era for marketing in general (Barger & Labrecque, 2013; Seric et al., 2014). As Ewing (2009) suggests, the permission-based marketing, where the consumer is the sole one in power, is the future of marketing communications, which is also expected to affect the development of IMC. Finally, globalisation and the rapid increase of products and services were also mentioned as accelerating reasons in IMC's appreciation in today's business world (Hackley & Kitchen, 1998; Luck & Moffatt, 2009; Batra & Keller, 2016).

The appreciation of multiple stakeholders and their relationship with IMC, as discussed in detail by Moriaty (1994, 1997), Schultz and Patti (2009) and Moriarty and Schultz (2012), is also considered an important factor in IMC's emergence. The consumer in general and the loyal consumer in particular are no longer regarded as the main focus of marketing communications, with more internal and external audiences being increasingly valued as key to IMC's success (Kliatchko, 2008; Keller, 2016). The company-wide communications idea, based on the multiple touch points' principle and combined with the improved understanding for various stakeholder groups' influence, appears to be an increasingly acknowledged argument that can lead to the wider appreciation of IMC (Moriarty, 1994; Schultz & Kitchen, 2000b; Duncan, 2002; Barger & Labrecque, 2013; Keller, 2016). Since the emergence of new technological advances, such as CRM systems, new communications channels and social media, appreciating, understanding and communicating with various stakeholders groups has been attracting additional attention within the IMC literature (Naik & Peters, 2009; Owen & Humphrey, 2009; Valos et al., 2010; Ivanov, 2012; Barger & Labrecque, 2013; Seric et al., 2014). Based on the fact that, macro economically, *'a company exists within a value field of stakeholder interactions*' whose groups often overlap, and through them and their support, brand equity is created (Moriarty, 1997, p. 7), IMC as a company-wide process could assist in ensuring a coherent and consistent brand message at all times.

The driving force behind the introduction and implementation of IMC in a company is an additional topic widely discussed within literature. The client, or the marketing management of the client company in more detail, is presented as the main initiator of IMC in the marketplace (Caywood & Ewing, 1991; Kallmeyer & Abratt, 2001; Kitchen et al., 2004a; Eagle et al., 2007; Schultz et al., 2016). The leadership behind the process of integration though is the reason behind an existing debate that will be discussed in the following section.

Another issue that has received significant interest within the literature is the benefits of IMC. It is repeatedly argued that a carefully and strategically chosen combination of marketing communications and promotion tools can produce a greater return than any one of those tools used in isolation (Moriarty, 1993; Stammerjohan et al., 2005; Reinold & Tropp, 2012; Seric et al., 2014; Batra & Keller, 2016). This return is measured both in terms of behavioural and consumer impact, and in terms of financial benefits (ROI). Smith and Taylor (2004) suggest that such a synergy between various elements of the communications mix can achieve better results in a more cost-effective way. Pickton and Broderick (2001) also suggest that synergy can prove economic for the company in terms of cost, time and effort. This synergy has been supported with empirical investigation (Ewing et al., 2001; Naik & Raman, 2003; du Plessis, 2005; Tsai, 2005; Seric et al., 2014) and leaves little room for scepticism.

Alongside the synergy effect, the 'one voice' concept is also regarded as a benefit IMC can bring in marketing communications programmes. Beard (1997) underlines that academics, even when disagreeing on the definition of IMC, seem to appreciate that a strong, consistent and coherent message by a company is more valuable than a number of incoherent ones. Duncan and Everett (1993) examine the topic in more detail suggesting various terms that can describe the concept such as 'orchestration', 'consistent voice' and 'seamless communication'. The fast multiplication of media and the introduction of new online media in recent years, combined with the changes in media's power in consumers' lives, have highlighted the growing importance of the 'one-voice' approach (Peltier et al., 2003; Naik & Peters, 2009; Valos et al., 2010; Ivanov, 2012; Lauska et al., 2014). As it is argued, when all marketing communications efforts share the same 'look, sound and feel', successful integration can be achieved (Schultz, 2000, 2001; Reinold & Tropp, 2012; Kitchen & Tourky, 2015). As a result, IMC can assist in both achieving 'one-voice' within messages and harvesting the synergy among the selected marketing communications and promotion tools (Kitchen & Tao, 2005; Eagle et al., 2007; Schultz et al., 2007, 2013).

Kitchen and Schultz (1999), Pickton and Broderick (2001), Kitchen et al. (2008) and Gambetti and Schultz (2015) suggest that the benefits an organisation can have from synergy and coherence in its marketing communications have been the driving force behind IMC's appreciation and implementation. Ewing et al. (2001), Atkinson (2003), Naik and Raman (2003), Reid (2003), Han et al. (2004), du Plessis (2005), Tsai (2005), Reinold and Tropp (2012) and Luxton et al. (2015) examine the benefits of IMC that include a stronger behavioural and consumer impact, better control over marketing and communications budget, higher campaign and communications effectiveness, stronger brand personality, fewer brand misconceptions, and better market and financial performance of a brand. These benefits can be considered the reason why IMC has been advocated as a necessity for the future of an organisation by academics such as Han et al. (2004), Kitchen et al. (2004a), Kitchen et al. (2008), Moriarty and Schultz (2012), Kitchen and Tourky (2015) and Keller (2016).

Finally, the barriers and challenges IMC is met with have been examined by various academics such as Duncan and Everett (1993), Moriarty (1994), Eagle and Kitchen (2000), Ewing et al. (2000), Schultz (2000, 2001), Pettigrew (2000/2001) and Dmitrijeva and Batraga (2012). Duncan and Everett (1993), Phelps et al. (1996), Rose (1996), Kitchen et al. (2004a) and Schultz et al. (2016) mention that there are four issues that are prevailing in the business world, which constitute the four main barriers for IMC. These barriers include the lack of cross-disciplinary managerial skills and the existence of egos and 'territory-protection' arguments, especially between different discipline agencies (Awad, 2009; Schultz & Patti, 2009). Power, coordination and control issues, as well as organisational, leadership and cultural differences have also been identified as hindering factors in IMC's future (Moon & Franke, 2000; Han et al., 2004; Ebren et al., 2005). These issues can be located in relationships developed between clients and agencies, among different specialised agencies and even within the same organisation. In each occasion, one or a combination of the above-mentioned issues has been acting as an impediment in IMC's implementation or progress (Dmitrijeva & Batraga, 2012; Homburg et al., 2015). Additional obstacles include time and resources restrictions and lack of flexibility on behalf of both the client and the agency, as well as deficiency in indispensable tools, such as detailed customer databases and measurement techniques (Han et al., 2004; Eagle et al., 2007; Awad, 2009; Dmitrijeva & Batraga, 2012). The way these issues can be addressed and the level in which they can affect IMC have been discussed, without, however, reaching an agreement, and since they exceed the purpose of this study, they will not be further discussed.

Key Debates

The main debates regarding IMC can be presented from either a practical or a theoretical point of view. The former includes measurement, structural and leadership issues, while the latter involves the main theoretical debate on IMC's originality and appreciation. Both practical and theoretical disagreements will be presented in this section.

First, even though measurement is considered to be one of the most important matters in IMC's future, with the need for further improvement on the area being repeatedly underlined (Ewing et al., 2000; Ebren et al., 2005; Vantamay, 2011; Reinold & Tropp, 2012; Kamboj & Rahman, 2015) a clear answer on how or who should measure IMC and its effects has yet to be provided within the literature available. A number of tools have been suggested, such as attitudinal and communication measures according to Keller (1996) and financial and behavioural values according to Schultz (1995). More recently, methods such as ROCI, return-on-customer-investments, ROTPI, return-on-touch-point-investment and ROBI, return-on-brand-investment were also suggested by Kliatchko (2005), Schultz and Schultz (2005) and Ewing (2009), respectively. None of the above-mentioned methods, nevertheless, has received unanimous support (Reinold & Tropp, 2012; Luxton et al., 2015; Munoz-Leiva et al., 2015). At the same time, as Ewing et al. (2000), Eagle et al. (2007), Kitchen et al. (2008) and Awad (2009) argue, it has yet to be clarified who, the client or the agency, should bear the responsibility and cost of the measurement of IMC. Similarly, the literature available does not clarify which party should be in charge of the development and use of customer databases (Eagle et al., 2007; Vantamay, 2011; Esposito, 2013).

Second, organisational and structural issues, as well as leadership, coordination and control matters have been discussed within the literature available, without nevertheless presenting a clear answer. When the question of who integrates is being asked there appear to be very dissimilar responses given. Centralisation or decentralisation of communication responsibilities seems to be the main concern of academics such as Schultz (1992), McArthur and Griffin (1997), Low and Mohr (1999), Low (2000) and Vernuccio and Ceccotti (2015). On the one hand, researchers such as McArthur and Griffin (1997) and Low (2000) suggest that centralisation could be an easy and applicable way to implement integration. For example, when an individual marketing manager, often referred to as the *Integration Czar* (as Schultz named the potential role in 1992), is in charge of all possible marketing communications functions (advertising, product publicity, sales promotion, packaging and direct marketing). On the other hand, researchers such as Phelps et al. (1996) and Low and Mohr (1999) reach a contradicting conclusion. According to their studies, integration can be achieved by the decentralisation of communication responsibilities and the *'alignment through a consensus decision-making approach or team structure'* (Cornelissen, 2003, p. 225). However, at the same time, scholars such as Beverland and Luxton (2005) expressed a third argument that rather than deciding on a centralised or decentralised approach, it is expected that various organisations might develop a mixed structural style that best fits their needs in regards with IMC's implementation. As Eagle and Kitchen (2000) and Eagle et al. (2007) argue, the centralisation question has yet to be answered.

Leadership, coordination and control issues have also attracted various opposing arguments. Who leads, who coordinates and who controls the integration process has created a rather heated debate within the IMC-focused literature, which has yet to reach a common conclusion; is it the client or any of the agencies involved (Cornelissen, 2003; Swain, 2004; Homburg et al., 2015; Gambetti & Schultz, 2015). Studies conducted by Eagle and Kitchen (2000), Atkinson (2003), Han et al. (2004), Kitchen et al. (2004a), Eagle et al. (2007), Awad (2009) and Esposito (2013) have examined the issue providing conflicting suggestions while arguing that egos and agency 'turf battles' are obstructing this search for a common view. As a result, a more collaborative style of integration has yet to be adopted or even examined in further detail (Phelps et al., 1996; Beverland & Luxton, 2005; Vernuccio & Ceccotti, 2015).

Apart from the practical debates in need of additional attention, the IMC literature appears to be limited in answering the key theoretical debate as well. IMC's originality debate that derives from the uncertainty of locating IMC within marketing has yet to be provided with a clear answer. While a number of academics have claimed that IMC is a strategic combination of areas such as relationship marketing, brand management and communications systems (Baker & Hart, 2008; Thorson & Moore, 2013; Armstrong et al., 2014; Percy, 2014; Schultz et al., 2014; Batra & Keller, 2016; Keller, 2016; Kitchen, 2016), scholars such as Spotts et al. (1998), Cornelissen and Lock (2000), Fahy and Jobber (2012), Shimp and Andrews (2012) and Barger and Labrecque (2013) still claim that IMC is nothing more than a practical tool that has always been used by advertisers and marketers. As a result, some researchers have argued that IMC is only the existing marketing communications concepts repackaged and presented with new and attractive definitions but with a noticeable lack of rigorous theory behind them (Spotts et al., 1998; Shimp & Andrews, 2012; Barger & Labrecque, 2013). With Cornelissen (2001, 2003) arguing that there have been few attempts at formalising the term in order to create a rather vague notion around it, which has ulterior motives. For example, he argues, by some academics, who have 'jumped the gun' to present IMC as a panacea for various organisational difficulties, based on the fear of addressing future challenges in the business world.

On the other hand, however, scholars such as Duncan and Caywood (1996), Schultz (1996), Gambetti and Schultz (2015) and Vernuccio and Ceccotti (2015) have argued that what differentiates IMC from traditional marketing communication theories and practices is the element of strategy it contains, which distinguishes it as a new and developed discipline. IMC is not just a marketing communications process but a strategic business process (Schultz & Schultz, 1998; Schultz et al., 2014; Kitchen, 2016) which has the potential to restructure marketing and communications and remove the boundaries between them (Porcu et al., 2012; Tafesse & Kitchen, 2015). This on-going argument, which originates from the lack of identifying where IMC fits within the overall marketing literature, is the main reason behind this heated debate on IMC and is one of the most researched issues on the subject (Kliatchko, 2008; Kerr & Patti, 2015; Munoz-Leiva et al., 2015).

This debate, however, does not appear to reflect on the popularity of IMC, which as studies by Han et al. (2004), Kitchen et al. (2004a), Dmitrijeva and Batraga (2012), Esposito (2013) and Kliatchko and Schultz (2014) suggest is still believed to be *'the future of marketing communications'* (Han et al., 2004, p. 35) and *'on the agenda of all marketers'* examined (Kliatchko & Schultz, 2014, p. 386). The way in which IMC is implemented (Kitchen et al., 2004a; Eagle et al., 2007; Dmitrijeva & Batraga, 2012; Schultz et al., 2016), however, does not suggest that IMC's strategic nature or potential argued by Porcu et al. (2012), Schultz et al. (2013), Gambetti and Schultz (2015) and Kerr and Patti (2015) is in fact appreciated, as it will be further discussed later in this chapter.

It could be argued that the only clear answer to this originality debate and the practical debates discussed above, as well as to claims such as the one made by Madhavaram et al. (2016, p. 335) that *'IMC remains a controversial and theoretically underdeveloped domain within the marketing literature'*, could be provided through additional research and engaged scholarship studies on IMC's appreciation and implementation.

Conclusion

Overall, as the synthesis of the literature review so far has shown, the extensive focus on IMC's theoretical appreciation has obstructed scholars from researching IMC in practice, which, in turn, has resulted in the current relatively limited literature on the topic. Having discussed the theoretical appreciation of IMC in this chapter, the following chapter will focus on its practical appreciation and application, by exploring the perceptions and implementation of IMC according to the existing literature.

Notes

1. More than 87% of the pieces examined in this literature review (239 out of 273 peer-reviewed studies).
2. Only 15% of the IMC-focused pieces in this literature review were published after 2010 (41 out of the 273 peer-reviewed studies).
3. Less than 13% of the pieces examined in this literature view (34 out of 273 peer-reviewed studies) – full list provided in Appendix 4.
4. Fourteen out of the thirty-four studies (5% of the overall IMC-focused pieces examined in this literature review).
5. Twenty of the thirty-four studies (7% of the overall IMC-focused pieces examined in this literature review).
6. E.g. *'A sample of 500 persons was selected from Advertising Age's communications or marketing managers who worked for a "client"'* in Duncan and Everett (1993, p. 32) and *'companies that had publicly traded since at least 1987'* in Phelps et al. (1996, p. 220).
7. Brand equity is defined as *'the differential effect of brand knowledge on consumer response to the marketing of the brand'* (Keller, 1993, p. 1).

References

Ahmed, P. K. & Rafiq, M. (1995) 'The role of internal marketing in the implementation of marketing strategies', *Journal of Marketing Practice: Applied Marketing Science*, 1 (4) 32–51.
Armstrong, G., Adam, S., Denize, S. & Kotler, P. (2014) *Principles of marketing*, Sydney: Pearson.
Atkinson, C. (2003) 'Integration still a pipe dream for many', *Advertising Age*, 10 (1) 47.
Awad, T. A. (2009) IMC – An Egyptian advertising agency perspective. In P. D. Jawahar (Ed.) *Contemporary issues in management research*, (pp. 71–91), New Delhi: Excel Books.
Baker, M. & Hart, S. (2008) *The marketing book*, London: Routledge.
Barger, V. A. & Labrecque, L. (2013) 'An integrated marketing communications perspective on social media metrics', *International Journal of Integrated Marketing Communications*, 5(1) 64–76.
Barnes, B. E. (2001) 'Integrated brand communication planning: Retail applications', *Journal of Marketing Communications*, 7 (1) 11–17.
Batra, R. & Keller, K. L. (2016) 'Integrating marketing communications: New findings, new lessons and new ideas', *Journal of Marketing*, 80 (6) 122–145.
Beard, F. (1997) 'IMC use and client-ad agency relationships', *Journal of Marketing Communications*, 3 (4) 217–230.
Beverland, M. & Luxton, S. (2005) 'The projection of authenticity: Managing integrated marketing communications through strategic decoupling', *Journal of Advertising*, 34 (4) 103–116.
Burmann, C. & Zeplin, S. (2005) 'Building brand commitment: A behavioural approach to internal brand management', *Journal of Brand Management*, 12 (4) 279–300.
Caywood, C. & Ewing, R. (1991) 'Integrated marketing communications: A new master's degree concept', *Public Relations Review*, 17 (3) 237–244.
Cornelissen, J. P. (2001) 'Integrated marketing communications and the language of marketing development', *International Journal of Advertising*, 20 (4) 483–498.
Cornelissen, J. P. (2003) 'Change, continuity and progress: The concept of integrated marketing communications and marketing communications practice', *Journal of Strategic Marketing*, 11 (4) 217–234.
Cornelissen, J. P. & Lock, A. R. (2000) 'Theoretical concept or management fashion? Examining the significance of IMC', *Journal of Advertising Research*, 40 (5) 7–16.
Cova, B. (1997) 'Community and consumption: Towards a definition of the "linking value" of product or services', *European Journal of Marketing*, 31 (3/4) 297–316.
De Chernatony, L. (2001) 'A model for strategically building brands', *The Journal of Brand Management*, 9 (1) 32–44.
Dmitrijeva, K. & Batraga, A. (2012) 'Barriers to integrated marketing communications: The case of Latvia (small markets)', 8th International Strategic Management Conference, 21–23 June 2012, Barcelona, Spain.
du Plessis, E. (2005) *The advertised mind: Ground-breaking insights into how our brains respond to advertising*, London: Kogan Page.
Duncan, T. R. (2002) *IMC: Using advertising and promotion to build brands* (International Edition), New York: The McGraw-Hill.
Duncan, T. R. & Caywood, C. (1996) 'The concept, process, and evolution of integrated marketing communication'. In E. Thorson & J. Moore (Ed.) *Integrated communication: Synergy of persuasive voices*, (pp. 13–34), Mahwah, NJ: Lawrence Erlbaum Associates.

Duncan, T. R. & Everett S. E. (1993) 'Client perceptions of integrated communications', *Journal of Advertising Research*, 32 (3) 30–39.

Duncan, T. R. & Moriarty, S. E. (1998) 'A communication-based marketing model for managing relationships', *The Journal of Marketing*, 56 (2) 1–13.

Eagle, L. & Kitchen, P. J. (2000) 'IMC, brand communications, and corporate cultures: Client / advertising agency co-ordination and cohesion', *European Journal of Marketing*, 34 (5/6) 667–686.

Eagle, L., Kitchen, P. J. & Bulmer, S. (2007) 'Insights into interpreting integrated marketing communications: A two-nation qualitative comparison', *European Journal of Marketing*, 41 (7/8) 956–970.

Ebren, F., Kitchen, P. J., Aksoy, S. & Kaynak, E. (2005) 'Probing integrated marketing communications (IMC) in Turkey', *Journal of Promotion Management*, 11 (1) 127–151.

Esposito, A. (2013) 'Insights about integrated marketing communication in small-and-medium-sized Italian enterprises', *Business Systems Review*, 2 (1) 80–98.

Ewing, M. T. (2009) 'Integrated marketing communications measurement and evaluation', *Journal of Marketing Communications*, 15 (2/3) 103–117.

Ewing, M. T., de Bussy, N. M. & Caruana, A. (2000) 'Perceived agency politics and conflicts of interest as potential barriers to IMC orientation', *Journal of Marketing Communications*, 6 (1) 107–119.

Ewing, M. T., Du Pleiss, E. & Foster, C. (2001) 'Cinema advertising re-considered', *Journal of Advertising Research*, 41 (1) 78–85.

Fahy, J. & Jobber, D. (2012) *Foundations of marketing*, London: McGraw-Hill Education.

Gabrielli, V. & Balboni, B. (2010) 'SME practice towards integrated marketing communications', *Marketing Intelligence & Planning*, 28 (3) 275–290.

Gambetti, R. C. & Schultz, D. E. (2015) 'Reshaping the boundaries of marketing communication to bond with consumers', *Journal of Marketing Communications*, 21 (1) 1–4.

Geissler, G. L. (2001) 'Building customer relationships online: The web site designers' perspective', *Journal of Consumer Marketing*, 18 (6) 488–502.

Gurau, C. (2008) 'Integrated online marketing communication: Implementation and management', *Journal of Communication Management*, 12 (2) 169–184.

Hackley, C. & Kitchen, P. (1998) 'IMC: A consumer psychological perspective', *Marketing Intelligence & Planning*, 16 (3) 229–235.

Han, D., Kim, I. & Schultz, D. E. (2004) 'Understanding the diffusion of integrated marketing communications', *Journal of Advertising Research*, 44 (1) 31–45.

Hoffman, D. L., Novak, T. P. & Chatterjee, P. (1995) 'Commercial scenarios for the web: Opportunities and challenges', *Journal of Computer-Mediated Communication*, 1 (3). Available at www.ascusc.org/jcmc /v011/issue3/hoffman.html (accessed March 3, 2022).

Holt, D. B. (2002) 'Why do brands cause trouble: A dialectical theory of consumer culture and branding', *Journal of Consumer Research*, 29 (1) 70–90.

Homburg, C., Vomberg, A., Enke, M. & Grimm, P. H. (2015) 'The loss of the marketing department's influence: Is it really happening? And why worry?', *Journal of the Academy of Marketing Science*, 43 (1) 1–13.

Hutton, J. G. (1996) 'Integrated relationship-marketing communications: A key opportunity for IMC', *Journal of Marketing Communications*, 2 (3) 191–199.

Ivanov, A. E. (2012) 'The internet's impact on integrated marketing communication', *Procedia Economics and Finance*, 3 (1) 536–542.

Kallmeyer, J. & Abratt, R. (2001) 'Perceptions of IMC and organizational change among agencies in South Africa', *International Journal of Advertising*, 20 (3) 361–380.

Kamboj, S. & Rahman, Z. (2015) 'Marketing capabilities and firm performance: Literature review and future research agenda', *International Journal of Productivity and Performance Management*, 64 (8) 1041–1067.
Keegan, W., Moriarty, S. E. & Duncan, T. R. (1992) *Marketing, branding*, Hoboken, NJ: Prentice Hall.
Keller, K. L. (1996) Brand equity and integrated communication. In J. Moore & E.Thorson (Eds.) *Integrated marketing communications*, (pp. 113–142), Mahwah, NJ: Lawrence Erlbaum Associates.
Keller, K. L. (2016) 'Unlocking the power of integrated marketing communications: How integrated is your IMC program?', *Journal of Advertising*, 45(3), 286–301.
Kerr, G. F. & Patti, C. H. (2002) 'Integrated marketing communications (IMC): Where to from here' in *Australian and New Zealand Marketing Academy (ANZMAC) 2002 Conference Proceedings*, 2381–2387.
Kerr, G. F. & Patti, C. (2015) 'Strategic IMC: From abstract concept to marketing management tool', *Journal of Marketing Communications*, 21 (5) 317–339.
Kitchen, P. J. (2016) Is IMC "marketing oriented"? In L. Petruzzellis & R. S. Winer (Eds.) *Rediscovering the essentiality of marketing* (pp. 441–442), New York: Springer International Publishing.
Kitchen, P. J. & Burgmann, I. (2010) *Integrated marketing communication*, Hoboken, NJ: John Wiley & Sons, Ltd.
Kitchen, P. J. & Schultz, D. E. (1999) 'A multi-country comparison of the drive for IMC', *Journal of Advertising Research*, 39 (1) 21–38.
Kitchen, P. J. & Tao, L. (2005) 'Perceptions of integrated marketing communications: A Chinese ad and PR agency perspective', *International Journal of Advertising*, 24 (1) 51–78.
Kitchen, P. J. & Tourky, M. (2015) *Integrated communications in the postmodern era*, Hampshire: Palgrave Macmillan.
Kitchen, P. J., Brignell, J., Li, T. & Jones, G. S. (2004b) 'The emergence of IMC: A theoretical perspective', *Journal of Advertising Research*, 44 (1) 19–30.
Kitchen, P. J., Kim, I. & Schultz, D. E. (2008) 'Integrated marketing communication: Practice leads theory', *Journal of Advertising Research*, 48 (4) 531–546.
Kitchen, P. J., Schultz, D. E., Kim, I., Han, D. & Li, T. (2004a) 'Will agencies ever "get" (or understand) IMC?', *European Journal of Marketing*, 38 (11/12) 1417–1436.
Kliatchko, J. (2005) 'Towards a new definition of integrated marketing communications (IMC)', *International Journal of Advertising*, 24 (1) 7–34.
Kliatchko, J. (2008) 'Revisiting the IMC construct: A revised definition and four pillars', *International Journal of Advertising*, 27 (1) 133–160.
Kliatchko, J. G. & Schultz, D. E. (2014) 'Twenty years of IMC: A study of CEO and CMO perspectives in the Asia-Pacific region', *International Journal of Advertising*, 33 (2) 373–390.
Kotler, P. (2000) *Marketing management* (10th ed.), London: Prentice Hall International.
Laurie, S. & Mortimer, K. (2011) "IMC is dead. Long live IMC': Academics' versus practitioners' views', *Journal of Marketing Management*, 27 (13/14) 1464–1478.
Lauska, D., Laurie, S. & Mortimer, K. (2014) The management of corporate personality: An IMC perspective. In *Proceedings of the 47th Academy of Marketing Conference, AM 2014: Marketing Dimensions: People, Places and Spaces*, Bournemouth: Academy of Marketing.
Low, G. S. (2000) 'Correlates of integrated marketing communications', *Journal of Advertising Research*, 40 (3) 27–39.

Low, G. S. & Mohr, J. J. (1999) 'Setting advertising and promotion budgets in multi-brand companies', *Journal of Advertising Research*, 39 (1) 67–78.
Luck, E. & Moffatt, J. (2009) 'IMC: Has anything really changed? A new perspective on an old definition', *Journal of Marketing Communications*, 15 (5) 311–325.
Luxton, S., Reid, M. & Mavondo, F. (2015) 'Integrated marketing communication capability and brand performance', *Journal of Advertising*, 44 (1) 37–46.
Madhavaram, S., Badrinarayanan, V. & Bicen, P. (2016) Integrated marketing communication (IMC): conceptual and theoretical lacunae, foundational premises, and framework. In K. K. Kim (Ed.) *Celebrating America's pastimes: Baseball, hot dogs, apple pie and marketing?* (pp. 335–336), New York: Springer International Publishing.
Manoli, A. E. & Hodgkinson, I. R. (2019) 'The implementation of integrated marketing communication (IMC): Evidence from professional football clubs in England', *Journal of Strategic Marketing*, 28 (6) 542–563.
McArthur, D. & Griffin, T. (1997) 'A marketing management view of integrated marketing communications', *Journal of Advertising Research*, 37 (5) 19–27.
Moon, Y. S. & Franke, G. R. (2000) 'Cultural influences on agency practitioners' ethical perceptions: A comparison of Korea and the US', *Journal of Advertising*, 29 (1) 51–65.
Moriarty, S. & Schultz, D. E. (2012) Four theories of how IMC works. In S. Rodgers & E. Thorson (Eds.) *Advertising theory* (pp. 491–505), New York: Routledge.
Moriarty, S. E. (1993) The circle of synergy: Theoretical perspectives and an evolving IMC research agenda. In E. Thorson & J. Moore (Eds.) *Integrated communication: Synergy of persuasive voices*, (pp. 343–363), Mahwah, NJ: Lawrence Erlbaum Associates.
Moriarty, S. E. (1994) 'PR and IMC: The benefits of integration', *Public Relations Quarterly*, 39 (3) 38–44.
Moriarty, S. E. (1997) 'IMC needs PR's stakeholder focus', *Marketing News*, 31 (11) 7.
Muñoz-Leiva, F., Porcu, L. & Barrio-García, S. D. (2015) 'Discovering prominent themes in integrated marketing communication research from 1991 to 2012: A co-word analytic approach', *International Journal of Advertising*, 34 (4) 678–701.
Naik, P. A. & Peters, K. (2009) 'A hierarchical marketing communications model of online and offline media synergies', *Journal of Interactive Marketing*, 23 (4) 288–299.
Naik, P. A. & Raman, K. (2003) 'Understanding the impact of synergy in multimedia communications', *Journal of Marketing Research*, 40 (4) 375–388.
Ouwersloot, H. & Duncan, T. (2008) *Integrated marketing communications*, London: McGraw-Hill Education.
Owen, R. & Humphrey, P. (2009) 'The structure of online marketing communication channels', *Journal of Management and Marketing Research*, 2, 54–62.
Peltier, J. W., Schibrowsky, J. A. & Schultz, D. E. (2003) 'Interactive integrated marketing communication: Combining the power of IMC, the new media and database marketing', *International Journal of Advertising*, 22 (1) 93–116.
Percy, L. (2014) *Strategic integrated marketing communications*, New York: Routledge.
Pettigrew, A. M. (2001) 'Management research after modernism', *British Journal of Management*, 12 (1) 61–S70.
Pettigrew, L. S. (2000/2001) 'If IMC is so good, why isn't it being implemented?: Barriers to IMC adoption in corporate America', *Journal of Integrated Communications*, 11 (1) 29–37.
Phelps, J. E., Harris, T. E. & Johnson, E. (1996) 'Exploring decision-making approaches and responsibility for developing marketing communications strategy', *Journal of Business Research*, 37 (3) 217–223.

Phelps, J. E., Plumley, J. & Johnson, E. (1994) 'Integrated marketing communications: Who is doing what?' In K. W. King (Ed.) *Proceedings of the 1994 Conference of the American Academy of Advertising* (pp. 143–145), Athens, GA: University of Georgia.

Pickton, D. & Broderick, A. (2001) *Integrated marketing communications*, Essex: Pearson Education.

Porcu, L., del Barrio-García, S. & Kitchen, P. J. (2012) 'How integrated marketing communications (IMC) works? A theoretical review and an analysis of its main drivers and effects/¿Cómo funciona la Comunicación Integrada de Marketing (CIM)? Una revisión teórica y un análisis de sus antecedentes y efectos', *Comunicación y sociedad*, 25 (1) 313–348.

Rafiq, M. & Ahmed, P. K. (2000) 'Advances in the internal marketing concept: Definition, synthesis and extension', *Journal of Services Marketing*, 14 (6) 449–462.

Reid, M. (2002) 'Building strong brands through the management of integrated marketing communications', *International Journal of Wine Marketing*, 14 (3) 37–52.

Reid, M., Johnson, T., Ratcliffe, M., Skrip, K. & Wilson, J. (2001) 'Integrated marketing communications in the Australian and New Zealand wine industry', *International Journal of Advertising*, 20 (2) 239–262.

Reinold, T. & Tropp, J. (2012) 'Integrated marketing communications: How can we measure its effectiveness?', *Journal of Marketing Communications*, 18 (2) 113–132.

Rose, P. B. (1996) 'Practitioner opinions and interests regarding integrated marketing communications in selected Latin American countries', *Journal of Marketing Communications*, 2 (3) 125–139.

Schultz, D. E. (1992) 'Integrated marketing communications: The status of integrated marketing communications programs the US today', *Journal of Promotion Management*, 1 (1) 99–104.

Schultz, D. E. (1993a) 'Integrated marketing communications: Maybe definition is in the point of view', *Marketing News*, January 18.

Schultz, D. E. (1993b) 'We simply can't afford to go back to mass marketing', *Marketing News*, February 15.

Schultz, D. E. (1995) 'The six scariest letters in the marketing alphabet', *Marketing News*, No. 20, November 6.

Schultz, D. E. (1996) 'IMC has become a global concept', *Marketing News*, 30 (5) 6.

Schultz, D. E. (2000) 'Structural flaws dash marcom plans', *Marketing News*, 34 (3) 14.

Schultz, D. E. (2001) 'Campaign approach shouldn't exist in IMC', *Marketing News*, 35 (5) 11–13.

Schultz, D. E. (2004) 'IMC receives more appropriate definition', *Marketing News*, 38 (15) 8–9.

Schultz, D. E., Chu, G. & Zhao, B. (2016) 'IMC in an emerging economy: The Chinese perspective', *International Journal of Advertising*, 35 (2) 200–215.

Schultz, D. E., Kerr, G., Kim, I. & Patti, C. (2007) 'In search of a theory of integrated marketing communication', *Journal of Advertising Education*, 11 (2) 21–31.

Schultz, D. E., Kim, I. & Kang, K. (2014) Integrated marketing communication research. In H. Cheng (Ed.) *The handbook of international advertising research* (pp. 455–483), London: Wiley Blackwell.

Schultz, D. E. & Kitchen, P. J. (1997) 'Integrated marketing communications in US advertising agencies: An exploratory study', *Journal of Advertising Research*, 37 (5) 7–18.

Schultz, D. E. & Kitchen, P. J. (2000b) A response to 'Theoretical concept or management fashion?', *Journal of Advertising Research*, 40 (5) 17–21.

Schultz, D. E. & Patti, C. H. (2009) 'The evolution of IMC: IMC in a customer driven marketplace', *Journal of Marketing Communications*, 15 (2–3) 75–84.
Schultz, D. E., Patti, C. H. & Kitchen, P. J. (2013) *The evolution of integrated marketing communications: The customer-driven marketplace*, London: Routledge.
Schultz, D. E. & Schultz, H. F. (1998) 'Transitioning marketing communication into the twenty-first century', *Journal of Marketing Communications*, 4 (1) 9–26.
Schultz, D. E. & Schultz, H. F. (2004) *IMC: The next generation*, New York: McGraw-Hill.
Schultz, D. E., Tannenbaum, S. I. & Lauterborn, R. F. (1993) *Integrated marketing communications: Putting it together and making it work*, Lincolnwood: NTC Business Books.
Seric, M., Gil-Saura, I. & Ruiz-Molina, M. E. (2014) 'How can integrated marketing communications and advanced technology influence the creation of customer-based brand equity? Evidence from the hospitality industry', *International Journal of Hospitality Management*, 39 (1) 144–156.
Shimp, T. A. & Andrews, J. C. (2012) *Advertising promotion and other aspects of integrated marketing communications* (9th ed.), Mason: Cengage Learning.
Smith, P. R. & Taylor, J. (2004) *Marketing communications: An integrated approach*, London: Kogan Page Publishers.
Spotts, H. E., Lambert, D. R. & Joyce, M. L. (1998) 'Marketing déjà vu: The discovery of integrated marketing communications', *Journal of Marketing Education*, 20 (3) 210–218.
Stammerjohan, C., Wood, C. M., Chang, Y. & Thorson, E. (2005) 'An empirical investigation of the interaction between publicity, advertising, and previous brand attitude and knowledge', *Journal of Advertising*, 34 (4) 55–67.
Swain, W. N. (2004) 'Perceptions of IMC after a decade of development: Who's at the wheel, and how can we measure success?', *Journal of Advertising Research*, 44 (1) 46–65.
Tafesse, W. & Kitchen, P. J. (2015) 'IMC–an integrative review', *International Journal of Advertising*, 1–17.
Thorson, E. & Moore, J. (2013) *Integrated communication: Synergy of persuasive voices*, New York: Psychology Press.
Tsai, S. P. (2005) 'Integrated marketing as management of holistic consumer experience', *Business Horizons*, 48 (5) 431–441.
Valos, M. J., Ewing, M. T. & Powell, I. H. (2010) 'Practitioner prognostications on the future of online marketing', *Journal of Marketing Management*, 26 (3–4) 361–376.
Van de Ven, A. H. (2007) *Engaged scholarship: A guide for organizational and social research*, Oxford: Oxford University Press.
Vantamay, S. (2011) 'Performances and measurement of integrated marketing communications (IMC) of Advertisers in Thailand', *Journal of Global Management*, 1 (1) 1–12.
Vernuccio, M. & Ceccotti, F. (2015) 'Strategic and organisational challenges in the integrated marketing communication paradigm shift: A holistic vision', *European Management Journal*, 33 (6) 438–449.
Wang, A. (2008) 'The effects of integrating advertising and product publicity on web usability', *Journal of Website Promotion*, 3 (1–2) 84–101.

Chapter 3

Integrated Marketing Communications Perceptions and Implementation

Introduction

The synthesis of the literature review discussed in the previous chapter offered a more detailed view of IMC, by exploring the state of its literature and the theoretical appreciation it has received. It also revealed a number of areas lacking substantial research regarding IMC. First, IMC's implementation overall is under-researched, with more studies focusing on its theoretical aspects. As a result, practitioners' perceptions of IMC are also understudied, in line with the overall lack of engaged scholarship noted. It is these two areas that will be discussed in this chapter, along with the marketing communications practices that are associated with IMC's implementation and finally, IMC in sport in general and football in particular, in an attempt to underline the limited research on the subject domain and appreciate the need for further study.

Practitioners' Perceptions of IMC

As it was mentioned in the previous chapter, limited research exists on practitioners' perceptions of IMC. These perceptions have been studied through the examination of practitioners' views on IMC and what it represents, and will be discussed in this section in detail. Given that literature on practitioners' perceptions has been limited on the examination of various narrow samples (using 3–25 case studies) in a small number of countries (half of which are developed and English-speaking), the findings of the review of these studies cannot be extended to all marketing professionals or marketing agencies in the countries examined, or be perceived as representative of the current status of IMC worldwide. Their examination, however, can provide some valuable insights to practitioners' perceptions of IMC, which informs its implementation. At the same time, as Gould (2004, p. 66) pointed out: *'particular practitioner interpretations are just as important as general theoretical ones'*.

As far as definitions are concerned, practitioners were presented with the earlier one developed by the AAAA (Schultz, 1993a). Their reaction to the definition *'appears to be of some agreement but not of actual conviction'*

DOI: 10.4324/9781003140238-3

(Schultz & Kitchen, 1997, p. 12), or as Kitchen and Schultz (1999, p. 26) suggest: '*the definition of IMC was supported but not overwhelmingly*'. The lack of strong agreement by the practitioners in these studies is caused, according to their arguments, by the limited emphasis on the consumer and product centric nature of IMC, as well as by the complete absence of measurement or quantifiable analysis of the term.

Overall, there seems to be a stronger agreement that IMC is '*the coordination of communication activities*' than '*a strategic brand business process*' (Kitchen et al., 2004a, p. 1426). In more detail, the delivery of unified messages is, according to the practitioners, more representative of what IMC is, than a development and direction tool to brand strategy, or a means to organise the actual business or firm. Surprisingly, even though IMC as the '*coordination of communications disciplines*' appears to find advertising agency practitioners (in the UK and New Zealand – Eagle et al., 2007, p. 961) in strong agreement, the '*coordination of advertising and PR programmes*' is not regarded as equally important (Eagle et al., 2007, p. 961). Kitchen et al. (2004a) claim that this phenomenon might owe its existence to the popular *turf wars* between different disciplines' agencies that were presented above as a key challenge to IMC's implementation.

Practitioners' comments appear to evolve around the same basic principles of what IMC should be, providing the reader with a clearer picture of their perceptions. First, the consumer and product centric nature of IMC is underlined by most practitioners as one of its fundamental elements (Schultz & Kitchen, 1997; Kitchen & Schultz, 1999; Reid, 2003; Eagle et al., 2007). The consumer in general and the loyal consumer in particular are presented as the starting point of the whole process (Han et al., 2004; Kliatchko & Schultz, 2014). Second, the results-oriented aspect of IMC is emphasised, presenting the need for measurability or quantification analysis to be included in the definition (Ewing et al., 2000; Han et al., 2004; Eagle et al., 2007; Schultz et al., 2016). Its cost-effectiveness is also underlined not only as a result of the discipline overlap but also as an important drive for quantitative results measurement and evaluation (Kitchen & Schultz, 1999; Kitchen et al., 2004a). Third, IMC's audience is addressed in various ways. The importance of both internal and external audience is put forward, in alignment with the emphasis on the connection between IMC and relationship marketing (Kitchen & Tao, 2005; Awad, 2009; Dmitrijeva & Batraga, 2012). The multiple points of contacts are also mentioned in later studies, where the attention is drawn to additional stakeholder groups (Eagle & Kitchen, 2000; Esposito, 2013; Kliatchko & Schultz, 2014).

The creativity needed in order for IMC to be implemented is underlined as an important element that the definition seems to have missed, according to practitioners (Schultz & Kitchen, 1997; Kitchen & Schultz, 1999). Practitioners suggest that integrating all messages requires a level of creativity, from both a practical and an executional point of view, which is currently not acknowledged in its definition. Both IMC's strategic and tactical nature are mentioned by the practitioners, but more emphasis tends to be drawn on its practical aspects and outcomes. Notably, IMC's importance as a strategic business process is met with a strong agreement (e.g. Eagle et al., 2007; Kitchen et al., 2008; Kliatchko & Schultz, 2014; Schultz et al., 2016), while in Kitchen and Schultz' study (1999) in advertising agencies in India, it was the practitioners that added the word *strategic* to the original definition provided to them. Finally, the *'how'* factor is being portrayed as an important element of IMC, that, especially in later studies, is believed to be crucial in facilitating its implementation (Dmitrijeva & Batraga, 2012; Esposito, 2013; Schultz et al., 2016).

Interestingly, the examination of these studies suggests that most of the current trends in new and social media are absent from practitioners' views. That could be because the majority of the studies analysed were conducted more than a decade ago, resulting in the exclusion of what is now perceived as a ground-breaking change factor in marketing (Shankar & Hollinger, 2007; Keller, 2009; Shankar & Balasubramanian, 2009) and in IMC (Gurau, 2008; Barger & Labrecque, 2013; Seric et al., 2014).

IMC's Implementation

Apart from analysing practitioners' perceptions of IMC, the studies involving practitioners' participation also examined IMC's implementation, providing valuable insights to the extent to which IMC is in fact applied in the geographic areas investigated. As it was mentioned above, these insights are limited by the lack of empirical research on IMC's implementation, which has been emphasised repeatedly by academics such as Kliatchko and Schultz (2014), Schultz et al. (2016), Tafesse and Kitchen (2016) and Ewing et al. (2000, pp. 107–108) who argued that:

> While the conceptualisation of integrated marketing communications (IMC) ... is well documented, ... Detailed work on its practical implementation is less prolific.

Examining the extent to which IMC is implemented in practice is therefore limited on the number of geographic areas, as well as on the nature of the companies examined. In fact, in the studies examining IMC's implementation, the companies and agencies researched are selected based on factors such as size, market share or profitability, with the researchers mostly opting for the bigger and more advanced organisations in each region (Kitchen et al., 2008; Kliatchko & Schultz, 2014). These factors need to be taken into consideration when examining IMC's implementation.

According to the research available, IMC appears to be on the agenda of all marketing agencies and most client companies that have been included in the studies (Kitchen & Schultz, 1999; Eagle & Kitchen, 2000; Kitchen et al., 2004a; Kitchen et al., 2008; Kliatchko & Schultz, 2014; Schultz et al., 2016). The services they provide and the amount of time and money clients are willing to invest in IMC differ both between countries and between different disciplines' agencies; nevertheless, both numbers seem to be increasing. According to practitioners, interest on IMC is expected to grow rather rapidly within the next few years

(Han et al., 2004; Dmitrijeva & Batraga, 2012; Schultz et al., 2016), which underlines the need for further study on IMC and its implementation. Based on the fact that a decline in IMC-focused publications has been noted, this need for further research appears to be unanswered.

A cross analysis of the studies would suggest that the vast majority of the organisations researched are implementing IMC, but only on an executional or tactical level. This assertion is made, since a number of the studies, such as the ones by Han et al. (2004), Kitchen et al. (2004a), Kitchen et al. (2008) and Kliatchko and Schultz (2014), use the IMC development stages to identify the extent to which IMC is implemented and thus pinpoint the IMC level or stage to which the companies belong, based on each stage's criteria. Kitchen and Schultz (1999) further developed the study of the IMC levels by introducing the stages in IMC development, which links the IMC levels or stages with the criteria through which a company's practices can indicate the level or stage where it belongs. According to the empirical studies on IMC's implementation that are using the IMC stages (such as Han et al., 2004; Kitchen et al., 2004a; Kitchen et al., 2008; Kliatchko & Schultz, 2014), it appears that the majority of the organisations examined are in fact in stages one and two, 'tactical coordination of marketing communications' and 'redefining the scope of marketing communications', respectively (Figure 3.1).

An additional method to identify the level or stage of IMC to which each company belongs would be to use Kiatchko's (2008) interplay between the IMC levels and pillars. In his work, this interplay between the levels and pillars of IMC is introduced, which suggests that the emphasis placed by a company on the content, channels, stakeholders or results of marketing communications indicates the IMC level in which it belongs. It is argued that all four pillars may be present in each of the four levels of IMC, but with one pillar emphasised more at each level. According to Kiatchko (2008), level 1 emphasises content, level 2 channels, level 3 stakeholders and level 4 results. Since the interplay was presented after most of the studies examining practitioners' views had been conducted, it has not been used as an IMC level identification method yet. As it will be discussed later on in this study, the present research is using both Kitchen and Schultz' (1999) and

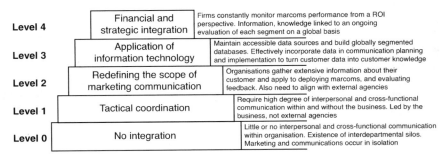

Figure 3.1 Five levels of IMC (adapted from Schultz and Schultz, 1998, p. 18).

Kliatchko's (2008) methods to classify the organisations examined (football clubs) in IMC levels.

The empirical studies on IMC's implementation that are using the IMC stages do not provide additional details on the number of the client or agency organisations that belong in each level; however, the reluctance to progress to the more advanced levels is repeatedly emphasised (Kitchen & Schultz, 1999; Kitchen et al., 2004a; Eagle et al., 2007). In fact, as it was often described, practitioners '*displayed a remarkable proclivity to be anchored*' in the early stages (Eagle et al. 2007, p. 965), and do not provide the researchers with evidence of endeavours to progress integration further. The word '*anchored*' is actually used repeatedly by the academics studying IMC's implementation. For example, the word is used by Kitchen and Schultz (1999, pp. 34–35) who state that:

> *The majority of firms are anchored in either stage 1 or stage 2 scenarios. Some are moving into stage 3, but very few (a handful in today's world) have moved to stage 4*

and by Kitchen et al. (2004a, p. 1433) who argue that companies '*appear to be anchored in stages 1 and 2 of IMC development*'.

A study by Kliatchko and Schultz (2014, p. 386) suggests that even after 20 years of IMC research (as their study's title underlines) the vast majority of the companies '*are definitely well within levels 1 and 2 in the way they practice IMC*'. In their research, it is argued that the large multinational companies might be considered as part of level 3, while only a few of the large global firms meet the criteria for level 4. As the analysis suggests, even though IMC is widely recognised for its potential and, as academics claim, change is expected in the marketplace, IMC's implementation in reality still remains in the early stages.

Unlike early studies on the topic, such as the one conducted by Rose (1996), which suggested that IMC had not been adopted fully by the marketplace (with practitioners yet to be convinced on the idea of integration), later studies, such as the ones by Kliatchko and Schultz (2014) or Schultz et al. (2016), categorically argue that all organisations examined implement IMC, even on a tactical level. It can therefore be argued that the marketplace is in fact progressing and that IMC is gradually being adopted by more organisations. However, Kliatchko and Schultz' (2014) and Schultz et al.'s (2016) argument on IMC's widespread implementation is worth examining further.

According to their findings, all companies examined (which represent the most successful or larger client and agency firms in each country) can be placed within the four IMC levels, with the vast majority of the organisations concentrated on levels 1 and 2. One could argue that the examination of a less uniform sample of client and agency organisations (which could include smaller and less successful companies) would possibly yield more diverse results regarding integration. A more diverse sample could potentially include organisations that do not practice integration and thus do not meet the criteria needed in order to fit in any of the above-mentioned IMC levels. Consequently, a question could be raised on the applicability of the four IMC levels in examining a more diverse sample, such as a full sector of an industry, which would consist of organisations of varying sizes and success levels. It can therefore be suggested that the levels or stages of IMC might not be able to depict the IMC implementation or lack of it in these organisations accurately.

In other words, the four IMC levels framework can currently identify the extent to which IMC is implemented, but cannot capture a possible question on whether IMC is in fact implemented. In order for a wider appreciation of IMC's implementation to be achieved, the question behind the examination of the levels or stages of IMC needs to be reformed, so that the focus is shifted to both whether a company can fall under any of the suggested levels and which one of them.

If a company does not implement IMC and cannot be accounted as belonging in any of the four levels, suggested by Schultz and Schultz (1998), an additional level has to be created in order for this to be captured, something that Manoli and Hodgkinson (2019) have also touched upon in their work. The author of this book suggests for a level or stage zero to be added preceding level 1 that can illustrate the stage in which a company that is not implementing IMC belongs to. The five levels of IMC framework are better presented in Figure 3.1. The arrow next to the figure demonstrates the phases organisations go through in their efforts to implement IMC, from no practice of integration to financial and strategic integration. As Kitchen and Schultz (1999) explain in their work, the stages or levels are not rigid and their boundaries are not inflexible and definite. Likewise, level 0 does not have strictly defined boundaries, which means that the companies that are captured within it might demonstrate practices that cross over with level 1. The overall practice within each company, however, is one that can be better described as not practising integration.

Adding level 0 to Kliatchko's (2008) interplay of levels and pillars of IMC would enhance this interplay with an extra level, in which all pillars may be present, but none is emphasised more than the others. In more detail, level 0 describes the stage in which a company does not practice or attempts to practice any integration of the marketing and communications elements. Following Kliatchko's (2008) study's suggestions, level 0 would describe the stage in which consistency within the content of the messages of the organisation is not achieved (content), the channels through which the organisation communicates are not coordinated (channels), the target audience of the organisation is not researched or understood (stakeholders) and the marketing and communications efforts' results are not measured (results).

Based on this interplay of the pillars and the five levels of IMC, if the emphasis of an organisation in regard to marketing communications can be identified, the stage or level of IMC in which this organisation belongs to can be also pinpointed. The updated interplay between the levels and pillars of IMC could then be used in order to categorise more diverse companies, such as the ones comprising a full industry sector, to the five levels of IMC. The five IMC levels and their interplay with the IMC pillars are used in this study, as it will be presented in more detail in Chapter 6.

Additional research is required in order for the five IMC levels and their interplay to be investigated. Further research could also shed light on the reasons behind this restriction of IMC's implementation to stages 1 and 2 that has been repeatedly mentioned (Kitchen & Schultz, 1999; Han et al., 2004; Kitchen et al., 2004a; Eagle et al., 2007; Kliatchko & Schultz, 2014; Schultz et al., 2016). According to these studies, a number of reasons could be considered as possible factors such as the confusion on understanding what IMC is, the absence of a clear and widely-respected measurement process and the continuous debate on who leads and controls the integration process (Han et al., 2004; Kitchen et al., 2004a; Dmitrijeva & Batraga, 2012). According to Eagle et al. (2007, p. 966), this reluctance or anchoring in the early stages of IMC's implementation could be traced back to the driving force of integration, since it is suggested that:

> *Despite this apparent anchoring location this does not mean that the full potential of IMC has not been recognised or that it is deliberately ignored. It is just that ad agencies will do only as they are instructed by the client organisations.*

Since the clients are sitting on the drivers' seat of integration (Caywood & Ewing, 1991), agency executives, who have been the main focus of the available research on IMC's implementation, have been merely following their lead, or occasionally lack of it. Additional research focusing on clients is therefore required in order for IMC's implementation to be examined in more detail. As it is suggested by Eagle et al. (2007, p. 967):

> *The spotlight of research attention now needs to be turn away from ad agencies, for at best the light they shed is borrowed from the clients they serve. Focus on clients may reveal just where IMC is.*

This suggestion to examine client and agency organisations separately and appreciate the client as the driving force of integration (that could be potentially 'accused' of hindering IMC's implementation) has been taken into consideration in this study. The following section will introduce and examine the *practitioners' strategy paradox* in order to present and further investigate IMC's appreciation by practitioners and the way it has informed its implementation.

The *Practitioners' Strategy Paradox*

As it was presented in the IMC's implementation section above, an inconsistency exists between the way in which IMC is appreciated by the practitioners in theory and the way in which it is implemented in practice. In more detail, as the practitioners' perception section suggests, practitioners appreciate the strategic value of IMC, but as it was shown in the IMC's implementation section above, their application of IMC remains on a merely executional level. This inconsistency has been encountered and noted by academics conducting research on IMC's implementation (such as Caywood & Ewing, 1991; Kitchen et al., 2004a; Eagle et al., 2007; Dmitrijeva & Batraga, 2012; Schultz et al., 2016); however, no attempt has been made to define the phenomenon or to examine it in more detail, with the exception of Manoli and Hodgkinson (2019).

As it is argued in this study, most academics appear to focus on the 'best-case' scenario of integration, neglecting any other possible scenarios. The author of this book, in line with her approach of a more critical engaged scholarship and following on the footsteps of Manoli and Hodgkinson (2019), can draw additional attention on these scenarios, starting with the *practitioners' strategy paradox*, which can be defined as:

> *the discrepancy between the theoretical support of IMC's strategic nature and the lack of practical evidence of strategy in its implementation.*

This paradox could be considered one of the key elements behind IMC's lack of progress over the last few years. As scholars have argued, IMC in practice still remains in levels 1 and 2, with little or no evidence of endeavours to progress to levels 3 and 4 (Kitchen et al., 2004a; Kitchen & Tao, 2005; Eagle et al., 2007; Dmitrijeva & Batraga, 2012), where the true benefits of IMC can be appreciated according to Kliatchko (2008). In other words, despite the widely recognised belief among practitioners that IMC has more than operational value and is in fact a strategic concept and process (Kitchen & Schultz, 1999; Eagle et al., 2007; Kitchen et al., 2008; Kliatchko & Schultz, 2014; Schultz et al., 2016), its implementation today remains predominantly at an executional level, with marketers still relying on the methods and processes they have been using before the emergence of IMC.

Linking the integration scenarios presented above with Schultz and Schultz' (1998) four IMC levels framework, an additional observation can be made. Since IMC is implemented strategically and to its full potential only on level 4, the scenario of full strategic integration can be studied in organisations that belong in this final level. Consequently, the *practitioners' strategy paradox*, which suggests that IMC is not implemented strategically, can be observed in companies belonging in any other level (levels 1, 2 and 3), according to Kitchen and Schultz' (1999) analysis.

At the same time, according to Eagle et al. (2007, p. 958) practitioners:

> *display a superficial philosophical commitment to it (IMC), but maintain continued reliance on existing forms of promotional juxtaposition.*

and alter their practice of IMC in order to fit their specific talents, capabilities and needs. Eagle et al. argue that practitioners are still campaign and project focused, trying to achieve the goals set on a short-term scale. Therefore, the continuity suggested through IMC's strategic implementation is not in fact considered a priority in their efforts, mainly because long-term planning remains a rather uncommon practice, irrespectively of its importance regarding a company's brand and corporate positioning (Schultz, 2001; Reid, 2002, 2003).

This anchoring in their practices, however, emphasises the paradox defined above, since practitioners claim to believe in the strategic nature of IMC (Kitchen & Schultz, 1999; Eagle et al., 2007; see section 2.5, p. 38). Consequently, examining this paradox raises the question of intention behind this lack of strategy regarding IMC's implementation. This question can be then traced back to scholars' claims that practitioners do not truly understand IMC, regardless of their statements (Dmitrijeva & Batraga, 2012; Schultz et al., 2016), that their level of appreciation of the theory has not reached an adequate level of maturity (Rose, 1996; Han et al. 2004; Kitchen & Tao, 2005), or that their demonstrated belief that IMC as a strategic nature is nothing more but *'superficial'* and *'philosophical'* (Kitchen et al., 2004a; Eagle et al., 2007, p. 958). This question of intention has to be addressed in order for the reasons behind the paradox to be examined. In other words, the question that needs to be investigated is whether the *strategy paradox* exists intentionally or unintentionally.

According to Eagle and Kitchen (2000, p. 683) an additional factor that can justify why the paradox exists unintentionally should be considered:

> *Respondents (both client and agency marketers) felt that IMC has significant potential for the future but that progression up a fairly steep learning and developmental curve was needed, coupled with significant client-side restructuring.*

As a result, it can be argued that the paradox exists unintentionally, while the practitioners are in the process of achieving strategic integration. While the organisations are within this transitional state or learning and development curve, strategic integration cannot be achieved, despite the practitioners' knowledge and appreciation of IMC's potential.

The possible answers to the question of intention, according to the literature available, can be summarised as:

- unintentionally due to the lack of knowledge and understanding of IMC (Rose, 1996; Han et al. 2004; Kitchen & Tao, 2005; Dmitrijeva & Batraga, 2012; Schultz et al., 2016),
- unintentionally while the organisations are in the learning and transitioning curve (Eagle & Kitchen, 2000), and
- intentionally, in which the practitioners are fully aware of the potential of IMC but are still reluctant to implement it fully (Kitchen & Schultz, 1999; Kitchen et al., 2004a; Eagle et al., 2007).

All three possible reasons behind the paradox will be explained below, in relation to the possibility of reaching strategic integration.

Unintentionally due to the Lack of Knowledge

The following information has to be taken into consideration regarding the unintentional claim due to the lack of concise knowledge of IMC. First, the majority of the practitioners, according to the literature, have stated that they do not feel they have truly captured what IMC is and what it entails (Han et al., 2004; Schultz et al., 2016). As a result, questions can be raised regarding the practitioners' agreement on various statements that represent IMC such as '*strategic brand business process*' discussed above. Interestingly, in Han et al.'s study (2004, p. 35) all agency and client marketers viewed IMC as a necessity in the marketplace, despite the fact that 1.8% of the agency marketers and 20.2% of the client marketers did not know what IMC is. In other words, practitioners might state that they agree with the strategic nature of IMC, while in reality not possessing adequate knowledge of what IMC is, or without having a consensus on what they view IMC as (Laurie & Mortimer, 2011). In this case, their inability to progress further to the next stages of IMC's implementation can be considered unintentional.

However, Kitchen et al. (2004a, p. 1433) argue that '*there is strong evidence that agency practitioners know what IMC is and how it can be operationalised on behalf of the clients*' (referring to UK advertising and PR agency marketers). This complements Han et al.'s (2004, p. 35) suggestion that agency practitioners' understanding is better than clients'.

On the other hand, Dmitrijeva and Batraga (2012) suggest that the IMC concept is not truly understood by client marketers (in the Latvian market), especially in smaller organisations. Rose (1996, p. 137) adds that client marketers in Latin America '*haven't reached the same level of conviction as agency practitioners; it (IMC) is not yet as important to them*'. Taking this evidence into consideration, client and agency practitioners should be examined separately in relation to the unintentional claim behind this paradox.

According to the studies available which suggest that practitioners are not fully aware of what IMC is, it could be claimed that client practitioners have unintentionally been '*glued*' to applying IMC only at an executional level, due to their lack of understanding and appreciation of the strategic nature of IMC. At the same time, and despite agency practitioners' understanding and appreciation, IMC's implementation on their behalf has been obstructed by the fact that clients are driving the integration process. As Schultz and Kitchen (1997, p. 15) argue: '*agencies, no matter how skilled or capable, simply can't integrate a client's marketing communications programs unless the client leads the way*'.

Since clients are leading the integration and in this case, in fact obstructing it from reaching a more strategic level (by insisting on a tactical integration), it could be argued that this is linked to the original claim that formed the paradox. As a result, a vicious circle is created in which the paradox is caused by the lack of knowledge that still drives IMC's implementation and impedes it from reaching a strategic level.

Unintentionally While on Transitional Stage

As Eagle and Kitchen (2000) suggested, a less documented reason behind the anchoring of practices to a non-strategic level is not related to the lack of knowledge on behalf of client or agency practitioners. In fact, it can be argued that knowledge and appreciation of IMC's full potential exists and could be even considered the drive for integration as far as this claim is concerned. In this case, the paradox seems to exist while the organisation is in the process of transitioning in order to be able to fully implement IMC. Consequently, while the client or agency organisation is in this learning and development curve, the paradox exists, but only for the duration of this transitional stage.

It could be argued, therefore, that the paradox exists for a potentially limited amount of time and consequently will cease to exist once this transitional phase is over. It could also be suggested that when the learning and development curve is over, the organisation will be able to overcome the paradox and implement IMC strategically. Eagle and Kitchen (2000) emphasise that both agency and client organisations will have to go through a difficult reformation process, which might require a significant and more laborious restructuring project from the clients' side, in order for strategic integration to be achieved. This restructuring phase resembles the organisational redesign suggested by Pettigrew (2000/2001), Schultz and Schultz (2004) and Christensen et al. (2008a) in order for any structural barriers to be overcome, and as a result, for strategic implementation of IMC to be achieved. Unfortunately, more information on this transitional stage is not provided in the studies, which could suggest that additional research on the topic is needed in order for light to be shed on its characteristics and duration. This need for further research on the matter comes in direct contrast with the decline in IMC-focused publications that was noted in the previous chapter.

Intentionally due to Reluctance

As far as the intentional claim is concerned, Eagle et al. (2007, p. 958) claim that marketers demonstrate nothing more but a *'superficial'* and *'philosophical'* attitude towards the strategic nature of IMC, while intentionally opting for already known and applied practices. This approach has not been studied further; however, taking into consideration the fact that clients are driving integration (Caywood & Ewing, 1991; Kallmeyer & Abratt, 2001; Kitchen et al., 2004a; Eagle et al., 2007; Schultz et al., 2016), it could be argued that agency practitioners' reliance is nothing more but the execution of clients' orders and, thus, this dependence is in reality unintentional on their behalf. Nevertheless, and regardless of whether the marketers are employed by an agency or a client organisation, the intentional claim sheds light on an area that is also under-researched, the existence or lack of willingness and motivation to implement IMC strategically.

As it was discussed in the previous chapter, there exist a number of challenges and obstacles to IMC's implementation, which could be considered the reasons behind this reluctance. For example, the lack of a clear measurement process whose cost and leadership would be supported by either the agency or the client organisation (Eagle et al., 2007; Awad, 2009; Vantamay, 2011). Additionally, it can be suggested that this reluctance can be traced back to the arguments of lack of cross-disciplinary skills of both client and agency marketers reported by Moriarty (1994). In her work it was argued that since practitioners do not possess the required skills, they choose to apply methods and techniques that they feel comfortable with, and thus select already applied practices and avoid strategic integration. Consequently, the campaign focus that produces quick and easy results is maintained and preferred, over the long-term strategic cross-discipline approach (Schultz, 2001). Finally, the lack of resources, time and effort to be invested in conducting the changes needed within each organisation that could foster strategic integration has been noted as an additional factor that could make practitioners reluctant in implementing IMC (Eagle et al., 2007). This decision could therefore suggest that practitioners would intentionally overlook the merits of strategic integration (Smith & Taylor, 2002).

Additional research is needed in order to pinpoint and understand any other possible factors that could be causing the paradox intentionally, which would also assist in identifying ways to overcome it. Examining the intentional claim would require thorough research on practitioners' practices and rationale behind their choices, as well as details on organisational factors of influence (e.g. organisational structure) that could underline the power relations guiding the individuals in deciding on whether and to what extent to integrate.

From the data available, it could be suggested that the question of intention behind the paradox cannot be answered without additional research on the topic. Examining the paradox in more detail could provide information on its parameters, the reasons behind it and the ways in which this discrepancy can be addressed and overcome. Based on the various dissimilarities originating from the nature of each role a marketer has (agency or client), it is also expected that examining the paradox separately for clients and for agencies would provide clearer answers. Taking the fact that the clients are driving integration (Kallmeyer & Abratt, 2001; Eagle et al., 2007; Schultz et al., 2016) into consideration, it can be argued that examining client practitioners would allow for richer insights in explaining the paradox, especially regarding its unintentional existence and the vicious circle of integration.

Taking all the above into consideration, it can again be argued that IMC's appreciation and implementation remain understudied, with academic research on the matter still focusing on a rather limited sample and pointing to a single integration scenario, *full strategic integration*. Even though an inconsistency exists between the way in which IMC is appreciated and implemented in reality, the *practitioners' strategy paradox*, an additional integration scenario which was defined and discussed in this section, has not been studied in detail before. Subsequently, the question of intention behind it has not been explored, potentially impeding the progress of implementing IMC. Based on the narrow focus of the literature available, it could be argued that additional research on a more diverse

48 Perceptions and Implementation

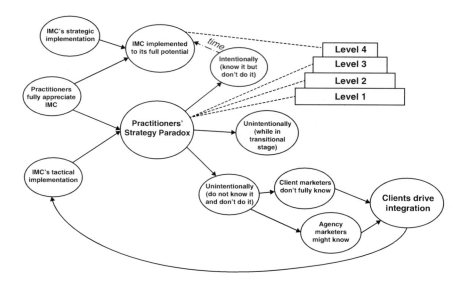

Figure 3.2 Interplay between integration scenarios and IMC levels.

sample, such as a full industry sector, could help identify additional scenarios that are yet to be detected and studied.

In order to summarise the integration scenarios and the discussion on them and link them with the IMC levels discussed in the previous chapter, Figure 3.2 offers a more detailed understanding of IMC's implementation in practice. Figure 3.2 illustrates this interplay between the scenarios and the IMC levels in which they can be studied. As it can be seen in the figure, the additional analysis on the question of intention behind the paradox is added, in order for the potential to progress to strategic integration from the unintentional transitional stage over a period of time to be demonstrated. As an antithesis, the vicious circle of integration, presented at the bottom of the figure, does not lead the organisations to *full strategic integration*, but returns them to IMC's tactical implementation and therefore to the *practitioners' strategy paradox*.

Figure 3.2 allows us to appreciate the complexity of the integration scenarios, as well as the need for further research on the topic, due to the fact that the majority of the literature available has been focusing on the areas that are presented on the top right of the figure. It is thus suggested that developing more holistic frameworks, by further expanding the focus of the existing ones, can assist in the future examination of IMC's appreciation and implementation.

In order for more light to be shed on practical aspects of integration, the focus of the following section will be drawn on the ways in which IMC is implemented, while identifying and underlining the marketing communications practices it is associated with.

IMC and Marketing Communications Management

As the review of the existing research on the topic illustrated, various marketing communications actions and processes have been linked with IMC. These in other words represent the means or ways through which marketing communications can (or should) be managed for IMC to be implemented. This is to say that these marketing communications practices can be considered an *advanced* or *enhanced* version of relatively common marketing communications practices, which assist, promote and even represent what integration is in practice. While the association that these practices bear with IMC has not been extensively explored, it is worth noting that such an exploration would be of particular importance in better comprehending and highlighting them and their link with integration, and could even lay the foundation and support further research on the area and in the wider issue of IMC's actual implementation by agency and client practitioners.

First, as it was mentioned earlier, practitioners have been focused on campaigns creation and projects completion, with their emphasis mainly placed on results (Schultz, 2000, 2001; Schultz & Patti, 2009). Reid (2003), Lauska et al. (2014), Batra and Keller (2016) and Keller (2016) suggested that a more complex brand development process through these task-oriented activities would allow marketers to continue their practices, while enhancing the brand equity entwined with IMC. Such a process would require the integration of a number of functions and consequently a number of individuals, who would all assist in the development, management and implementation of each task (Beverland & Luxton, 2005; Vernuccio & Ceccotti, 2015; Manoli, 2020).

Using a customer relationship management system or database (CRM) is presented as an important tool in this process, since it allows for the brand development process to focus on the appropriate target audience that can assist in making it successfully audience-centric (Gummesson, 2002; Schultz & Patti, 2009; Schultz et al., 2013). Based on the outside-in focus of IMC, it is expected that using customer data and understanding the target audience selected when a campaign, project or task is being developed can ensure that any marketing communications messages created on behalf of the organisation will have the maximum effect possible, while being coherent with the overall brand (Proctor & Kitchen, 2002; Kitchen et al., 2004b; Luck & Moffatt, 2009; Keller, 2016). According to Kliatchko (2008) the content of the messages also needs to be appropriate for the channels selected, in order to achieve the best possible results with the target audience. CRM could therefore assist in creating and fostering long-term message exchange, or conversation, with the selected stakeholders, which can, in turn, lead to an enhanced loyalty towards the brand and a long-term relationship with them (Kerr & Patti, 2002, 2015; Manoli, 2016; Manoli & Kenyon, 2018).

More importantly, this process would demand that any promotion on behalf of an organisation would be connected with the overall strategy and objectives of the organisation (Luck & Moffatt, 2009; Porcu et al., 2012; Manoli & Hodgkinson, 2017). Consequently, any new marketing or communication message would have to be aligned with the overall strategy, while ensuring that the objectives set match the overall objectives of the organisation. This, in turn, would be followed with regular updates on the overall strategy and objectives, in order for new information or changes to be captured and incorporated within them (Reid, 2002; Lauska et al., 2014; Kitchen & Tourky, 2015; Manoli & Hodgkinson, 2017). As a result, any brand messages created would be consistent with each other and coherent with the overall marketing communication strategy of the organisation. Reid (2002) argues that following such a process and, thus, managing integrated marketing communications would enable the companies to build a strong brand.

It is also suggested that in order for this consistency on brand messages to be achieved, the process should include a number of individuals from different functions who could discuss and review the planning and executing of marketing communications (Reid, 2003; Jenkinson, 2006; Shimp & Andrews, 2012; Keller, 2016). This group of individuals could help ensure that a more holistic view is achieved, while appreciating the specialisation and strategic value of each function (Swain, 2004). At the same time, a polyphony of views would allow for any misconceptions regarding the implementation of the brand strategy to be minimised (Gabrielli & Balboni, 2010; Keller, 2016). Gabrielli and Balboni argue that companies have been gradually introducing the idea of focus groups in marketing communications executing rather than planning, with their role mainly focusing on the final result of each message and, in more detail, its brand meaning. It could be argued that introducing focus groups earlier in this process could support a more thorough and strategic brand consistency.

As it can be seen through the marketing communications messages development process analysis, having an overall marketing communications strategy is believed to be a key factor in achieving strategic integration. As Christensen et al. (2008a, 2008b) and Moriarty and Schultz (2012) suggest, creating an appropriate brand strategy that is linked with relevant brand objectives can help an organisation achieve strategic integration. In more detail, a clear and concise strategy is required, which should be communicated in detail to all individuals within an organisation, in order to ensure that it is understood and appreciated.

Additionally, a number of objectives that complement the strategy should be created and, in turn, communicated to the individuals within the organisation. These objectives should be created centrally in an attempt to cover all areas / functions of the organisation (Christensen et al., 2008b; Keller, 2016). Individual function-specific elements can be included in these objectives, in order to guide the pertinent functions. These objectives set should be linked with the organisation's brand while maintaining a coherency cross-functionally (Schutlz & Kitchen, 2000a; Kitchen, 2016). Appropriate measurement systems should be linked to these objectives according to Reid et al. (2003), in order for information on customer/stakeholder perception to be collected. It is underlined that these measurements should exceed mere sales figures and instead focus on aspects of brand equity such as brand strength and brand perception. Connecting the objectives with appropriate measurement techniques can assist the organisation in understanding whether the desired results are being achieved, while acquiring feedback on the practices followed (Schultz & Schultz, 1998, 2004; Moriarty & Schultz, 2012). Additionally, it can even assist in possibly identifying any potential errors or areas in need of improvement. This focus on results of marketing communications can be considered an indication of an organisation achieving strategic integration as Kiatchko (2008) argued. As a result, the focus on measurement suggested by Reid (2003) aligns with Kliatchko's interplay between level 4 and results suggested in the latter's study.

A topic that has been emphasised numerous times is the existence of collaborative cross-functional communication, in order to ensure that the functions and individuals within an organisation communicate openly and are able and willing to co-operate (Mohr et al., 1996; Swain, 2004; Gabrielli & Balboni, 2010; Porcu et al., 2012; Manoli & Hodgkinson, 2021). It is suggested that improved cooperation and channels of open communication should be encouraged both culturally and managerially within organisations. In fact, it is underlined that communication should exist both on a formal and an informal level in order for stronger relationships to be built between employees, which can enhance collaboration (Moriarty, 1997; Ferdous, 2008; Moriarty & Schultz, 2012). These relationships and open communication can then prove beneficial in the process of planning and executing marketing communications campaigns, since they allow for information to be shared and for constructive feedback to be offered (Moriarty, 1994; Rouziès et al., 2005; Gambetti & Schultz, 2015). Supporting collaborative communication can also assist in overcoming any interdepartmental silos that have been identified as one of the key barriers hindering IMC's implementation (Christensen et al., 2008a, 2008b; Vernuccio & Ceccotti, 2015).

It is emphasised that organisational culture holds a crucial role in supporting and facilitating coordination and collaboration among employees, and should therefore be designed, altered or reinforced accordingly (Kelemen & Papasolomou-Doukakis, 2004). Culture has in fact been identified as one of the key barriers in implementing IMC, since it appears to have hindered the appreciation of strategic integration by both agency and client marketers (Eagle & Kitchen, 2000; Han et al., 2004; Dmitrijeva & Batraga, 2012; Homburg et al., 2015). It can consequently be suggested that drawing additional attention in implementing the appropriate culture of communication and collaboration can assist in achieving strategic integration.

Moreover, the practice of *'orchestrating'* all promotional tools and activities at different brand levels was emphasised, in response to the rather popular practice of coordinating the marketing communications tools only on a tactical level (McArthur & Griffin, 1997; Luck & Moffatt, 2009; Keller, 2016). The orchestration practice suggested underlines that additional emphasis should be placed on the effects each tool can have, not only on the merely tactical communication but also on the organisation's overall brand (Tsai, 2005; Lauska et al., 2014; Seric et al., 2014). Orchestrating on higher brand levels can ensure that brand consistency exists within all marketing communications efforts and activities, as strategic integration suggests (Pickton & Broderick, 2001; Shimp, 2007; Fill, 2009; Tafesse & Kitchen, 2015). Ensuring the consistency of messages promoted through different parts of the company can guarantee that the execution of the overall marketing communications strategy is consistent, while promoting and safeguarding the organisation's brand. At the same time, such an orchestration would require for each contact point of the organisation to be fully understood, regarding both its strategic value and the possible target audiences it can attract (Cornelissen, 2001; Ouwersloot & Duncan, 2008; Schultz et al., 2013).

In addition, and in order for the brand to be communicated and represented accurately and appropriately, the importance of training and information sharing is underlined (Reid, 2003). It is suggested that all employees of a company should be given adequate information and updates on the brand, in order for them to be able to understand it and represent it appropriately (Seric et al., 2014; Luxton et al., 2015). Informative training should be also provided, in order for any misconceptions to be minimised, while ensuring that coherency exists within the company (Madhavaram et al., 2005; Homburg et al., 2015). Regular updates should follow the training, in order for new information to be also communicated to the employees. According to Madhavaram et al.'s (2005) and Seric et al.'s (2014) studies, managing IMC can be considered a critical component of brand equity, which can only be achieved when the people in charge of representing the brand are following the appropriate strategy and are well-informed regarding the effects of their actions. As Eagle and Kitchen (2000, p. 677) argue *'responders endorsed the overriding objective desired by all participants as being "brand guardians", but noted that considerable education, re-education, training or upskilling was required'*. According to their research, in order for the brand to be represented accordingly and for the employees to act as *'brand guardians'*, extensive training within each organisation is considered imperative.

Finally, while as Eagle and Kitchen (2000, p. 683) claim that *'no structure was seen as being inherently superior to any other'*, the organisational structure is still considered a key factor that can assist or hinder strategic integration. As it was discussed earlier in this chapter, centralisation was originally presented as an easy and efficient way of integrating marketing communications. As Schultz (1992) suggested, integration can be achieved by simply placing an individual in charge of controlling all marketing communications functions (advertising, product publicity, sales promotion, packaging and direct marketing) and, thus, acting as an *Integration Czar*. McArthur and Griffin (1997) and Low (2000) supported this view and examined companies in which this structure was adopted in order to ensure that all communications were aligned.

On the other hand, Phelps et al. (1996) and Low and Mohr (1999) suggested that a more decentralised approach would allow for collaboration between individuals to drive and manage integration. Their views that were later also supported by Cornelissen (2003) focus on a team decision-making process which enables more employees to take responsibilities regarding their marketing communications practices. Through Phelps et al.'s (1996) and Low and Mohr's (1999) research it is argued that, although companies are keen to allocate responsibilities regarding their communication strategy to managers, it is common that the final line of actions and strategy development process will take place through a collective team work and decisions alignment. The study the researchers conducted in a number of US-based companies provided them with evidence that this method is being followed and considered successful.

However, it could be suggested that rather than opting for a centralised or decentralised approach, organisations might adopt a rather mixed style that would suit their needs regarding integration, as Beverland and Luxton argue (2005). As Gurau (2008, p. 172) suggests, each organisation has established different marketing communications structures under a distinctively diverse marketing communication culture. It is, therefore, *'impossible to design an implementation model that generally fits all firms'*. Consequently, it is argued that there are no clear suggestions provided by academics on which organisational structure enhances IMC's application, since integration can be driven and implemented irrespectively of the approach selected (Vernuccio & Ceccotti, 2015). As a result, and regardless of academics failing to pinpoint whether centralisation or decentralisation of marketing communications responsibilities is more efficient in regard to IMC's implementation, it can be argued that any structure selected has to support strategic integration.

Based on the importance these practices have in strategic integration, it could be argued that further research on them would enhance the existing literature on IMC and possibly assist in IMC's appreciation and application by practitioners. In other words, it is suggested that additional engaged scholarship studies focusing on these practices and their link with IMC could deepen our understanding of IMC and its implementation, and potentially bridge this important knowledge transfer gap. It is the significance of these practices for the progress of IMC that informed this study, which will aim to investigate them and potentially develop our understanding of them, while studying the practices through their application in the football industry. The particular sector selected in this study in regard to IMC and the very limited attention it has received in regard to the study of IMC within it will be presented below.

IMC in Sports / Football

As it was discussed in this and the previous chapter, even though IMC has attracted considerable attention in regard to its theoretical appreciation, its implementation in various sectors has not been adequately researched. A few academics have examined IMC's implementation in a limited number of sectors, such as the wine (Reid et al., 2001) and the supermarket industry (McNeil, 2012), while Low's (2000) study attempted a cross industry analysis of marketing managers in US companies. As it was underlined earlier, these sector-specific studies focus on a limited number of companies in each sector, which are selected based on their success and size.

Unfortunately, the sport industry has received considerably less attention compared to other sectors, with significantly limited studies focusing on the topic. Batchelor and Formentin (2008) examined the re-branding process of the National Hockey League (NHL) in a study that focuses more on the details of the 'My NHL' campaign, rather than the strategic design behind it. Kinney (2014) studied the University of South Alabama's (American) Football Program, in an attempt to examine whether the way its communications function was ran resembled the concept behind the theory of excellence in public relations or IMC. The case study focuses on the managerial practices which according to Kinney bear a great resemblance to the theory of excellence. Watkins (2014) attempts to examine the link between sports branding and IMC, through a survey on National Basketball Association (NBA) fans; however, the study focuses only on the use of social networking sites and a comparison between them. Farrelly, Quester and Burton (1997), Dewhirst and Davis (2005), Smolianov and Aiyeku (2009), Kelly and Whiteman (2010), Kinney (2010) and Micu and Pentina (2014) conducted research on IMC in which sport sponsorship is examined as a marketing communications tool. Viewed from the perspective of the sponsor, the sports organisation or the athlete, their studies do not provide the reader with an evaluation or understanding of IMC and its strategic value, but rather use sport sponsorship as an example of an additional tool which can be incorporated in the IMC mix.

In reality it could be argued that only three studies have focused purely and more holistically on IMC in sport. One was conducted by Hopwood (in Beech & Chadwick, 2007) and focuses on the sport integrated marketing communications mix (SIMCM), its characteristics and the advantages and disadvantages of each element. Emphasis is also placed on the benefits of adopting a fully integrated marketing communications strategy and its managerial implications and challenges in sports. Within her study, the peculiarity of the sport industry is presented in order to assist the reader in appreciating the potential differences noted. Dos Santos' (2019) work also focuses on IMC and its tactical operation in sport. In his work, various sport case studies on different sport contexts (e.g., athletes, cities) are presented, examining how IMC is implemented through the analysis of their current practices. Finally, the study conducted by Manoli and Hodgkinson (2019), which set the basis for this book, examines the implementation of IMC in football clubs. Through the study, the idea of integration scenarios is discussed, which this book extends further as Chapter 7 will present.

Conclusion

The synthesis of the literature review presented in this chapter allowed for thorough insights to be provided in practitioners' appreciation of IMC, as well as its implementation through the investigation of the considerably small number of studies available on the topic, and an even smaller number focusing on sport in general and football in particular. This investigation allowed for IMC's implementation anchoring on a non-strategic level to be highlighted, which, in turn, led to the discussion of integration scenarios that will be explored further in Chapter 7.

References

Awad, T. A. (2009) IMC – An Egyptian advertising agency perspective. In P. D. Jawahar (Ed.) *Contemporary issues in management research*, (pp. 71–91), New Delhi: Excel Books.

Barger, V. A. & Labrecque, L. (2013) 'An integrated marketing communications perspective on social media metrics', *International Journal of Integrated Marketing Communications*, 5 (1) 64–76.

Batchelor, B. & Formentin, M. (2008) 'Re-branding the NHL: Building the league through the "My NHL" integrated marketing campaign', *Public Relations Review*, 34 (2) 156–160.

Batra, R. & Keller, K. L. (2016) 'Integrating marketing communications: New findings, new lessons and new ideas', *Journal of Marketing*, 80 (6) 122–145.

Beech, J. & Chadwick, S. (2007) *The marketing of sport*, Harlow: Pearson Education.

Beverland, M. & Luxton, S. (2005) 'The projection of authenticity: Managing integrated marketing communications through strategic decoupling', *Journal of Advertising*, 34 (4) 103–116.

Caywood, C. & Ewing, R. (1991) 'Integrated marketing communications: A new master's degree concept', *Public Relations Review*, 17 (3) 237–244.

Christensen, L. T., Firat, F. A. & Torp, S. (2008a) 'The organisation of integrated communications: Toward flexible integration', *European Journal of Marketing*, 42 (3/4) 423–452.

Christensen, L.T., Morsing, M. & Cheney, G. (2008b) *Corporate communications: Convention, complexity and critique*, London: Sage.

Cornelissen, J. P. (2001) 'Integrated marketing communications and the language of marketing development', *International Journal of Advertising*, 20 (4) 483–498.

Cornelissen, J. P. (2003) 'Change, continuity and progress: The concept of integrated marketing communications and marketing communications practice', *Journal of Strategic Marketing*, 11 (4) 217–234.

Dewhirst, T. & Davis, B. (2005) 'Brand strategy and integrated marketing communication (IMC): A case study of Player's cigarette brand marketing', *Journal of Advertising*, 34 (4) 81–92.

Dmitrijeva, K. & Batraga, A. (2012) 'Barriers to integrated marketing communications: The case of Latvia (small markets)',*8th International Strategic Management Conference, 21–23 June 2012, Barcelona, Spain.*

Dos Santos, M. A. (2019) *Integrated marketing communications, strategies, and tactical operations in sports organizations*. Hersey, USA: IGI Global.

Eagle, L. & Kitchen, P. J. (2000) 'IMC, brand communications, and corporate cultures: Client / advertising agency co-ordination and cohesion', *European Journal of Marketing*, 34 (5/6) 667–686.

Eagle, L., Kitchen, P. J. & Bulmer, S. (2007) 'Insights into interpreting integrated marketing communications: A two-nation qualitative comparison', *European Journal of Marketing*, 41 (7/8) 956–970.

Esposito, A. (2013) 'Insights about integrated marketing communication in small-and-medium-sized Italian enterprises', *Business Systems Review*, 2 (1) 80–98.

Ewing, M. T., de Bussy, N. M. & Caruana, A. (2000) 'Perceived agency politics and conflicts of interest as potential barriers to IMC orientation', *Journal of Marketing Communications*, 6 (1) 107–119.

Farrelly, F. J., Quester, P. G. & Burton, R. (1997) 'Integrating sports sponsorship into the corporate marketing function: An international comparative study', *International Marketing Review*, 14 (3) 170–182.

Ferdous, A. S. (2008) 'Integrated internal marketing communication (IIMC)', *The Marketing Review*, 8 (3) 223–235.

Fill, C. (2009) *Marketing communications; Interactivity, communities and content*, Essex: Pearson Education.

Gabrielli, V. & Balboni, B. (2010) 'SME practice towards integrated marketing communications', *Marketing Intelligence & Planning*, 28 (3) 275–290.

Gambetti, R. C. & Schultz, D. E. (2015) 'Reshaping the boundaries of marketing communication to bond with consumers', *Journal of Marketing Communications*, 21 (1) 1–4.

Gould, S. J. (2004) 'IMC as theory and as a poststructural set of practices and discourses: A continuously evolving paradigm shift', *Journal of Advertising Research*, 44 (1) 66–70.

Gummesson, E. (2002) 'Relationship marketing in the new economy', *Journal of Relationship Marketing*, 1 (1) 37–57.

Gurau, C. (2008), 'Integrated online marketing communication: Implementation and management', *Journal of Communication Management*, 12 (2) 169–184.

Han, D., Kim, I. & Schultz, D. E. (2004) 'Understanding the diffusion of integrated marketing communications', *Journal of Advertising Research*, 44 (1) 31–45.

Homburg, C., Vomberg, A., Enke, M. & Grimm, P. H. (2015) 'The loss of the marketing department's influence: Is it really happening? And why worry?', *Journal of the Academy of Marketing Science*, 43 (1) 1–13.

Jenkinson, A. (2006) 'Planning and evaluating communications in an integrated organisation', *Journal of Targeting, Measurement and Analysis for Marketing*, 15 (1) 47–64.

Kallmeyer, J. & Abratt, R. (2001) 'Perceptions of IMC and organizational change among agencies in South Africa', *International Journal of Advertising*, 20 (3) 361–380.

Kelemen, M. & Papasolomou-Doukakis, I. (2004) 'Can culture be changed? A study of internal marketing', *The Service Industries Journal*, 24 (5) 121–135.

Keller, K. L. (2009) 'Building strong brands in a modern marketing communications environment', *Journal of Marketing Communications*, 15 (2/3) 139–155.

Keller, K. L. (2016) 'Unlocking the power of integrated marketing communications: How integrated is your IMC program?', *Journal of Advertising*, 45 (3) 286–301.

Kelly, L. & Whiteman, C. (2010) 'Sports sponsorship as an integrated marketing communications tool: An Australian sponsor's perspective', *Journal of sponsorship*, 4 (1) 26–37.

Kerr, G. F. & Patti, C. H. (2002) 'Integrated marketing communications (IMC): Where to from here' in *Australian and New Zealand Marketing Academy (ANZMAC) 2002 Conference Proceedings*, 2381–2387.

Kerr, G. F. & Patti, C. H. (2015) 'Strategic IMC: From abstract concept to marketing management tool', *Journal of Marketing Communications*, 21 (5) 317–339.

Kinney, L. (2010) 'An IMC strategy for introducing game-day jersey sponsorships to American sports leagues', *International Journal of Integrated Marketing Communications*, 2 (2) 44–53.

Kinney, L. (2014) 'IMC or ET?', *International Journal of Integrated Marketing Communications*, 6 (1) 52–62.

Kitchen, P. J. (2016) Is IMC "marketing oriented"? In L. Petruzzellis & R. S. Winer (Eds.) *Rediscovering the essentiality of marketing* (pp. 441–442), New York: Springer International Publishing.

Kitchen, P. J., Brignell, J., Li, T. & Jones, G. S. (2004b) 'The emergence of IMC: A theoretical perspective', *Journal of Advertising Research*, 44 (1) 19–30.

Kitchen, P. J., Kim, I. & Schultz, D. E. (2008) 'Integrated marketing communication: Practice leads theory', *Journal of Advertising Research*, 48 (4) 531–546.

Kitchen, P. J. & Schultz, D. E. (1999) 'A multi-country comparison of the drive for IMC', *Journal of Advertising Research*, 39 (1) 21–38.

Kitchen, P. J., Schultz, D. E., Kim, I., Han, D. & Li, T. (2004a) 'Will agencies ever "get" (or understand) IMC?', *European Journal of Marketing*, 38 (11/12) 1417–1436.

Kitchen, P. J. & Tao, L. (2005) 'Perceptions of integrated marketing communications: A Chinese ad and PR agency perspective', *International Journal of Advertising*, 24 (1) 51–78.

Kitchen, P. J. & Tourky, M. (2015) *Integrated communications in the postmodern era*, Hampshire: Palgrave Macmillan.

Kliatchko, J. (2008) 'Revisiting the IMC construct: A revised definition and four pillars', *International Journal of Advertising*, 27 (1) 133–160.

Kliatchko, J. G. & Schultz, D. E. (2014) 'Twenty years of IMC: A study of CEO and CMO perspectives in the Asia-Pacific region', *International Journal of Advertising*, 33 (2) 373–390.

Laurie, S. & Mortimer, K. (2011) "IMC is dead. Long live IMC': Academics' versus practitioners' views', *Journal of Marketing Management*, 27 (13/14) 1464–1478.

Lauska, D., Laurie, S. & Mortimer, K. (2014) The management of corporate personality: An IMC perspective. In *Proceedings of the 47th Academy of Marketing Conference, AM2014: Marketing Dimensions: People, Places and Spaces*, Bournemouth: Academy of Marketing.

Low, G. S. (2000) 'Correlates of integrated marketing communications', *Journal of Advertising Research*, 40 (3) 27–39.

Low, G. S. & Mohr, J.J. (1999) 'Setting advertising and promotion budgets in multi-brand companies', *Journal of Advertising Research*, 39 (1) 67–78.

Luck, E. & Moffatt, J. (2009) 'IMC: Has anything really changed? A new perspective on an old definition', *Journal of Marketing Communications*, 15 (5) 311–325.

Luxton, S., Reid, M. & Mavondo, F. (2015) 'Integrated marketing communication capability and brand performance', *Journal of Advertising*, 44 (1) 37–46.

Madhavaram, S., Badrinarayanan, V. & McDonald, R. (2005) 'Integrated marketing communication (IMC) and brand identity as critical components of brand equity strategy', *Journal of Advertising*, 34 (4) 69–80.

Manoli, A. E. (2017) Media relations in English football clubs. In J. J. Zhang & Pitts, B. G. (Eds.) *Contemporary sport marketing: Global perspectives*. (pp. 120–138), London: Routledge.

Manoli, A. E. (2020) 'Brand capabilities in English premier league clubs', *European Sport Management* Quarterly 20 (1) 30–46.

Manoli, A. E. & Hodgkinson, I. R. (2017) 'Marketing outsourcing in the English premier league: The right holder/agency interface', *European Sport Management Quarterly*, 17 (4) 436–456.

Manoli, A. E. & Hodgkinson, I. R. (2019) 'The implementation of integrated marketing communication (IMC): Evidence from professional football clubs in England', *Journal of Strategic Marketing*, 28 (6) 542–563.

Manoli, A. E. & Hodgkinson, I. R. (2021) 'Exploring internal organisational communication dynamics in the professional football industry', *European Journal of Marketing*, 55 (11) 2894–2916.

Manoli, A. E. & Kenyon, J. A. (2018) Football and marketing. In S. M. Chadwick, P. Widdop, D. Parnell & C. Anagnostopoulos (Eds.) *Routledge handbook of football business and management*, (pp. 88–100), Oxon: Routledge.

McArthur, D. & Griffin, T. (1997) 'A marketing management view of integrated marketing Communications', *Journal of Advertising Research*, 37 (5) 19–27.

McNeil, L. S. (2012) 'Sales promotion in the supermarket industry: A four country case comparison', *The International Review of Retail, Distribution and Consumer Research*, 22 (3) 243–260.

Micu, A. C. & Pentina, I. (2014) 'Integrating advertising and news about the brand in the online environment: Are all products the same?', *Journal of Marketing Communications*, 20 (3) 159–175.

Mohr, J. J., Fisher, R. J. & Nevin, J. R. (1996) 'Collaborative communication in interfirm relationships: Moderating effects of integration and control', *The Journal of Marketing*, 60 (3) 103–115.

Moriarty, S. E. (1994) 'PR and IMC: The benefits of integration', *Public Relations Quarterly*, 39 (3) 38–44.

Moriarty, S. E. (1997) 'IMC needs PR's stakeholder focus', *Marketing News*, 31 (11) 7.

Moriarty, S. & Schultz, D. E. (2012) Four theories of how IMC works. In S. Rodgers & E. Thorson (Eds.) *Advertising theory* (pp. 491–505), New York: Routledge.

Ouwersloot, H. & Duncan, T. (2008) *Integrated marketing communications*, London: McGraw-Hill Education.

Pettigrew, L. S. (2000/2001) 'If IMC is so good, why isn't it being implemented?: Barriers to IMC adoption in corporate America', *Journal of Integrated Communications*, 11 (1) 29–37.

Phelps, J. E., Harris, T. E. & Johnson, E. (1996) 'Exploring decision-making approaches and responsibility for developing marketing communications strategy', *Journal of Business Research*, 37 (3) 217–223.

Pickton, D. & Broderick, A. (2001) *Integrated marketing communications*, Essex: Pearson Education.

Porcu, L., del Barrio-García, S. & Kitchen, P. J. (2012) 'How integrated marketing communications (IMC) works? A theoretical review and an analysis of its main drivers and effects/¿Cómo funciona la Comunicación Integrada de Marketing (CIM)? Una revisión teórica y un análisis de sus antecedentes y efectos', *Comunicación y sociedad*, 25 (1) 313–348.

Proctor, T. & Kitchen, P. (2002) 'Communication in postmodern integrated marketing', *Corporate Communications: An International Journal*, 7 (3) 144–154.

Reid, M. (2002) 'Building strong brands through the management of integrated marketing communications', *International Journal of Wine Marketing*, 14 (3) 37–52.

Reid, M. (2003) 'IMC–performance relationship: Further insight and evidence from the Australian marketplace', *International Journal of Advertising*, 22 (2) 227–248.

Reid, M., Johnson, T., Ratcliffe, M., Skrip, K. & Wilson, J. (2001) 'Integrated marketing communications in the Australian and New Zealand wine industry', *International Journal of Advertising*, 20 (2) 239–262.

Rose, P. B. (1996) 'Practitioner opinions and interests regarding integrated marketing communications in selected Latin American countries', *Journal of Marketing Communications*, 2 (3) 125–139.

Rouziès, D., Anderson, E., Kohli, A. K., Michaels, R. E., Weitz, B. A. & Zoltners, A. A. (2005) 'Sales and marketing integration: A proposed framework', *Journal of Personal Selling & Sales Management*, 25 (2) 113–122.

Schultz, D. E. (1992) 'Integrated marketing communications: The status of integrated marketing communications programs the US today', *Journal of Promotion Management*, 1 (1) 99–104.

Schultz, D. E. (1993a) 'Integrated marketing communications: Maybe definition is in the point of view', *Marketing News*, January 18.

Schultz, D. E. (2000) 'Structural flaws dash marcom plans', *Marketing News*, 34 (3) 14.

Schultz, D. E. (2001) 'Campaign approach shouldn't exist in IMC', *Marketing News*, 35 (5) 11–13.

Schultz, D. E., Chu, G. & Zhao, B. (2016) 'IMC in an emerging economy: The Chinese perspective', *International Journal of Advertising*, 35(2) 200–215.

Schultz, D. E. & Kitchen, P. J. (1997) 'Integrated marketing communications in US advertising agencies: An exploratory study', *Journal of Advertising Research*, 37 (5) 7–18.

Schultz, D. E. & Kitchen, P. J. (2000a) *Communicating globally. An integrated marketing approach*, London: Macmillan.

Schultz, D. E. & Patti, C. H. (2009) 'The evolution of IMC: IMC in a customer driven marketplace', *Journal of Marketing Communications*, 15 (2–3) 75–84.

Schultz, D. E., Patti, C. H. & Kitchen, P. J. (2013) *The evolution of integrated marketing communications: The customer-driven marketplace*, London: Routledge.

Schultz, D. E. & Schultz, H. F. (1998) 'Transitioning marketing communication into the twenty-first century', *Journal of Marketing Communications*, 4 (1) 9–26.

Schultz, D. E. & Schultz, H. F. (2004) *IMC: The next generation*, New York: McGraw-Hill.

Seric, M., Gil-Saura, I. & Ruiz-Molina, M. E. (2014) 'How can integrated marketing communications and advanced technology influence the creation of customer-based brand equity? Evidence from the hospitality industry', *International Journal of Hospitality Management*, 39 (1) 144–156.

Shankar, V. & Balasubramanian, S. (2009) 'Mobile marketing: A synthesis and prognosis', *Journal of Interactive Marketing*, 23 (2) 118–129.

Shankar, V. & Hollinger, M. (2007) 'Online and mobile advertising: Current scenario, emerging trends, and future directions', *Marketing Science Institute Report*, 07–206.

Shimp, T. A. (2007) *Integrated marketing communications in advertising and promotion* (7th ed.), Mason: Thomson Higher Education.

Shimp, T. A. & Andrews, J. C. (2012) *Advertising promotion and other aspects of integrated marketing communications* (9th ed.), Mason: Cengage Learning.

Smith, P. R. & Taylor, J. (2004) *Marketing communications: An integrated approach*, London: Kogan Page Publishers.

Smolianov, P. & Aiyeku, J. F. (2009) 'Corporate marketing objectives and evaluation measures for integrated television advertising and sports event sponsorships', *Journal of Promotion Management*, 15 (1/2) 74–89.

Swain, W. N. (2004) 'Perceptions of IMC after a decade of development: Who's at the wheel, and how can we measure success?', *Journal of Advertising Research*, 44 (1) 46–65.

Tafesse, W. & Kitchen, P. J. (2015) 'IMC–an integrative review', *International Journal of Advertising*, 36 (2), 210–226.

Tsai, S. P. (2005) 'Integrated marketing as management of holistic consumer experience', *Business Horizons*, 48 (5) 431–441.

Vantamay, S. (2011) 'Performances and measurement of integrated marketing communications (IMC) of advertisers in Thailand', *Journal of Global Management*, 1 (1) 1–12.

Vernuccio, M. & Ceccotti, F. (2015) 'Strategic and organisational challenges in the integrated marketing communication paradigm shift: A holistic vision', *European Management Journal*, 33 (6) 438–449.

Watkins, B. (2014) 'An integrated approach to sports branding: Examining the influence of social media on brand outcomes', *International Journal of Integrated Marketing Communications*, 6 (2) 30–40.

Chapter 4

Marketing Strategy, Marketing Goals and Internal Communication

Introduction

In order for IMC's implementation to be examined, the practices that represent integration in practice as they have been identified by the literature will be examined below. First, an examination of the existence of marketing strategy and marketing related targets or goals within the clubs will be presented. Second, cross-functional communication within each club in either a formal or an informal way will be studied, followed by a discussion on interdepartmental silos, allowing us insights to how and to what extent IMC is being implemented in practice.

Marketing Strategy and Goals

A topic that emerged early on through the examination of football clubs' marketing practices is the element of strategy in marketing communications. Based on the link between strategy and IMC that was discussed extensively in Chapter 2 (Schultz & Schultz, 1998, 2004; Kliatchko, 2005, 2008; Porcu et al., 2012; Manoli & Hodgkinson, 2019) and in order for the author to be able to examine this further, additional inquiries were made on the marketing or marketing communications strategy each club has, as well as the marketing goals set within it. Investigating the shared patterns among the clubs can further assist in understanding strategic marketing communications as they are perceived and implemented by the clubs, which can further contribute in comprehending the extent to which integration occurs among them.

A clarification needs to be made, that the aim of this analysis is not to assess the existing marketing strategies and goals set in each club, or the potential success they might have. On the contrary, the analysis is conducted in order for patterns to be identified that will allow the author to assess whether and to what extent is IMC implemented within EPL clubs.

Marketing Strategy

A number of patterns appear to occur regarding the existence and content of marketing strategies in EPL clubs.

First, when inquired about the existence of a marketing or a marketing communications strategy, six clubs stated that there is no current strategy in place within the organisations.

> *It's something we learn over the years that we cannot do. We spend that much time reacting to requests that we don't get the time to plan and stick to the original strategy. We follow the same patterns throughout the last years instinctively. Our fans trust us, this is our unofficial strategy. It has worked for us. And when you get to this level and you're an established Premier League club, you don't really need a strategy.*

As the quote shows two main reasons were presented by the interviewees as their rationale behind this lack of a strategy. First, the fast and unpredictable nature of the industry that requires the clubs to re-act and does not allow for a plan to be set in place and followed. Second, the misconception that the identity of the club is that strong that it does not require a marketing strategy in order to promote it. This mistaken belief could be linked with a lack of understanding of the use and value of a marketing strategy (Christensen et al., 2008a, 2008b; Keller, 2009; Manoli & Hodgkinson, 2017; Manoli & Kenyon, 2018), which could be, in turn, connected to misconceptions on branding and brand management (Gabrielli & Balboni, 2010; Manoli, 2020). As the brand management section in this chapter will further discuss, misconceptions on what a brand is and how it can be affected by proper and strategic brand management are evident in the same six clubs. These misconceptions could be also potentially traced back to the marketing employees' knowledge, understanding and experience of marketing theory and practice and would be in line with an overall lack of integration practice.

An additional four clubs mentioned that an overall marketing strategy exists, but it is neither updated every year nor detailed enough to guide the clubs throughout each season, as the following quote shows.

> *There is one (marketing strategy), but not rigid, not really. There is a strategy for the remaining of the season, but we cannot plan things, as you know, we just look at things and how to promote them.*

One of these four clubs explained that the person in charge of designing and leading the implementation of the marketing strategy had left in the beginning of the season, and on their absence, the team continued without a clearly set plan for that season. The unpredictability of the industry was presented again as the main reason behind this lack of focus on the marketing strategy.

An additional seven clubs stated that a marketing strategy is designed in the beginning of the season and kept as consistent as possible throughout; however its focus tends to be around sales. Getting people in the stadium on a matchday was in fact presented as their main marketing strategy.

We've got a very big stadium to fill, so that is our main strategy. Our marketing strategy focuses towards this task and getting people in the stadium is a very challenging thing to do. Smaller projects are also included in the strategy, such as selling season tickets, the season cards for the new stadium, and then individual campaigns for smaller things.

As this quote illustrates, these clubs tend to be commercially focused, following a marketing strategy that comprises mostly of commercial elements, while lacking marketing components.

Overall, marketing strategy is a topic that does not attract considerable attention within any of the above-mentioned 11 clubs. On the contrary, a rather lax and more commercially focused plan appears to guide the clubs throughout each season. This lack of a detailed marketing focused plan could be linked with the lack of appreciation of the marketing function and its value as something more than a commercial tool, which has been considered one of the main hindering factors of strategic marketing since the emergence of relevant marketing literature (Kotler & Levy, 1969; Trustrum, 1989; Manoli & Hodgkinson, 2021).

Moreover, eight clubs referred to a wider company strategy that is carefully designed in the beginning of each season and is then filtered down to the members of the marketing team. This overall club strategy is designed by the heads of the departments and agreed to by the higher management of the club before each season begins. Once it has been approved, it is broken down into individual department or team strategies that are then managed by the head of each department. The marketing strategy is therefore a fraction of the overall club strategy, which ensures that coherency exists within each club.

This marketing strategy tends to include various elements such as growing the brand both nationally and internationally, and increasing fan engagement. Commercial elements are not absent, however, with raising commercial revenue being one of the most prominent components of each season's marketing strategy. In fact, all eight clubs mentioned that raising revenue and increasing sales is part of their marketing strategy.

Overall, these eight clubs appeared to be following a more coherent and consistent practice regarding their marketing strategies which derives from the overall strategy of each club, suggesting that integration occurs to some extent (Duncan & Mulhern, 2004; Gould, 2004; Kitchen & Tourky, 2015). Gradually moving towards a separation of marketing specific and commercial elements within it could be then considered as a step forward in IMC's implementation (Jones et al., 2004; Swain, 2004; Shimp & Andrews, 2012).

Finally, the remaining five clubs gave a more detailed description of how the strategy is set and agreed before each season begins, which resembles the process described by the eight clubs above. After the heads of the departments have met and decided on an overall club-wide strategy for the season, the higher management's approval is requested. Once the approval is given, the overall strategy is divided into a number of smaller function specific strategies. The heads of the departments are then provided with the strategies that they are in charge of. For example, marketing in one of these clubs is not only in charge of the marketing strategy but also of the fan engagement strategy, the customer relations strategy, the campaigns strategy and the international social media strategy. According to the interviewee of this club:

> We set out an initial strategy, what we're trying to achieve and how we're going to achieve it. And in the beginning of the year we set our priorities, and for each priority we have a strategy to achieve it.

When discussing what the marketing strategy entails, these five clubs did not mention any revenue or sales elements, and instead talked about their brand, its national and international awareness, strength and growth, as well as fan engagement. As the following section on marketing goals will also demonstrate, these clubs appear to have clearer targets set than the ones belonging in any other level, followed by a well-defined evaluation process. As it will be discussed, the goals and evaluation process is agreed on with the relevant employees, suggesting that this well-structured and organised approach is implemented in a collaborative way, which can have a positive effect on the employees and the way in which they are able to represent the organisation's brand (Rafiq & Ahmed, 2000; Burmann & Zeplin, 2005).

The practices followed in these clubs regarding the marketing strategy and the way it is designed and structured allow the author to suggest that the element of strategy in marketing communications is in fact appreciated by them. Strategic plans are set for a number of business functions that allow for a coherent and consistent strategy to be implemented throughout the clubs, which closely resemble the suggestions made by Pickton and Broderick (2001), Ouwersloot and Duncan (2008) and Kitchen and Tourky (2015) on IMC planning.

Marketing Goals

Having examined the existence and content of marketing strategies among the clubs, the discussion will now focus on the establishment and focus of marketing goals. Clubs were asked about the marketing goals they set for each season, regarding both their content and their assessment. Planning, goal setting and evaluating the achievement of marketing targets were presented by Jenkinson (2006) as key aspects in organisations that practice integration. According to his work, the question that should be asked to marketers is not whether marketing objectives are set, but how they are set. However, bearing in mind that the present study was conducted on a wider range of organisations than normally examined, the inquiry on the marketing goals commenced with questions on whether they are set and what they entail. A number of patterns exist among the 30 clubs, which will be presented below.

Before the patterns among the clubs regarding their goals are discussed, an additional point has to be underlined. All 30 clubs mentioned the word sales when discussing the goals of their team. Regardless of their team being part of the commercial arm of the club, all interviewees highlighted the importance their role holds as a direct or indirect support in driving revenue for the club. Football match attendances, season ticket sales and membership sales were brought up by all clubs as part of the overall clubs' and individual teams' objectives, with some placing more emphasis on them than others. Even if their marketing or marketing and communications strategy does not include raising commercial revenue directly, according to the interviewees, assisting in achieving the club's overall commercial goals is, in fact, part of their objectives.

First, six clubs claimed that there are no marketing objectives or goals set for them and their departments for each season, with a number of reasons given to justify this. Even though the lack of direct leadership was brought up by all six clubs, it was the individual members' experience on the role that was presented as the main reason why clear and well-defined marketing goals are not set.

> *We have been in the club for many years and know exactly what to do. We do not need annual targets to do our job.*

As another interviewee added:

> *There is not a set of targets and we all have to do the best we can. We do quite a lot and maybe that is why. Since we do quite well I guess we don't need them. There is no problem though, we don't work on commission.*

As the quotes illustrate, the employees experience and proficiency in their job was presented as the main reason against setting marketing targets.

The speed by which things change in each club was also mentioned by the interviewees as a hurdle against goal setting. The fact that the marketing team is in some cases different from the commercial team made an interviewee question why they would need goals and targets, since that is the commercial team's job.

> *We are here to support the commercial team, they are the ones with the targets they have to hit. We are here to provide support and that does not require hitting targets or setting goals.*

This mistaken belief on the nature and content of targets might be an additional hurdle to the existence and potential future introduction of marketing goals within the club (Chelladurai & Chang, 2000; Baker & Hart, 2008).

Finally, a justification for the lack of goals that will also be mentioned and further discussed in the brand management analysis section that follows is the misconception practitioners have on the club's brand and its strength. This misconception can be better illustrated through the following quote:

> *When you get to this level and you're an established Premier League club, there is no point really. There's no need to target to get your message out there. Our brand is such that we always surpass the targets anyway'.*

An additional 11 clubs that referred to a rather lax and commercially focused plan instead of a marketing strategy in the previous section, presented the author with a similar picture when asked about their marketing goals. Consequently, the sales goals were presented as the marketing goals of these clubs. As the interviewees suggested, since their role entails providing support to the commercial department, their goals involve assisting in the commercial goals as well.

An interviewee's answer on the inquiry about any separate marketing goals was:

> *No, purely because a lot of it is irrelevant really, which is weird from me to say coming from a marketing background. It's very much depending on the result on the pitch. If things are not going well, everything about the brand is lost, so marketing targets wouldn't matter, only sales targets would.*

The way in which the brand of these clubs is managed will be discussed further in a following section on brand management. However, their misconception on the ways in which marketing actions can affect the brand (as the above interviewee's quote suggests), contradicts academics' views on brand equity that have identified an important direct analogy between the two (Keller, 1993, 2009; Batra & Keller, 2016). It also suggests that the value of marketing goals and objectives has yet to be fully appreciated (Moriarty, 1997; Jenkinson, 2006).

As expected from the discussion on the existence of a marketing strategy discussed in the previous section, an additional eight clubs presented the author with a more structured approach in terms of their marketing planning and goal setting. Commercial elements were also included in their targets, with sales or direct assistance to sales being incorporated in their goals. As it was underlined, their role is a support function to the commercial team and since the organisation in which they work is a commercial operation, increasing the revenue is part of their goals.

In more detail, membership seems to be an area marketing teams are particularly focused on, with membership sales mentioned by most of these eight clubs, and *'getting people through the door on a matchday'* being the close second. When discussing their goals further, an interviewee's answer was:

> *We have revenue targets on what to achieve. Money is for us the best form of measuring. Everything we do, we have to check the response it has on people, how much revenue we generate, how does it activate.*

All eight clubs, however, mentioned other marketing goals as well, including strengthening the brand of the club internationally and *'creating hospitality products that would match the new brand position of the club'*. One of these eight clubs made a distinction between the national and international goals set, clarifying that international objectives include brand awareness and the use and appreciation of the social media channels by local users, while national goals tend to focus more on revenue.

It can be argued that these eight clubs appear to understand and appreciate the planning process that can allow for marketing communications actions to be carried out in an organised and structured way (Jenkinson, 2006). Setting marketing goals demonstrates the clubs' planning process which can be linked with the foundations needed in order for IMC to be implemented, while indicating that there is still room for development in order for a more strategic approach to be adopted (Porcu et al., 2012; Kitchen & Tourky, 2015).

Finally, the remaining five clubs presented the author with a well-structured approach to setting and evaluating marketing goals. According to them, the strategy set in the beginning of each season is then filtered down to each team, and subsequently to each individual member, so that clear objectives are set and communicated to them. These objectives are then evaluated often throughout the season to ensure that the plan is followed, the targets are met and the individual or individuals in charge of them are working efficiently. The goals are sometimes broken down to weekly sets, in order for this appraisal to take place more often. KPIs were mentioned by all five clubs when referring to the goals, since they assist them in the appraisal process that examines whether the goals set were met.

The words *'processes'*, *'systems'* and *'structure'* were also mentioned by these clubs, underlying the emphasis they place on their well-defined and well-organised approaches to marketing planning and goal setting. The objectives and goals these clubs set are according to them:

> Smart, quantifiable, measurable and time sensitive. We're looking for hard figures that we can track.

When inquired more about the goals and their evaluation, one of the interviewees gave the following answer:

> By analysing the data we understand exactly the outcomes of that campaign and that marketing activity we did, so that we know if we're meeting our weekly goals, so that we can measure our success against this objective, etc.

This traceability, as well as the way in which marketing targets are broken down into individuals' targets, allows for a consistency and a coherency within marketing to be ensured, through the setting of the appropriate marketing goals. This, in turn, allows for the foundations to be set in order for a company-wide implementation of IMC to be achieved, as Reid (2003) and Lauska et al. (2014) argued in their work.

One of these five clubs provided the author with additional details on how the evaluation process takes place, while emphasising that assessing the results is a priority for the company. The importance placed on the results could be considered as an indication of the IMC level in which the club belongs to and thus allows the author to suggest that IMC in implemented throughout the club on a strategic level (as argued by Kliatchko, 2008).

Even though evaluating the marketing targets set exceeds the purpose of this study and will therefore not be discussed further, it will be noted that out of the 30 clubs asked, less than half of them answered affirmatively. Details on how this evaluation process takes place were not provided. However, KPIs were often mentioned, as well as fan surveys, especially when assessing brand awareness.

Having examined the existence and content of both marketing strategies and marketing goals, a number of patterns have been identified. From the lack of marketing planning and misconceptions on a company's brand, to multiple well-defined and measurable marketing strategies and goals, the variations among clubs demonstrate the discrepancy in marketing communications practices within the sector (EPL), while allowing the author to identify the patterns that impede or assist respectively in the implementation of IMC.

Cross-Functional Communication vs Silos

In order for the interdepartmental relations and cross-functional communication within the clubs to be discussed, attention needs to be drawn to the fact that a number of different organisational structures were observed among the clubs studied, with marketing being a separate department, a sub-team of the commercial department or a joint team with the communications department. These structures define the departmental proximity between marketing and communications, placing them individually, in separate teams or under the same team.

Regardless of the structure under which each club operates, however, a number of topics emerged during the interviews that indicate the level of communication between teams. Since, the topic of interdepartmental or cross-functional communication or '*tearing down partitions*' as Tsai (2005, p. 440) suggested, is a fundamental component in the strategic planning and implementation of IMC (Gambetti & Schultz, 2015; Kitchen, 2016), it is therefore expected to shed light in understanding the clubs' integration practices. From informal interpersonal relations to formal interdepartmental meetings, the way in which the marketing and communications teams are in contact will be discussed in this section. Moreover, interdepartmental silos, a related topic that also emerged through the interviews as the result of poor communication, will be examined in detail.

Formal vs Informal Communication

'*Collaborative communication*' (Mohr et al., 1996, p. 103) and the effects it can have on integration have attracted considerable attention among academics, which encouraged the author to investigate it further. When examining the relationship between marketing and communications teams in each club, the vast majority (90%) of the clubs used the phrase 'we talk with each other every day' to describe it. The three clubs that did not use this or any phrase that might suggest that there is frequent communication between the two teams, used the words silos or 'islands' to describe the relationship between the marketing and the communication teams, as it will be further discussed below.

As the above commonly used quote suggests, the vast majority of the clubs imply that an informal aspect exists in cross-functional communication between the marketing and communications teams, which can be better illustrated in the following quotes.

> We talk all the time, since we practically sit together. Their desks are next to ours, so we don't even need to pick up the phone. We will put things on an email only if we want something to be formal; Otherwise, I can just turn my chair and ask them something.
>
> We talk every day, all the time. We are part of the same team, better yet part of the same club. There's a formal relationship, of course, we have to work together to do our job, but it's not the formality that defines our relationship. We are all colleagues and most of us are friends after all these years working here.

As both quotes show, the members of the marketing and the communications teams appear to be in frequent communication with each other. The informality of the communication between them is also evident through their quotes, which present their relationship as a well-functioning and even a friendly one. Formal communication was mentioned by the interviewees as well, but with a significantly smaller frequency than informal communication. The factors enhancing this cross-functional communication, according to the interviewees, are the interpersonal relationships between individuals, the layout of the offices, and the overall culture of the organisation, as well as the processes set out by the heads of each department and the higher management of the club (CEO/COO/Chairman). Nevertheless, the importance of each of these factors, as well as the balance between formal and informal communication varies. Similarities, however, can be observed within the clubs as it will be further examined below.

First, one club drew the picture of seamless communication between the marketing and the communication teams. Both on a formal and an informal way, the two teams, according to the interviewee are in constant communication. According to the interviewee, the frequent communication between the marketing and the communications teams, both on an informal and on a formal basis, is considered to be part of the employees' jobs. Communication and collaboration between the teams are not only considered desired but also required in order for the marketing and communications tasks to be completed appropriately.

Interdepartmental relationships are encouraged through a carefully designed process by the directors of marketing and communications, in order for communication and collaboration to be nurtured. More details on this process were not provided; However, it was underlined that a number of interdepartmental meetings take place on a weekly basis that reinforce teamwork and openness between employees. The layout of the offices between the two teams was also presented as a factor that enhances communication. Nevertheless, it was highlighted that it is the culture of the organisation and the processes in place that ensure seamless communication between the two teams. This could suggest that organisational culture and leadership have in fact enhanced collaborative communication as it was advocated by Ferdous (2008) and Porcu et al. (2012), and that seamless cross-functional communication is currently in place in this particular club.

Second, four clubs presented the author with a similar picture as the one described above, where members of the two teams communicate with each other frequently, both formally and informally. One of the clubs underlined that the structure of the organisation was in fact recently changed in order for communication between the teams to be enhanced.

Formal meetings are in place in all four clubs, in which members of the two teams exchange information, especially in regard to upcoming projects. Nevertheless, these meetings do not cover the full spectrum of interaction between the two teams. Informal communication is encouraged as well, since it can prove invaluable, as the following quote demonstrates.

> *This is a fast pace environment and things change very quickly. You have to be flexible, adaptable and able to react immediately.*

The promptness of informal communication, as the quote shows, allows this club to respond quickly and is therefore encouraged within it.

The culture of the organisations, the frequent meetings set in order to ensure a formal process of interaction, and the layout of the offices (geographical proximity between the two teams' desks) were presented as the main reasons behind the enhanced communication between marketing and communications. Interpersonal friendly relations were not mentioned by the interviewees as a key factor, but it was made clear that communicating openly and frequently is part of the role of each employee.

Third, eight clubs presented the author with a less structured approach regarding interdepartmental communication. Even though the interviewees claim to 'talk to each other every day', as already mentioned, the communication between the two teams appears to be predominantly on an informal basis. Informal ways of communication regularly replace formal procedures, as the quote presented in the beginning of this section shows, which allows the employees to interact quicker and easier but with a less structured and organised approach.

Interdepartmental formal meetings take place every one or two weeks, however, not all members of both teams are asked to participate in them. The culture of the organisations appears to encourage communication between the employees, but in a less passionate and methodical way than what was described by the five clubs discussed above.

Only two of these eight clubs mentioned the proximity of the employees' desks as a factor boosting communication. On the contrary, the teams directors' personality, views and practices were presented as the key factors behind fostering open communication between the two teams.

> It all changed when X (Head of Communications) joined the club. Not only is he exceptional in his job, but he made sure that we all talk to each other regularly. Before him, it was a project-based, one-way street. If we wanted something we could go to them, but that didn't mean that they would come to us to give us information.

In other words, as the above-mentioned quote shows, leadership appears to hold a key role in fostering collaborative communication, even when the overall organisational culture does not place adequate emphasis on it (McGrath, 2005a, 2005b). Consequently, it could be argued that, as Kelemen and Papasolomou-Doukakis (2004) suggest, had these clubs' culture been altered or reinforced accordingly, interdepartmental collaborative communication would have been better supported and facilitated.

Moreover, 11 clubs do not seem to have seamless communication between the marketing and the communication teams, regardless of the interviewees' initial claim. The original statement 'we talk to each other every day' can in fact be replaced with the more detailed and accurate statement:

> We work closely, but talk every day only when there is a project or task in which we need each other's help.

Informal communication is encouraged between employees; however, it is not encountered as often as in the clubs discussed above. Formal interdepartmental meetings are arranged by the directors of the teams, but their frequency varies from once a week to once a month. As it was also suggested by the eight clubs presented above, not all members are invited to these meetings, with the junior members of both teams rarely attending. In fact, in four of these 11 clubs, it is only the directors of the departments that participate in these meetings. As a result, the remaining members of the teams have no formal process encouraging them to communicate with their colleagues from other teams, hindering the overall horizontal communication within the organisation (Mohr et al., 1996).

Informal communication between the employees is fostered by the layout of the offices and the regular projects that require collaboration. Teams directors' leadership was not mentioned by the interviewees as an important factor in enhancing communication; however, the 'overall friendly atmosphere of the office' was underlined as a key influence in informal relations between members of different teams by three of these 11 clubs.

Finally, seven of the 11 clubs admitted that the relationship between the marketing and the communication team is not always on favourable terms. Friction between the teams occurs often, which according to interviewees is caused by the differing direct targets and overall scope each team has. This friction can cause miscommunication between the teams and obstruct their collaboration as Christensen et al. (2008a, 2008b) argue. More details on this friction and the effects it has on the clubs will be discussed in the following section examining interdepartmental silos.

Finally, the remaining six clubs presented the author with a contrasting image to seamless communication between the two teams. In fact, marketing and communication teams in the clubs do not seem to communicate or collaborate, unless a project obliges them to. When the teams need to work together, the communication between them was presented as focused solely on the task in hand. In these clubs, informal communication is favoured over formal due to its promptness and efficiency, according to the interviewees, especially between the junior members of the teams.

> *If you can get to him (Press Officer) directly, then you can get things done. You can just go to him and nip in and get things done. If it's something bigger, then the Heads get involved and it becomes more formal.*

Formal interdepartmental meetings are rarely organised in these six clubs, and as a result horizontal communication within the organisation is not facilitated at any stage, as one interviewee argued:

> *There has not been a meeting between us in the last five years that I have been here. Interestingly enough, I was told one will be planned at the end of the season.*

In five of these clubs the marketing and communication teams are based in separate offices or even in separate buildings (marketing team based in the stadium and communications team based in the training ground), which hinders any informal communication further. Moreover, each team's directors' leadership or the club's overall culture was not mentioned as factors that enhance communication between the teams. In fact, the projects that require the teams to collaborate appear to be the only factor that obliges members of the two teams to communicate with each other. Seamless communication does not seem to exist in any of these six clubs that presented the author with the existence of silos or *'islands'* within them (Rouziès et al., 2005; Ferdous, 2008). These silos will be further discussed in the following section.

Interdepartmental Silos

As the previous section on communication between the clubs' marketing and communications teams showed, considerable discrepancies exist among the clubs. While some clubs appear to have established open channels of communication between the two teams, and some encourage informal communication, 13 clubs

Marketing Strategy and Communication 73

seem to follow a different pattern. These 13 clubs presented the author with a more segregated approach between the two teams, which is characterised by obstructed and limited communication, affecting the overall collaboration between marketing and communications. In more detail, these clubs suggested the existence of silos or *'islands'* between the teams that hindered any open dialogue between them.

Emphasis was placed by the interviewees on the fact that the relationship between the teams was often a *'one-way street'*, in which requests were made by one team to the other, without an inquiry or interest on the second team's opinion or views on the matter. Members of the two teams in the above-mentioned clubs appear to collaborate with each other only when a project requires them to, and, according to the interviewees, in a less enthusiastic way. Friction can be created between the two teams that often do not feel they operate like they are part of the same club.

This phenomenon appears to be more intense in five of these clubs, where the two teams are often located in different buildings, hindering the communication between their members further. Nevertheless, even when marketing and communications teams share the same office and are also under the same department, such as in one of these clubs, internal silos exist and hinder the collaboration between the two teams.

According to the interviewees, the existence of these silos could be traced back to the primary distinction between the practical roles of different function teams, such as communications and marketing. As it was emphasised by the interviewees that identify silos in the clubs they work for, segregating the two teams is based on the dissimilar purpose each team was originally created for and further enhanced by the different people selected to populate them. In more detail, communications is a team that consists primarily of journalists who create content for the club's various media and are in charge of speaking directly to the fans through the club's own media or the Press. Most of them are, according to the interviewees, not only passionate football supporters but also loyal fans of the club they work for.

> *You are talking to the clubs' experts when talking to the fans, so in order to be heard and believed you need to be an expert yourself. We are trustworthy because we are experts and we know everything inside out.*

Their goal, according to the interviewees, is to write stories and make sure they voice the players', managers' and administrations' opinion to the Press.

On the other hand, the marketing team is created in order to primarily support the commercial arm of the club. The aim of the team is, according to the interviewees, to aid in creating revenue and assist in boosting sales. Their involvement in commercial activities represents the majority of the tasks they undertake, according to the interviewees of these 13 clubs, even when the marketing team is in fact considered to be part of the marketing and communications department (fan engagement and customer relationship management activities were also presented as commercial activities by these clubs). As it was pointed out by one interviewee, the fundamental distinction is how these teams are perceived and can be better explained in the following quote:

> *Communications people are journalists and football fans. They know the club, the history, the players. They know the voice of the club because they are the voice of the club, or they have been for many years. They might not understand the overall strategy of the club, but they know what the club is all about. On the other hand marketing people use corporate terms and numbers that cannot be understood by the fans. They don't know football and cannot think the way that football fans do. They are good marketers but they don't think football results, they think targets.*

This quote came from the Marketing and Communications Manager of a club, who is in charge of managing both the marketing and the communications teams.

These fundamental differences between the purpose and members of the two teams enhance the existence of silos and can create tension between them. However, apart from displeasing the employees (Ahmed & Rafiq, 1995; Rafiq & Ahmed, 2000), silos can have a direct damaging effect on the club's overall communication to the fans, as it was suggested. The inability to communicate and collaborate between the two teams proved to be harmful for a club's social media presence, as one of the interviewees suggested when the twitter account of the club which is managed by the media team was used by the marketing team without any checking of message that was promoted, resulting in fans' displeasure.

As the incident described by the interviewee suggests, silos can harm the club's communications significantly by damaging the consistency of the voice of the club. As it was discussed by Moriarty (1997), Duncan and Moriarty (1998), Duncan (2002), Keller (2016) and Manoli and Hodgkinson (2021) and such an inconsistency can harm the brand of the club and displease key stakeholders, such as the employees and the customers / fans. Most importantly, silos do not allow for open communication channels to be established, which would assist in a cross-functioning collaboration between the teams and an easily accessible flow of information within the organisation, as Christensen et al. (2008a, 2008b) suggested.

As it was underlined by four of these clubs, these silos are gradually being replaced with a more open, two-way communication platform between the teams. The main reasons behind this change, as argued by the interviewees, is the increasingly demanding marketing communications environment that requires quicker and better coordinated responses, and the organisational changes taking place within the clubs that include, but are not limited, to the replacement of the individuals leading these teams. In other words, it is both external and internal factors that could lead to interdepartmental silos being overcome (Duncan & Moriarty, 1998; Shimp, 2007).

Having examined the relations between marketing and communications teams among the clubs, a number of issues were identified. As the analysis above has demonstrated, significantly differing patterns exist, with the practices followed in some clubs contradicting the ways in which other clubs operate. While the overall image portrayed by the majority of the interviewees initially suggested a close relationship between the two teams, a number of clubs appear to be occupied by internal silos. These silos seem to not only create friction between the employees of the clubs but also affect the overall communication of the clubs, which can be harmful for the club's brand, as it will be further examined in the following section.

Conclusion

Examining the existence and form that marketing strategies and marketing goals take within the clubs, as well as the internal communication or interdepartmental silos that exist, allowed for insights in the marketing communications practices that represent the implementation of IMC. This examination, allowed for the wide disparities, as well as the similarities to be identified among the clubs studied, giving us a first glimpse to not only whether but also how and to what extent integration is being achieved in these client organisations.

References

Ahmed, P. K. & Rafiq, M. (1995) 'The role of internal marketing in the implementation of marketing strategies', *Journal of Marketing Practice: Applied Marketing Science*, 1 (4) 32–51.

Baker, M. & Hart, S. (2008) *The marketing book*, London: Routledge.

Batra, R. & Keller, K. L. (2016) 'Integrating marketing communications: New findings, new lessons and new ideas', *Journal of Marketing*, 80 (6) 122–145.

Burmann, C. & Zeplin, S. (2005) 'Building brand commitment: A behavioural approach to internal brand management', *Journal of Brand Management*, 12 (4) 279–300.

Chelladurai, P. & Chang, K. (2000) 'Targets and standards of quality in sport services', *Sport Management Review*, 3 (1) 1–22.

Christensen, L. T., Firat, F. A. & Torp, S. (2008a) 'The organisation of integrated communications: Toward flexible integration', *European Journal of Marketing*, 42 (3/4) 423–452.

Christensen, L. T., Morsing, M. & Cheney, G. (2008b) *Corporate communications: Convention, complexity and critique*, London: Sage.

Duncan, T. R. (2002) *IMC: Using advertising and promotion to build brands* (International Edition), New York: The McGraw-Hill.

Duncan, T. R. & Moriarty, S. E. (1998) 'A communication-based marketing model for managing relationships', *The Journal of Marketing*, 56 (2) 1–13.

Duncan, T. R. & Mulhern, F. (2004) A white paper on the status, scope and future of IMC. In *IMC Symposium, Northwestern University & University of Denver* (March 2004).

Ferdous, A. S. (2008) 'Integrated internal marketing communication (IIMC)', *The Marketing Review*, 8 (3) 223–235.

Gabrielli, V. & Balboni, B. (2010) 'SME practice towards integrated marketing communications', *Marketing Intelligence & Planning*, 28 (3) 275–290.

Gambetti, R. C. & Schultz, D. E. (2015) 'Reshaping the boundaries of marketing communication to bond with consumers', *Journal of Marketing Communications*, 21 (1) 1–4.

Gould, S. J. (2004) 'IMC as theory and as a poststructural set of practices and discourses: A continuously evolving paradigm shift', *Journal of Advertising Research*, 44 (1) 66–70.

Jenkinson, A. (2006) 'Planning and evaluating communications in an integrated organisation', *Journal of Targeting, Measurement and Analysis for Marketing*, 15 (1) 47–64.

Jones, G. S., Li, T., Kitchen, P. J. & Brignell, J. (2004) 'The emergence of IMC: A theoretical perspective', *Journal of Advertising Research*, 44 (1) 19–30.

Kelemen, M. & Papasolomou-Doukakis, I. (2004) 'Can culture be changed? A study of internal marketing, *The Service Industries Journal*, 24 (5) 121–135.

Keller, K. L. (1993) 'Conceptualizing, measuring, and managing customer-based brand equity', *The Journal of Marketing*, 57 (1) 1–22.

Keller, K. L. (2009) 'Building strong brands in a modern marketing communications environment', *Journal of Marketing Communications*, 15 (2/3) 139–155.

Keller, K. L. (2016) 'Unlocking the power of integrated marketing communications: How integrated is your IMC program?', *Journal of Advertising*, 45(3), 286–301.

Kitchen, P. J. (2016) Is IMC "marketing oriented"? In L. Petruzzellis & R. S. Winer (Eds.) *Rediscovering the essentiality of marketing* (pp. 441–442), New York: Springer International Publishing.

Kitchen, P. J. & Tourky, M. (2015) *Integrated communications in the postmodern era*, Hampshire: Palgrave Macmillan.

Kliatchko, J. (2005) 'Towards a new definition of integrated marketing communications (IMC)', *International Journal of Advertising*, 24 (1) 7–34.

Kliatchko, J. (2008) 'Revisiting the IMC construct: A revised definition and four pillars', *International Journal of Advertising*, 27 (1) 133–160.

Kotler, P. & Levy, S. J. (1969) 'Broadening the concept of marketing', *Journal of Marketing*, 33 (1) 10–15.

Lauska, D., Laurie, S. & Mortimer, K. (2014) 'The management of corporate personality: An IMC perspective', In: *Proceedings of the 47th Academy of Marketing Conference, AM2014: Marketing Dimensions: People, Places and Spaces*, Bournemouth: Academy of Marketing.

Manoli, A. E. (2020) 'Brand capabilities in English premier league clubs', *European Sport Management Quarterly* 20 (1) 30–46.

Manoli, A. E. & Hodgkinson, I. R. (2017) 'Marketing outsourcing in the English premier league: The right holder/agency interface', *European Sport Management Quarterly*, 17 (4) 436–456.

Manoli, A. E. & Hodgkinson, I. R. (2019) 'The implementation of integrated marketing communication (IMC): Evidence from professional football clubs in England', *Journal of Strategic Marketing*, 28 (6) 542–563.

Manoli, A. E. & Hodgkinson, I. R. (2021) 'Exploring internal organisational communication dynamics in the professional football industry', *European Journal of Marketing*, 55 (11) 2894–2916.

Manoli, A. E. & Kenyon, J. A. (2018) Football and Marketing. In S. M. Chadwick, P. Widdop, D. Parnell & C. Anagnostopoulos (Eds.) *Routledge handbook of football business and management*, (pp. 88–100), Oxon: Routledge.

McGrath, J. (2005a) 'IMC at a crossroads: A theoretical review and a conceptual framework for testing', *Marketing Management Journal*, 15 (2) 55–66.

McGrath, J. (2005b) 'A pilot study testing aspects of the integrated marketing communications concept', *Journal of Marketing Communications*, 11 (3) 191–214.

Mohr, J. J., Fisher, R. J. & Nevin, J. R. (1996) 'Collaborative communication in interfirm relationships: Moderating effects of integration and control', *The Journal of Marketing*, 60 (3) 103–115.
Moriarty, S. E. (1997) 'IMC needs PR's stakeholder focus', *Marketing News*, 31 (11) 7.
Ouwersloot, H. & Duncan, T. (2008) *Integrated marketing communications*, London: McGraw-Hill Education.
Pickton, D. & Broderick, A. (2001) *Integrated marketing communications*, Essex: Pearson Education.
Porcu, L., del Barrio-García, S. & Kitchen, P. J. (2012) 'How integrated marketing communications (IMC) works? A theoretical review and an analysis of its main drivers and effects/¿Cómo funciona la Comunicación Integrada de Marketing (CIM)? Una revisión teórica y un análisis de sus antecedentes y efectos', *Comunicación y sociedad*, 25 (1) 313–348.
Rafiq, M. & Ahmed, P. K. (2000) 'Advances in the internal marketing concept: Definition, synthesis and extension', *Journal of Services Marketing*, 14 (6) 449–462.
Reid, M. (2003) 'IMC–performance relationship: Further insight and evidence from the Australian marketplace', *International Journal of Advertising*, 22 (2) 227–248.
Rouziès, D., Anderson, E., Kohli, A. K., Michaels, R. E., Weitz, B. A. & Zoltners, A. A. (2005) 'Sales and marketing integration: A proposed framework', *Journal of Personal Selling & Sales Management*, 25 (2) 113–122.
Schultz, D. E. & Schultz, H. F. (1998) 'Transitioning marketing communication into the twenty-first century', *Journal of Marketing Communications*, 4 (1) 9–26.
Schultz, D. E. & Schultz, H. F. (2004) *IMC: The next generation*, New York: McGraw-Hill.
Shimp, T. A. (2007) *Integrated marketing communications in advertising and promotion* (7th ed.), Mason: Thomson Higher Education.
Shimp, T. A. & Andrews, J. C. (2012) *Advertising promotion and other aspects of integrated marketing communications* (9th ed.), Mason: Cengage Learning.
Swain, W. N. (2004) 'Perceptions of IMC after a decade of development: Who's at the wheel, and how can we measure success?', *Journal of Advertising Research*, 44 (1) 46–65.
Trustrum, L. B. (1989) 'Marketing: Concept and function', *European Journal of Marketing*, 23 (3) 48–56.
Tsai, S. P. (2005) 'Integrated marketing as management of holistic consumer experience', *Business Horizons*, 48 (5) 431–441.

Chapter 5

Communications Alignment and Brand Management

Introduction

This chapter will focus on the examination of the alignment of external communications of each club, as well as the brand management practices they follow. Since the link of both topics with IMC's implementation has been stressed throughout the existing literature on the topic, examining the practices of the clubs studied allows for a clear illustration to how integration is attempted or achieved, as it will be discussed below.

External Communications

The issue of communications alignment emerged when discussing the people or teams in charge of managing different channels of communications, including the CRM system and new social media. As it was uncovered through the interviews, tasks such as CRM system, website and social media management often fall under the remit of the marketing team; however, different patterns can be found. For example, the official social media accounts are managed by the marketing team in only six clubs, with the communications or media team leading their management in the rest. Moreover, a recent industry trend, according to four interviewees, is for additional commercial social media accounts to be created in order for the messages promoted from the club to be segregated based on their content. Following this practice, commercially focused messages can be separated from football-focused news, and be promoted through the new commercial social media accounts. These accounts are mainly managed by the commercial team, with the marketing team maintaining a limited input.

Based on this plethora of ways in which a club communicates, and the various people that appear to be managing the channels through which this communication takes place, the topic of communications alignment was brought into question. In other words, since several media are managed by different people (Manoli, 2016; Manoli & Hodgkinson, 2017), the interviewees were asked about the way in which an alignment of all communications is achieved in the clubs. This alignment would help achieve the 'one-voice' concept that can have a

DOI: 10.4324/9781003140238-5

direct effect on an organisation's brand (Keegan et al., 1992; Kotler, 2000; Keller, 2009, 2016).

The response given to this question was two-fold and triggered a discussion on both communications alignment through an *Integration Czar* (as originally suggested by Schultz, 1992) and brand management. Both topics will be presented in detail in this section since they represent the two perspectives of IMC as argued by Tsai (2005); IMC as strategic communications and IMC as strategic brand management.

Communications Alignment

The initial response of 83.33% of the interviewees (in 25 out of 30 clubs) is that communications alignment falls under the remit of one employee's job. The way in which they attempt or not attempt to align their communications will be discussed below.

Integration Czar

This employee the 25 interviewees referred to is either the marketing or the communications director, who is in charge of checking and approving any message that originates from the club. Their job entails controlling and ensuring that whatever is communicated is always aligned with the club's overall communications, which resembles Schultz' (1992) suggestion of introducing an *Integration Czar* within each organisation. The outward communications that are checked and controlled include, according to the interviewees, a wide spectrum of messages; from press releases sent directly to the media, or published on the club's own media, to group or individual emails sent by all departments within the club. Social media draw additional emphasis, since checking the communications that come from the club or the club's employees can even include the messages individual employees publish on their own social media accounts about the club, as the following quote demonstrates.

> That (alignment) is the job of the head of PR and communications. He will manage and have an overview of all the different communications messages that come from the club. He will monitor everything and make sure that all communications are consistent; our announcements, our posts, our emails, my twitter account, my facebook account. If we said something that has no relevance to the club or something that is controversial, if it's not consistent to what the club should say, he will pick this and change it.

It could be argued that such a control is difficult to be implemented in all one-to-one communications of the club, such as a sales discussion between a sales executive and a corporate client. Since such individual communications cannot be checked or approved by the person in charge, they could therefore potentially derail from the overall communications line of the club. Often detailed guidelines are created in order for this obstacle to be overcome, as it will be further discussed in the following section. These guidelines were mentioned by the clubs as an additional way in which the alignment can be achieved, which complements the checking process that was presented above.

The person in charge of ensuring that all communications are aligned is doing so in order to protect the club, by assuring that any outward communication is in line with what the club stands for, as the quote below illustrates.

> *Ninety-five percent of communication comes to my desk before it goes out, so there's a filtering process. People from other departments will have to come to my department before they get the ok to publicise something. Anyone who works for the club has to understand the club, what it is about and in other words be the club and behave likewise as well*

As it was suggested by the interviewees and is also underlined by the above quote, the employees of the club are expected to understand and respect that all communication messages need to be checked and approved by the above-mentioned person or team. Should the messages be considered inconsistent with the club, it is also expected that the changes suggested will be completed before a message is communicated.

An interviewee mentioned that respecting the approval or disapproval of the person in charge of aligning all communications has even led a club to bring a lucrative partnership agreement to an end at a very early stage. When the communication messages intended to announce and promote this club's partnership with a specific company were designed, they were then presented to the *Integration Czar* team as expected. In this occasion, however, the *Czar* team argued that should these messages be communicated to the media and public, they would contradict the identity and voice of the club. As a result of this contradiction, it was suggested that major alterations or even a cancellation of the agreement would be the most suitable solution. According to the interviewee, protecting the voice was and still is considered a priority for the club, which valued the opinion expressed and decided to withdraw from the original lucrative partnership with the company in question.

> *We were told that the club's voice and personality was built before we joined the club and that we should try our best to keep it consistent and strong. That voice will remain strong even after all of us have left, if we all try to support it. I can now say that it was the right call at the time.*

Placing a person or a team in charge of controlling, checking and approving all messages that are communicated from an organisation resembles the idea of an *Integration Czar* or central integration control, as discussed by Schultz (1992, 1993), which was originally met with enthusiasm by academics (Low, 2000). Nevertheless, it was soon replaced by the suggestion that a collaborative approach would be more beneficial for the organisation (Duncan & Everett, 1993). When Phelps et al. (1996, p. 221) examined the choice companies made regarding integration, the findings showed that organisations were gradually moving towards a more collaborative approach; however, the majority of them (69%) was still following the *Integration Czar* practice. As it can be seen through the analysis of the findings of this study, the *Integration Czar* appears to be a very popular practice in EPL football as well (followed by 83.33% of the clubs examined). Additionally, linking this practice with the centralisation versus decentralisation debate among academics (Low & Mohr, 1999; Beverland & Luxton, 2005; Gurau, 2008), as it was discussed in Chapter 2, it could be argued that centralisation better describes the current situation in EPL football clubs as presented in this section, given that all communications seem to be channelled through one central funnel that is then controlled by one person or a team.

Differences in Utilising an Integration Czar

Even though the above presented practice appears to be consistent within the 25 clubs, minor differences can be noted among them which will be presented below in more detail.

First, a difference appears to be in the detail in which one-to-one communication is being checked, with some clubs describing a meticulous scrutiny process that was presented as more detailed and thorough than a mere checking point procedure presented by others, with multiple variations existing in between the two extremes as well. Second, the concepts of collaboration and co-operation in aligning communications, instead of a mere checking point before a message is sent, were also mentioned by few of the interviewees. According to them, communications are checked by one person, however:

> *Collaborating and communicating with each other as much as we can enables us to get things right. We get everything checked by marketing and we also tend to send around an email to different departments to get it seen and approved by them as well.*

On the other hand, most of the clubs that follow the *Integration Czar* approach seem to respect the checking and controlling process, but do not refer to this process using the idea of collaboration. On the contrary, the opinion expressed by most is that:

> *It is a checking point. We send them most things and they check it. When it's approved, we get the ok and we push it out.*
>
> *There is a common understanding about our aims and objectives and how our messages should sound, but marketing and communications are different and it is difficult to make them (communications team) see what we want to come through. It is challenging to try and have the same tone of voice when talking about football and when talking about commercial.*

This second quote introduces the reader to the third difference between clubs identified, the potential problems the alignment of communications appears to have. While few clubs did not refer to any problems during the alignment process, a number of challenges in getting the tone of voice right in each message, as presented in the above quote, were mentioned by most clubs.

Inquiring on the success of the alignment process could provide the author with potentially subjective comments from the interviewees, bearing in mind that the alignment is managed by some of the individuals interviewed, which would thus not allow for a reliable conclusion to be reached. The problems or challenges encountered in the alignment, however, and the way in which they were mentioned by the interviewees suggests that additional research could be conducted on the topic in order to better capture potential challenges in the integration process within the clubs.

Finally, aligning the club's communications to ensure that the same tone of voice is used consistently throughout the club was appreciated as a demanding process by all clubs. It was in fact suggested that the process became particularly challenging since the multiplication of media, which often attract diverse and dissimilar fans. This diversity between the audiences of different media was presented as the main reason behind the creation of variations of the same tone of voice, in order to match diverse *'personalities'* of the club that can address fans in a way that better responds to them. According to the interviewees:

> *Everything we do gets to be checked and approved. But depending on the channel, we do get to change the tone of voice based on whether it is social media or website, because we have to match the personality we have built for the club on each medium. It is still the same tone of voice throughout the club, but comes in different tones to match each medium's personality.*

Once again, differentiations exist in the detail and consistency that is devoted in creating these diverse *'personalities'* that better match the fans on each medium, while using the same overall voice. Creating these *'personalities'* of the same voice resembles the effective application of IMC, as described by Schultz (2001), Porcu et al. (2012) and Kitchen and Tourky (2015), in which marketing communications successfully become audience-centric. According to the interviewees, few clubs presented this process as quite meticulous, while most of them did not present the author with information on whether such an attempt is made, while it could be argued that five clubs have yet to reach a point in which a coherent tone of voice is achieved, as it will be discussed below.

Communications Non-Alignment

The remaining five clubs which did not suggest that an employee or a team is in charge of aligning all communications, as discussed above (*Integration Czar*), presented the author with a different and rather contradicting pattern. According to them there is no attempt to align the communications generated by the club. On the contrary, these clubs argued that communications do not need to be aligned and that attempting to do so might 'harm' the club. Therefore the practice followed is that each medium is managed by a different person or team in each of these clubs, because that assists in maintaining each medium's individuality.

According to the interviewees, each medium has a different voice and often a different audience and by aligning what is communicated by the club resembles looking for a one-size-to-fit-all solution. As it was argued, such an attempt could potentially displease the fans who are looking for this individuality in order to identify themselves with the club. A quote by one of the interviewees suggests that:

> *The fans know the Press Officer, they know the Social Media Editor. They know how they speak, how they react. If we try to control their messages, the fans will know. Not only will we displease our employees who might feel they lost their voice, but we might also upset the fans who might think that they are not spoken to directly by the people they know.*

When asked whether they think that this polyphony of voices might confuse the audience, all five clubs responded categorically that the club's identity is very strong and cannot be easily mistaken for something else. As an interviewee argued:

> *All the fans have to do is check who the communications come from, what is the address, what is the emblem at the top of the message. If they see it's us, they know who we are. Even if a word is different, they will know it's us talking to them. That is the benefit of having such a strong identity.*

It could be argued that these five clubs do not seem to appreciate the link between aligning the communications of an organisation in order to create the 'one-voice' feeling, and the effect it can have on its brand, as it has been discussed by academics such as Duncan and Mulhern (2004), Gould (2004), Jones et al. (2004), Reid et al. (2005), Keller (2016) and Manoli and Hodgkinson (2019, 2021). In these occasions, the club's communications are viewed as an everyday task whose value is based more on its functionality rather than the effect it can have on the overall brand and identity of the club. On the contrary, the club's identity is considered to be a wider concept that cannot be affected by everyday routine actions, such as writing a Press release or posting a news bulletin on the club's official website. The club's identity in these occasions is considered to be strong, widely appreciated by the fans and therefore unaffected by most everyday actions.

The views expressed by these interviewees about the alignment of communications and its links to the club's identity are evident throughout the analysis of their practices. As their marketing communications practices show, there appears to be a number of misconceptions about the clubs' brand, its value and its management, as it will be discussed in the following section in more detail. These misconceptions can be considered a key barrier in IMC's implementation, which has not been captured so far by the relevant literature examining the topic (Duncan & Everett, 1993; Moriarty, 1994; Eagle & Kitchen, 2000; Schultz, 2000, 2001; Dmitrijeva & Batraga, 2012).

Having presented both ways in which communication is or is not aligned among the clubs, as well as any dissimilarities existing between clubs that follow similar processes, the second part of the interviewees' answer to the original question will be presented; brand management. The way in which the brand of each club is managed and safeguarded is, according to the interviewees, interlinked with the way in which communications are aligned. The two concepts complement each other in order for a better coherency within the organisation and consistency over time to be achieved, as it was argued by Tsai (2005) and will be further examined in the following section.

Brand Management

Three different aspects of brand management were included in the interviewees' answers on how the consistency of the club's communications is ensured; brand guidelines, brand training and brand control. As it will be presented in this section, different patterns seem to exist among the clubs in all three aspects examined, which are also interlinked in different ways, as it will be presented below in more detail.

Before the examination of the practices in each club begins, a noteworthy pattern identified will be noted. This second part of the interviewees' answers on the communications alignment question included the words '*brand guidelines*' in all the interviews conducted. According to the interviewees, all 30 clubs have brand guidelines which were mentioned and then presented in more detail to the author. The club's brand guidelines is a document of varying sizes that provides guidance on various topics regarding the brand, as Melewar (2003) suggests in his work. In order for a club's staff to be made aware of the brand guidelines, their contents and any updates on them over time, a process aptly referred to as training on the brand takes place (Melewar & Walker, 2003). At the same time, an additional system is organised, called brand control, through which the outward communications of a club are being '*policed*' in order to ensure that '*everything is on brand*', and thus the appropriate representation of the brand is safeguarded (Moriarty, 1994; Melewar & Walker, 2003; Manoli, 2020). Even though brand guidelines were mentioned by all clubs, their content, use, training and control differs vastly within the football clubs, which can justify why they were discussed and presented in more detail and with more enthusiasm by some interviewees than others.

First, five clubs indicated that the guidelines are being considered as the club's '*brand bible*' which is used, implemented and monitored by the marketing team that has the role of the club's '*brand police*'. As the interviewees suggested, the brand guidelines tend to be a rather lengthy document that offers thorough details and is updated regularly, in order to incorporate instructions and recommendations on various topics such as the use of the crest (when and how is it acceptable to use it), the official colours and fonts of the club, the suggested words and tone of voice when speaking on behalf of the club, and the acceptable clothes and decoration of any rooms associated with the club. As it was highlighted by the interviewees, particular attention is paid within the guidelines to offer detailed guidance on topics that might be ambiguous or potentially problematic, such as responding to fans' messages on social media. In these occasions details are provided on sample answers, which facilitate the employees to communicate on behalf of the club in a way that ensures the safeguarding of its brand.

> *We have brand guidelines that is a comprehensive bible that incorporates everything down to where you can and can't use our badge, which lines should surround the badge, where it can and cannot be placed on the page, etc. Also where is it used or even our tone of voice.*

The brand guidelines are updated regularly so that novel and emerging topics are addressed and already included aspects are '*refreshed*'. The most recent updates include guidance on how to speak on behalf of the club in each social medium and which imagery to use in social media videos. As these five interviewees underlined, since the clubs have also an international presence, the most updated brand guidelines include additional sections that cover topics regarding the international communications of each club. In these sections, additional emphasis is being drawn on the use of appropriate wording in outward communication that is aligned with the club's brand and identity, bearing in mind the discrepancy a translated message can have from the original. Following an update on the guidelines, the document is promoted to all members of staff who are, in turn, expected to consult it and comply with it in any future action.

The brand guidelines are not just provided to the employees of each club when they first join the organisation, but are on the contrary, a key part in an on-going education process. When a new employee joins one of these five clubs, a thorough induction to the brand guidelines is provided by a member of the marketing team, in order for the full details regarding the club's brand and its protection to be clarified. The employees are also provided with a copy of the brand guidelines that they are asked to consult in any outward communication they might engage. Additional training sessions or workshops are organised in these clubs in order for the brand guidelines and the regular updates on them to be communicated and clarified to all the employees. Particular attention is paid on employees working in the marketing, communications and commercial functions, since these departments tend to design and control most of the outward communication of the club. However, training is provided to all employees since, as it was underlined by the interviewees:

> *Even the recorded message on the phone says something about our brand, about our tone of voice. So, everyone working here has to know who we are, from the receptionist to the staff in the stadium store.*

Since the brand guidelines are communicated in a careful and detailed way to the employees, it is expected that all staff will comply with them in all occasions. Routine checks are performed by the marketing team, who as an interviewee argued acts as the '*brand police*', so that the compliance to the guidelines can be ensured. The person or team in charge of ensuring the alignment of the club's communication, as presented in the previous section (*Integration Czar*), is also the one in charge of these regular checks which certify that the brand is safeguarded and that the employees are adhering to the brand guidelines.

If the people in charge (the '*brand police*') deem that a message broadcasted is inconsistent with the brand values or could possibly prove tricky for the club's brand, it will be altered or removed. No incident of friction or lack of compliance was mentioned by the interviewees of these five clubs, who presented the author with an appreciation of the club's brand and its value, as the following quote shows.

> *If something is, or could potentially prove harmful, we are here to make sure that it is changed before it damages the brand in any way and everyone here knows that this is our job.*

The appreciation for the value of the brand and the effects its management can have on it, as they were expressed above, resemble the ideas expressed by academic such as Keegan et al. (1992), Barnes (2001) and Edelman (2010), who link IMC directly with a company's brand. In addition, focusing on the training and the control of the brand in order for its management and representation to be safeguarded can be considered an indicator of IMC's implementation in the clubs discussed above, according to Burmann and Zeplin (2005), Madhavaram et al. (2005) and Kitchen and Burgmann (2010).

Second, eight clubs presented the author with a similar, but rather downgraded version from the one described above. The brand guidelines in these clubs are also detailed documents that include advice and suggestions on how the brand should be represented. From the use of the badge to the imagery that can accompany an official message, the brand guidelines cover a number of areas. Social media attract additional attention in these clubs as well, with the latest updates including suggestions on how social media posts, answers to questions and videos should be structured and presented.

The marketing team in these clubs is also presented as the '*brand police*' that is in charge of writing and updating the document. However, the brand guidelines in these clubs do not seem to be that detailed regarding the tone of voice and one-to-one communication, as the ones presented above. Updates are occurring on a less regular basis, with the most recent ones concerning the club's brand representation on social media. The international presence of the clubs in regard to how the brand is represented was not mentioned by the interviewees, even though a number of these clubs have a substantial international fan base, as well as popular new and social media international accounts. The brand guidelines are communicated to all members of staff in these clubs, along with any new additions or revisions made on them. Nonetheless, what appeared to be missing was a clear control, guidance and leadership on the brand guidelines.

As it was suggested, even though the marketing team is in charge of the brand guidelines, a clear direction does not appear to be provided to the members of staff, who are instead trusted to comprehend and implement them without any training on them. The fact that no training is provided to them was justified by the interviewees by arguing that each employee has a high volume of work and they are capable of understanding and appreciating the guidelines without any additional training.

The guidelines are accessible to all employees through each club's intranet, a point that is underlined to all employees when joining the club. However, additional attention is placed on the employees of the marketing, communications and commercial departments who are also provided with a hard copy, as well as a hard copy of the updates when they occur. Checks on how the brand is represented take place less often than what was presented by the previous five clubs, since the clubs' belief is that they are doing a good job, as the following quote demonstrates.

> *That is one thing that we as a business have, we have a strong identity, a strong brand. Because of the nature of the business, even though we have many messages going out, we understand that we use the same tone of voice and represent the brand appropriately. In terms of consistency, continuity and the feel of the message, I think we manage that well enough. Could be better, but that comes down to the challenges of the business, the speed and turnout; There might be inconsistenciles.*

The lack of clear guidance and training can be seen through this quote, in which the employees' individual understanding is accepted as an adequate evaluation of the brand's representation. The lack of control is also apparent through this quote and is further justified through the employees' unsupported belief that the brand is represented appropriately. This quote underlines the belief of an already existing strength of the brand which enables the clubs to devote less attention in training and controlling its representation. In other words, since the identity and brand of the club are strong, less control is needed in order to maintain it. Based on the level in which these clubs belong, it could be suggested that in order for this potential misconception on the club's brand to be overcome, *'redefining the scope of marketing communication'*, as Kitchen and Schultz (1999, p. 34) named level 2 should be conducted and completed, leading to a more strategic implementation of IMC.

As it was underlined by the interviewees, an attempt is made for the brand guidelines that are currently used to be updated drastically, in order for the demanding communication needs of the EPL to be met. As the following quote demonstrates, the interviewees suggested that these changes will be designed based on the existing brand guidelines of some of the five clubs mentioned above.

> *This is why I need to rewrite the brand guidelines, because it (an update) doesn't happen all the time. They do not go into sufficient detail to help the communications team do their job with social media. We need a consistent tone of voice and brand representation in everything. We need the brand guidelines A and B have [the clubs' names have been redacted]. That is something we are working on.*

While the need for an update was underlined, as the quote illustrates, the interviewees did not indicate that attempts are being made in order to improve the brand guidelines' implementation and control as well, which differs substantially from what Melewar (2003) and Melewar and Walker (2003) suggest.

Moreover, 11 clubs mentioned the brand guidelines as a measure of control in order for the communications of the club to be aligned and the brand to be represented coherently; they nevertheless did not suggest that a similarly thorough document such as the one discussed by all clubs mentioned above existed. These interviewees argued that the brand guidelines offer suggestions on how to manage the brand of the club; however, since they are often outdated, the guidance provided can be at times unsuitable or unhelpful. For example, as it was suggested, handling social media seems to, often be missing from these guidelines, making it at times challenging for the employees. In these cases, details such as the tone of voice and the uniformity or coherency in the way fans are dealt with seems to also be absent from the guidelines.

On the contrary, these significantly smaller documents appear to focus on the representation of the club's badge (where and how it can be used) and the colours that the club can be associated with. These guidelines are often lacking some vital information regarding the club's brand representation and safeguarding, such as details on how the employees should be referring to the club (e.g. in cases in which a club's name consists of more than one word, and a number of variations of its name are popular among the media and the fans). These 11 clubs' interviewees highlighted that the brand guidelines are not sufficient and need updating, and as a result, improvements need to be made.

> *How do we spell our name; It's very long so we need to know how to spell it, how do we call ourselves (a number of variations of the name of the club were mentioned). We need a lot of detail in our brand guidelines and we need to add them.*

This interviewee provided the author with the following example that highlighted the point made on the variations in which the club's brand has been represented. The author was presented with three documents published by the club: a match programme, the club's official magazine and a brochure on the matchday hospitality packages available. While examining the covers of the three documents, an inconsistency was uncovered. Even though the badge of the club was used consistently in all three documents, the name of the club was presented with minor variations in each one of the documents. According to the interviewee, this incident took place before their appointment as the head of marketing and their assignment as the person in charge of ensuring all communications are aligned.

As the above-mentioned example illustrates, checking that the brand guidelines are adhered to does not take place regularly. Additionally, the brand guidelines are not shared with every employee of the club, unlike the practice followed in the clubs discussed above. The brand guidelines are not confidential; however, the employees belong in departments that are considered 'not relevant' to the club's brand such as the accounts or the security departments:

> *Do not need to read and follow the brand guidelines. It is not relevant to the job, so they don't really have to read it. It is there in the central hard drive if they ask for it, but they don't really need a copy of it on their desk.*

This suggestion that particular departments or functions bear little to no relevance to the organisation's brand contradicts the key aspect of IMC, as presented by Schultz and Schultz (1998, 2004), Kliatchko (2005, 2008) and Porcu et al. (2012) who argued that a holistic company-wide view of marketing communications should be followed.

Nevertheless, and despite the lack of controls on the brand, all interviewees were eager to argue that the brand is indeed appreciated by all members of staff in each club, since they are all able to fully comprehend the club's values and identity. This assessment was based on the interviewees' beliefs, who argued that understanding the brand is something that does not require training, but instead can be learned while performing your job.

> *We have pdf and power points illustrating the main things we should and shouldn't do, but nothing more. We try to follow what other people, more senior, have done. People who have been around for a long time. I rely on them to post something, but then it depends on what the club expects from us. You tend to learn things on the job.*

It was not clarified whether the updates that are scheduled to take place would include changes on the training and control of the brand. However, it could be argued that unless such a change is made, brand management and consequently IMC's implementation will keep encountering a high number of obstacles in these clubs (Ots & Nyilasy, 2015).

Finally, the remaining six clubs presented the author with a rather dissimilar view of the brand guidelines. The interviewees referred to the brand guidelines as a few pages of suggestions or rules on the club's crest, name and official imagery.

Details on how the crest should be used, such as where it should be placed on a page and which colours it should be matched with, are included but offered in a way that is mainly suitable for graphic designers (e.g. colours presented in codes, position of the crest given through coordinates). This was also in line with the interviewees suggestion that the brand guidelines are used by the designer or the designer agency that is employed by the club in order for the material created to be in accordance with the brand.

> *What we do is consistent because we use the same design agency consistently. Since they know our brand and the rules behind it, everything they create for us is consistent.*

As is evident, these clubs presented a coherency in the design as the main criterion in order for a brand to be appropriately represented. Similarly with the 11 clubs mentioned above, the guidelines are not confidential, but neither are they shared with all the employees of the club. In fact, very few people have access to them, since their use is mostly limited to the designer or design agency employed by the club. The guidelines are also provided to the club's partners' designers or design agencies, in order for guidance to be offered on their use of the club's emblem and brand. Since the guidelines entail only elementary information on the use of the designs and imagery, no efforts to update them were discussed, expect for the rare occasion in which a major change in the official colours or crest of the club occurs.

Concepts such as the tone of voice or the brand's representation on social media are absent from these brand guidelines. With no brand guidance on both one-to-one and mass communication through social media, it is solely the employees' responsibility to represent the brand accurately, something that was nevertheless presented as a relatively easy thing to do.

> *If you try to speak their language, you can speak to the fans and you can represent the brand.*

This rather simplistic view expressed by one of the interviewees highlights how these six clubs appear to be viewing brand management. A similar view was presented by all six interviewees, who all argued to have knowledge and understanding of the brand, without nevertheless any efforts to support their argument, assess their understanding or offer any training on the brand.

> *Nine out of ten times it's right. No one is making sure that what we're doing is right, but we might work pretty close to make sure it's consistent. However, that is just between our team, not a company-wide idea. It's just the understanding that we have, nothing more.*

As it was suggested, no training is provided to the members of staff in these clubs. Even departments that attract additional attention in other clubs, such as marketing, communications and commercial, appear to receive no training on how the brand should be represented. On the contrary, as the above quote illustrated, employees are expected to 'know' or 'understand' the brand.

As it was discussed in the communications alignment section, these same clubs do not seem to invest in controlling or checking outward communications. Likewise, the brand consistency of the club is not checked, which might occasionally lead to misrepresentations of the brand with potentially harmful effects, as the following quote illustrates:

> There have been occasions in which we missed the mark. A message went out from the ticketing side and we didn't get to check it. The social media editor posted something that was border-line out of order. But things happen.

According to one interviewee, the main factor that can influence and maybe accelerate the way in which the brand is managed and the brand guidelines are used, is the replacement of the individuals in charge of marketing and communications. The view expressed was that:

> Most of us have been around for a long time and done things in a specific way. However, times have changed and we do not seem to be responding right all the time. We need new people to come in and document important things like our brand and maybe train us on how it should be represented at all times.

Leadership and management are presented as potential solutions in improving the way in which the brand is managed, which has a direct effect on the way in which IMC is or is not implemented (Gronstedt, 1996; Eppes, 1998; Schultz & Kitchen, 2000; Luxton et al., 2015). It could be therefore suggested that unless a drastic change is made, the current lack of integration will not be overcome, limiting these six clubs in their current practices.

As it was discussed in this section, the way in which brands are managed differs drastically; from specific rules, guidance, on-going training and regular checks on all outward communications, to a lack of guidelines or suggestions and no training or control on how the brand is or should be represented.

Conclusion

Having examined external communications alignment and brand management, two marketing communications practices that are highly linked with strategic integration, as it was discussed earlier in the study, the way in which they are managed in EPL clubs was investigated carefully. The vast discrepancies in the alignment of a club's communications and managing its brand were investigated in this chapter, allowing for a detailed mapping of the practices encountered to take place, for insight to IMC's implementation to be provided and for our understanding on what IMC is to be deepened. Nevertheless, a closer look should be taken in order for the discussion on the current integration scenarios to be conducted. This investigation will be presented in the following chapter, which will discuss the interviewees' perception of IMC and its potential.

References

Barnes, B. E. (2001) 'Integrated brand communication planning: Retail applications', *Journal of Marketing Communications*, 7 (1) 11–17.

Beverland, M. & Luxton, S. (2005) 'The projection of authenticity: Managing integrated marketing communications through strategic decoupling', *Journal of Advertising*, 34 (4) 103–116.

Burmann, C. & Zeplin, S. (2005) 'Building brand commitment: A behavioural approach to internal brand management', *Journal of Brand Management*, 12 (4) 279–300.

Dmitrijeva, K. & Batraga, A. (2012) 'Barriers to integrated marketing communications: The case of Latvia (small markets)', *8th International Strategic Management Conference, 21–23 June 2012, Barcelona, Spain*.

Duncan, T. R. & Everett S. E. (1993) 'Client perceptions of integrated communications', *Journal of Advertising Research*, 32 (3) 30–39.

Duncan, T. R. & Mulhern, F. (2004) A white paper on the status, scope and future of IMC. In *IMC Symposium, Northwestern University & University of Denver* (March 2004).

Eagle, L. & Kitchen, P. J. (2000) 'IMC, brand communications, and corporate cultures: Client / advertising agency co-ordination and cohesion', *European Journal of Marketing*, 34 (5/6) 667–686.

Edelman, D. C. (2010) 'Branding in the digital age', *Harvard Business Review*, 88 (12) 62–69.

Eppes, T. E. (1998) 'Rebirth of an agency: Challenges and implications of operating in an IMC environment', *Journal of Integrated Communications* (1998–1999 edition) 28–38.

Gould, S. J. (2004) 'IMC as theory and as a poststructural set of practices and discourses: A continuously evolving paradigm shift', *Journal of Advertising Research*, 44 (1) 66–70.

Gronstedt, A. (1996) 'Integrated communications at America's leading total quality management corporations', *Public Relations Review*, 22 (1) 25–42.

Gurau, C. (2008), 'Integrated online marketing communication: Implementation and management', *Journal of Communication Management*, 12 (2) 169–184.

Jones, G. S., Li, T., Kitchen, P. J. & Brignell, J. (2004) 'The emergence of IMC: A theoretical perspective', *Journal of Advertising Research*, 44 (1) 19–30.

Keegan, W., Moriarty, S. E. & Duncan, T. R. (1992) *Marketing, Branding*, Hoboken, NJ: Prentice Hall.

Keller, K. L. (2009) 'Building strong brands in a modern marketing communications environment', *Journal of Marketing Communications*, 15 (2/3) 139–155.

Keller, K. L. (2016) 'Unlocking the power of integrated marketing communications: How integrated is your IMC program?', *Journal of Advertising*, 45(3) 286–301.

Kitchen, P. J. & Burgmann, I. (2010) *Integrated marketing communication*, Hoboken, NJ: John Wiley & Sons, Ltd.

Kitchen, P. J. & Schultz, D. E. (1999) 'A multi-country comparison of the drive for IMC', *Journal of Advertising Research*, 39 (1) 21–38.

Kitchen, P. J. & Tourky, M. (2015) *Integrated Communications in the Postmodern Era*, Hampshire: Palgrave Macmillan.

Kliatchko, J. (2005) 'Towards a new definition of integrated marketing communications (IMC)', *International Journal of Advertising*, 24 (1) 7–34.

Kliatchko, J. (2008) 'Revisiting the IMC construct: A revised definition and four pillars', *International Journal of Advertising*, 27 (1) 133–160.

Kotler, P. (2000) *Marketing management* (10th ed.), London: Prentice Hall International.

Low, G. S. (2000) 'Correlates of integrated marketing communications', *Journal of Advertising Research*, 40 (3) 27–39.

Low, G. S. & Mohr, J. J. (1999) 'Setting advertising and promotion budgets in multi-brand companies', *Journal of Advertising Research*, 39 (1) 67–78.

Luxton, S., Reid, M. & Mavondo, F. (2015) 'Integrated marketing communication capability and brand performance', *Journal of Advertising*, 44 (1) 37–46.

Madhavaram, S., Badrinarayanan, V. & McDonald, R. (2005) 'Integrated marketing communication (IMC) and brand identity as critical components of brand equity strategy', *Journal of Advertising*, 34 (4) 69–80.

Manoli, A. E. (2017) Media relations in English football clubs. In J. J. Zhang & B. G. Pitts (Eds.) *Contemporary sport marketing: Global perspectives*, (pp. 120–138), London: Routledge.

Manoli, A. E. (2020) 'Brand capabilities in English premier league clubs', *European Sport Management Quarterly*, 20 (1) 30–46.

Manoli, A. E. & Hodgkinson, I. R. (2017) 'Marketing outsourcing in the English premier league: The right holder/agency interface', *European Sport Management Quarterly*, 17 (4) 436–456.

Manoli, A. E. & Hodgkinson, I. R. (2019) 'The implementation of integrated marketing communication (IMC): Evidence from professional football clubs in England', *Journal of Strategic Marketing*, 28 (6) 542–563.

Manoli, A. E. & Hodgkinson, I. R. (2021) 'Exploring internal organisational communication dynamics in the professional football industry', *European Journal of Marketing*. 55 (11) 2894–2916.

Melewar, T. C. (2003) 'Determinants of the corporate identity construct: A review of the literature', *Journal of Marketing Communications*, 9 (4) 195–220.

Melewar, T. C. & Walker, C. (2003) 'Global corporate brand building: Guidelines and case studies', *Journal of Brand Management*, 11 (2) 157–170.

Moriarty, S. E. (1994) 'PR and IMC: The benefits of integration', *Public Relations Quarterly*, 39 (3) 38–44.

Ots, M. & Nyilasy, G. (2015) 'Integrated marketing communications (IMC): Why does it fail?', *Journal of Advertising Research*, 55 (2) 132–145.

Phelps, J. E., Harris, T. E. & Johnson, E. (1996) 'Exploring decision-making approaches and responsibility for developing marketing communications strategy', *Journal of Business Research*, 37 (3) 217–223.

Porcu, L., del Barrio-García, S. & Kitchen, P. J. (2012) 'How integrated marketing communications (IMC) works? A theoretical review and an analysis of its main drivers and effects/¿ Cómo funciona la Comunicación Integrada de Marketing (CIM)? Una revisión teórica y un análisis de sus antecedentes y efectos', *Comunicación y sociedad*, 25 (1) 313–348.

Reid, M., Luxton, S. & Mavondo, F. (2005) 'The relationship between integrated marketing communication, market orientation, and brand orientation', *Journal of Advertising*, 34 (4) 11–23.

Schultz, D. E. (1992) 'Integrated marketing communications: The status of integrated marketing communications programs the US today', *Journal of Promotion Management*, 1 (1) 99–104.

Schultz, D. E. (1993) 'Integrated marketing communications: Maybe definition is in the point of view', *Marketing News*, January 18.

Schultz, D. E. (2000) 'Structural flaws dash marcom plans', *Marketing News*, 34 (3) 14.

Schultz, D. E. (2001) 'Campaign approach shouldn't exist in IMC', *Marketing News*, 35 (5) 11–13.

Schultz, D. E. & Kitchen, P. J. (2000) *Communicating globally. An Integrated marketing approach*, London: Macmillan.

Schultz, D. E. & Schultz, H. F. (1998) 'Transitioning marketing communication into the twenty-first century', *Journal of Marketing Communications*, 4 (1) 9–26.

Schultz, D. E. & Schultz, H. F. (2004) *IMC: The next generation*, New York: McGraw-Hill.

Tsai, S. P. (2005) 'Integrated marketing as management of holistic consumer experience', *Business Horizons*, 48 (5) 431–441.

Chapter 6

Football Practitioners' Perceptions of Integrated Marketing Communications

Introduction

This chapter will focus on presenting the football practitioners' perceptions of IMC, in an attempt to showcase their understanding and appreciation of IMC and its potential. First the football clubs will be divided in IMC levels based in order to assist in the analysis that follows. Then the practitioners' perceptions will be presented, grouped together for level and thus allowing for a juxtaposition between IMC perceptions and implementation to be offered.

Classification of Clubs in IMC Levels

A number of points were identified and underlined in the analysis of the marketing communications practices encountered in each club, as it was presented in the previous chapters. This examination so far, however, was based on the author's analysis of the empirical research conducted using projective techniques (Haire, 1950). These techniques were used in the interviews in order for the interviewees to be encouraged to express their unbiased and honest opinions on how marketing communications is managed. The words *'integrated marketing communications'* were thus not mentioned but only towards the end of each interview, which sparked an additional discussion on IMC's current or potential implementation in EPL clubs.

This discussion about IMC provided the author with significantly diverse answers on a number of topics, including IMC's scope, potential to be implemented, implementation requirements, benefits and hurdles, which will be discussed in this section in more detail. The practitioners' views on the above-mentioned topics included a number of misconceptions regarding both the clubs' brand and IMC, which will be also presented in the analysis that follows.

Before the analysis begins, however, it will be noted that according to their answers only 60% of the interviewees (18 out of 30) know what IMC is, while the remaining 40% (12 out of 30) had not heard of the term before the interviews were conducted.

These percentages are based on the initial answer given to the question: *'Have you ever heard of Integrated Marketing Communications?'*, since the author's aim

DOI: 10.4324/9781003140238-6

was not to assess the participants' level of knowledge or understanding of IMC, or to create any discomfort to them during the interviews. Based on the initial answer provided by them to the above-mentioned question, additional queries on how they perceived IMC were asked, but not always answered clearly. On the contrary, even when an interviewee might have claimed that they had knowledge of IMC, their rather vague answer on what IMC is according to them could suggest that their actual understanding of IMC might be limited. This suggestion will be taken into consideration in the analysis that follows.

The fact that 40% of the club / companies within the sector (EPL) are not aware of IMC is in accordance with the opinions expressed by academics such as Rose (1996), Han et al. (2004) and Dmitrijeva and Batraga (2012) who have underlined that IMC is yet to be appreciated by the majority of the practitioners.

The interviewees' perceptions vary significantly, with similarities existing between clubs that follow similar patterns in their marketing communications practices, as they were discussed above. Based on the views encountered and the practices discussed above, the popular practice of categorising clubs to different IMC implementation levels took place, similarly to how it is encountered in IMC's implementation studies (e.g. in Han et al., 2004; Kitchen et al., 2004; Kitchen et al., 2008; Kliatchko & Schultz, 2014). This classification takes place in order for the organisations to be grouped in the corresponding IMC levels, based on their application of IMC, which assists in the analysis and discussion of the findings of the research. Following this popular practice and based on the focus of this study, the 30 clubs investigated were grouped in the five IMC levels introduced in Chapter 2. This categorisation of clubs in the five IMC levels took place based on the studies by Kitchen and Schultz (1999) and Kliatchko (2008).

First, using the interplay between the IMC pillars and the five IMC levels presented in Chapter 2, the 30 clubs composing the industry sector examined (EPL) were grouped in five categories, each one representing the level or stage of IMC in which the companies belong to. Scrutinising the data collected in this study enabled the author to identify the pillar on which emphasis was placed by each club, which allowed for this categorisation to take place. In more detail, one club which emphasised results was placed in level 4, four clubs that highlighted stakeholders were positioned in level 3, eight clubs focused on channels and were therefore considered level 2 and 11 clubs that appear to centre their efforts around content were grouped into level 1. Finally, the remaining six clubs that did not appear to place emphasis on any of the above-mentioned pillars were placed into the level 0 category, suggesting that they did not present the author with any evocation that integration was taking place.

In order for this classification to the five IMC levels to be cross-examined, an additional categorisation method was followed, which was originally presented by Kitchen and Schultz in 1999 and further developed by the same authors in 2001. Their studies list the criteria that can categorise companies in the IMC levels, by linking the marketing communications practices followed with the corresponding levels. By identifying the practices in the 30 clubs examined, as they were presented to the author by the interviewees, the classification conducted using Kliatchko's (2008) interplay was re-examined and confirmed.

In more detail, only one club appears to focus on results and evaluation, by monitoring the performance of their marketing communications practices using Key Performance Indicators (hereafter KPIs) that measure the return on their investment (ROI). Four clubs are placing additional emphasis on collecting, analysing and utilising databases, in order for the marketing communications practices to be informed by customer data. Eight clubs are in the process of developing similar databases by collecting information on their customers, which is only used on a rather elementary level, while focusing on the channels through which they communicate. Eleven clubs appear to be beginning the process of developing interpersonal and cross-functional communication, while attempting to foster inter-departmental relations and channels of communication, and placing emphasis on the content of their communications. Finally, six clubs present dissimilarities with all the above-mentioned practices followed, and on the contrary seem to be characterised by little or no interpersonal and cross-functional communication patterns and channels. In fact, it could be argued that marketing and communications in these clubs occur in isolation. As a result, these six clubs can be grouped in level 0, in which no integration is taking place.

Since each level is not rigid and its boundaries are not definite, not all companies belonging to each level – category, are implementing IMC the same way or to the same extent. On the contrary, it is expected that the companies within each level have differing practices that can sometimes overlap with other levels. The overall emphasis within each club, however, is the pillar of IMC that corresponds to the level in which it belongs, with the six clubs that comprise category-level 0 not placing emphasis on any of the four pillars.

According to this categorisation, 20% of the companies that comprise this industry sector (EPL) do not practice integration. While 80% of the companies implement IMC to some extent, the fact that a number of companies do not, allows the author to suggest the following. If the question asked when examining IMC in this study included grouping companies in the four levels of IMC as suggested by Schultz and Schultz (1998) and followed by academics who have studied IMC's implementation so far, the result of this categorisation could lead to false assumptions.

As it was discussed, this categorisation was conducted using the criteria of marketing communications practices and their emphasis, following the work of Kitchen and Schultz (1999, 2001) and Kliatchko (2008), in an attempt to interpret the analysis conducted above. As the analysis on the findings showed, a number of patterns were identified regarding the clubs' marketing communications practices and practitioners' perceptions, which indicated that different approaches and in this cases IMC levels existed. It is important to underline, however, that no other criteria, such as organisational structure, club size or playing success, were taken into consideration in order for this grouping to be conducted.

Using this categorisation of clubs in different levels, and combining it with the practitioners' views encountered, different scenarios can be identified in the five IMC levels. Due to these considerable differences in the perceptions expressed and the scenarios met, each level will be examined separately.

Perceptions in Level 0

All six level 0 clubs that do not practice integration, appear to have no knowledge of IMC and what it entails. All level 0 clubs are not aware of IMC, and therefore fall under the overall 40% of the clubs that had not even heard of the words '*integrated marketing communications*' before the interview was conducted.

When IMC was presented to them, most interviewees found it to be rather 'irrelevant' to EPL football, since, as it was argued, the quick pace of the football industry and the lack of proactivity within it would make IMC challenging if not impossible to be implemented.

This scepticism and disbelief expressed regarding IMC's potential implementation in the EPL could be traced back to their appreciation of polyphony in terms of each club's outwards communications. In fact, diversity and polyphony of the voices representing a club were presented as positive elements in football, since, according to the interviewees, they allow for personalised communications to take place, which enhance each club's brand. As it was mentioned earlier in this study, the way in which each club's brand is appreciated by its employees varies drastically; from a business wise process to an automatic, almost inherent idea that does not require effort.

While the former view was accompanied with details on how a brand is managed throughout each club and over time, the latter was presented as the reason why no efforts to manage a brand were needed by the clubs in question, followed by no assessments on how these decisions were evaluated, which could, in turn, raise a wider question on how the concept of branding is understood within these clubs (Ots & Nyilasy, 2015; Manoli, 2020). This, in turn, raises a question on the overall brand management throughout the club, which includes the everyday marketing communications practices, as they were discussed earlier in this study and the way in which they are linked with integration, or the lack thereof in level 0 clubs.

Surprisingly, following the author's brief explanation of IMC (based on Kliatchko's definition of 2008), one of these clubs claimed that it is an idea that is gradually introduced between individuals in the club, as the following quote shows.

> *I think we might be doing that, we are slowly getting there. Sometimes we do stuff instinctively, you don't think about it, you just do it and it works. So, if I think of something, I might ask my colleague who is sitting beside me. Maybe it's only within some colleagues, but we are currently trying to start communicating with each other more.*

This quote could suggest the beginning of integration within the club, even though there appears to be no knowledge of what IMC is. However, and based on the reluctance in the way in which the interviewee presented the author with the above quote (in his tone of voice and body expressions), it could be argued that the club is still not implementing IMC.

Taking all the above into consideration, and given that all level 0 clubs appear to have no knowledge of IMC, it can be argued that they are also unaware of the element of strategy IMC entails. The paradox could therefore be considered irrelevant to these clubs, since they do not in fact claim that they appreciate IMC on any level. Consequently, the integration scenario that could better represent these clubs would be the *no integration scenario*, suggesting that no integration occurs. This scenario can be studied when the practitioners do not have knowledge of IMC and there appears to be no implementation of IMC, as Manoli and Hodgkinson (2019) have also hinted in their study.

An additional question could be raised on whether the clubs' lack of knowledge on IMC could possibly be the initial reason behind their rather sceptical or even negative views towards its potential implementation in football. Further research would be required in order for this to be examined, since that could allow for IMC's implementation to progress.

Perceptions in Level 1

Level 1 clubs appear to be divided regarding the knowledge of IMC. According to the interviewees, six clubs had not heard of the term before, while only five knew what IMC is. Nevertheless, all level 1 clubs practice integration on a tactical level, as it can be seen through the examination of their marketing communications practices discussed in the previous sections of this chapter. As the analysis above demonstrated, integration processes and systems with an occasional club-wide mentality of collaboration are in fact followed in all level 1 clubs, even though the majority of them claim to have no knowledge of IMC.

Based on the reactions of the interviewees who claimed to have knowledge of IMC, it could be argued that their true understanding of what IMC entails can be brought into question. In fact, all five interviewees appeared to be rather uncomfortable in discussing their understanding of IMC, with the change in their tone of voice (shorter and sharper answers, often coughing to clear their throat) and body language (distancing themselves from the interviewee and moving on their seat) suggesting that it was a rather distressing topic of discussion. Additional information on their actual understanding of IMC was therefore not acquired, making their initial answer to the question the only evidence of their professed knowledge.

Based on this division regarding their knowledge of IMC, the two distinctive groups of level 1 clubs (level 1a and level 1b) will be presented separately below in order for their perceptions of IMC and the corresponding integration scenarios to be examined.

Perceptions in Level IA

When the author presented the six clubs of level 1a with a brief explanation of IMC (based on Kliatchko's definition of 2008), an unexpected response was given. All six clubs claimed that IMC is in fact implemented within the organisation:

The idea of an unintentional integration was emphasised by the interviewees, who argued that IMC evolved '*organically*' within each club, encouraging employees to work together in order to better manage the club's marketing communications messages. As a result, a rather unstructured, tactical integration is taking place, enhancing the collaboration among employees and the coordination and alignment of the messages produced and communicated by each club.

Taking both IMC's '*unintentional*' tactical implementation and the practitioners' lack of knowledge on IMC into consideration, an interesting practitioners' paradox can be identified. This *unintentional IMC implementation paradox* occurs when practitioners do not have knowledge of IMC, however, manage to implement it on a tactical level unintentionally (Manoli & Hodgkinson, 2019). The *unintentional paradox* identified differs from the *practitioners' strategy paradox*, due to the element of strategy missing from the equation. In these organisations the paradox exists because IMC's implementation is taking place '*unintentionally*' or '*organically*' according to the practitioners, and not because its value is recognised and appreciated.

The existence of this paradox and the unintentional emergence of IMC could be linked with the arguments of Schultz and Kitchen (2000b), Kliatchko and Schultz (2014) and Kitchen and Tourky (2015) who claim that applying integration is in fact inevitable, since it is a need deriving from today's demanding marketplace, which would underline the need for additional research on this paradox and its application.

This integration oxymoron presented through the *unintentional IMC implementation paradox* in the level 1a clubs can raise questions on the effectiveness of their marketing communications and integration efforts. Further research on the topic would allow for more rigor answers to be given to these questions.

> *We are a few steps behind to do (implement IMC) this fully, but we are working towards having that in the future. I saw a lot of initiatives to improve and I have been seeing a lot of things improving, it will happen eventually. We are trying to have integrated marketing communications informally, we try to keep everything aligned. But it is not a formal process we have at the club. We have improved lately and soon we'll get there.*

As the quote suggests and was underlined by all six clubs during the interviews, improvements have been made towards a more integrated approach, with the interviewees suggesting that IMC is a promising concept for football. One of the interviewees indicated that the change towards a more integrated approach was introduced following the replacement of the individual in charge of the management of the organisation (CEO) who emphasised the importance of strengthening the marketing communications of the club. According to the interviewee, the previous administration of the club had in fact hindered any integration efforts within the organisation, while imposing a rather micromanaging and compartmentalised system for all employees. As this example illustrates, leadership was mentioned as a differentiating factor that could foster or hinder any integration practices, which aligns with the views expressed by academics such as Ferdous (2008) and Porcu et al. (2012).

The element of strategy was not mentioned by any of these clubs. On the contrary, IMC was regarded as a management practice or a company-wide concept that is mainly performed on the executional side of marketing communications, as the level in which they belong would suggest. In other words, these clubs focus on the *'tactical coordination'* of marketing communications, as Kitchen and Schultz (1999, p. 34) suggested. Thus, it can be argued that since the interviewees do not know what IMC is, they are also unaware of its strategic nature, suggesting that neither the *full strategic integration* nor the *practitioners' strategy paradox* can be studied in these clubs. At the same time, and based on their marketing communications practices indicating a tactical implementation of IMC, the *no integration* scenario is also not applicable.

Therefore, the integration scenario that could be studied in these clubs is the *unintentional IMC implementation paradox*, which occurs when IMC is implemented unintentionally, while practitioners do not have knowledge of what IMC is. Based on the fact that this integration scenario has been only discussed by Manoli and Hodgkinson (2019), further research is needed in order for additional information on it to be acquired. Nevertheless, identifying it allows for attention to be brought on this under researched topic of practitioners' knowledge of IMC and how it can affect integration, which could provide valuable insight in shaping IMC's progress.

Perceptions in Level 1B

The remaining five clubs that claim to know what IMC entails, appear to be implementing it, but not to its full potential. According to the interviewees, IMC is understood and fully appreciated, including its strategic potential. Nevertheless, its implementation in the clubs examined resembles a rather tactical and not strategic application of IMC. According to the interviewees, steps of improvement are being taken; nevertheless the nature of the EPL obstructs the process of planning and is therefore hindering IMC's implementation.

> *If you compare where we are with where we were, you can say that we are improving. We are listening to each other more. We could have a more integrated relationship with our communications team, but we are now in better relations than before... But football is a weird industry, football fans are a weird set of customers.*

As a result and based on the interviewees' answers, the future of IMC's implementation is not presented as promising as academics have argued (Ouwersloot & Duncan, 2008; Ots & Nyilasy, 2015). On the contrary, since the nature and pace of the EPL have obstructed IMC's implementation so far, it could be expected that they will continue to hinder it.

Based on the varying answers this topic has received from the interviewees, it could be argued that this rather unfortunate future of IMC's implementation represents the opinion expressed by these particular clubs and not the universal view of the practitioners. As the following sections will better demonstrate, the answers given by practitioners in level 3 and 4 clubs contradict the level 1b clubs' view. In fact, based on the observations made by the author while the interviews with these level 1b clubs took place, it could be argued that their true knowledge and understanding of IMC could be questioned. The interviewees gave sharp short answers to the questions regarding their understanding of IMC and appeared rather uncomfortable to support their views. Consequently, taking this information into consideration, their lack of appreciation for IMC's strategic potential in football can be also brought into question.

As far as the *practitioners' strategy paradox* is concerned, it could be argued that these level 1b clubs are not only relevant in terms of observing the paradox in practice, but could be also considered the ideal subjects in order for the question of intention to be better examined. Based on the answer provided by these five clubs that know what IMC is and appreciate its strategic value, but are limiting their practices on the mere tactical implementation of IMC, the paradox exists unintentionally and is merely due to external factors. According to the interviewees, it is the nature of the EPL that does not allow for a more planned strategic approach to be followed. All five interviewees in fact used the word 'react' when describing the hurdles in IMC's implementation.

However, it could be argued that since a number of clubs have managed to progress their implementation practices closer to strategic integration, the nature of the EPL might not in reality be the defining factor. As it was discussed earlier in the previous chapter, the 11 clubs that belong in levels 2, 3 and 4 have managed to advance and exceed tactical integration, which is where the level 1 clubs focus. These clubs that are also part of the same industry sector face similar challenges as the one mentioned above, and are also asked to 'react', as the level 1b clubs argued. Their practices, nevertheless, suggest that the nature of the EPL was not a hurdle in implementing IMC to a more structured and even strategic way.

Based on the fact that the level 2, 3 and 4 clubs have managed to overcome the problems that are associated with the nature and pace of the EPL, it can be argued that the reason behind the level 1b clubs' limitation to a tactical integration is not unintentional, as it was presented to author. In this case, the interviewees are presenting the nature of the EPL as a justification behind this limitation, which in reality occurs intentionally. This intentional attachment to a tactical and non-strategic integration could be then traced back to their individual experience and training, as well as their personalities and their particular preference to set marketing communications practices (Duncan & Everett, 1993; Moriarty, 1994; Eagle & Kitchen, 2000; Ewing et al., 2000; Pettigrew, 2000/2001; Manoli & Hodgkinson, 2021).

On the other hand, based on the questions raised regarding their true knowledge and appreciation of IMC, this limitation to a tactical integration could in fact be unintentional but not due to external factors, as it was argued by the interviewees. The unintentional limitation to the paradox could be traced back to the practitioners' understanding of IMC's potential, regardless of their claims. Since the practitioners might not truly understand what IMC entails, they may be unable to progress its implementation to a strategic level. Consequently, they might be expected to drive strategic integration while in reality not truly understanding what that entails, which leads them to implement IMC on a tactical level, despite their claims of full appreciation of IMC's strategic potential. In other words, the conditions under which these clubs are being led to the *practitioners' strategy paradox* are the potentially limited actual appreciation or understanding of IMC's potential and, as a result, the tactical implementation of IMC. Additional research on these individual cases would allow for a more comprehensive answer to be given to this topic, which could lead to the question of intention behind their limitation to level 1 to be examined and to the conditions under which the clubs have reached the *practitioners' strategy paradox* to be investigated.

Perceptions in Level 2

All eight level 2 clubs appear to be in agreement regarding having knowledge of IMC and its strategic potential. It was additionally argued by the interviewees that IMC is implemented in these clubs, as the following quote shows.

> *I believe we do (implement IMC). We look at all channels, all connection points with our audience and think of the right way to communicate with them, above the line, below the line, using marketing, trying to pull a singular plan together.*

In fact, the interviewees in all level 2 clubs had used the word 'integrated' when discussing their current marketing and communications practices earlier in the interviews. A number of the interviewees presented the author with details on how IMC is implemented and were rather enthusiastic in discussing the practices followed. However, they all appeared to be rather sceptical regarding club-wide integration. As an interviewee argued:

> *As a concept I know it, but I have never come across an organisation that does it in reality. At the top level we do. We got a pretty good handle on the look and feel of anything that is related to the club. But in some things, especially on every day or one-to-one tasks, it is not possible to achieve it.*

As the quote shows, these clubs appreciate the strategic nature of IMC, but suggest that such an implementation would be impossible to be achieved. The interviewees appeared to be sceptical regarding strategic integration, with their arguments based on the nature of the EPL, while suggesting that other sectors might be able to implement it. These interviewees presented a number of challenges that affect IMC's implementation from reaching its full potential. The reactivity and fast pace of the industry were presented as the main reason behind this limitation, followed by the lack of human and financial resources (often due to recent relegation to a lower division of the sport) and the wide and varying demographics of football fans. The following quotes can illustrate the points made in more detail:

> It (IMC) helps from a brand point of view, but I don't think it's something we can plan. Clubs cannot do that. We do reactive marketing strategy as oppose to a well-planned integrated marketing strategy. When you don't have the budget you don't really have a lot to think about. For us, it's more a case of I'll do this, you do that. It's a case of get together and plan things every day. I think we're so obsessed with selling our tickets that we cannot have a 12 month plan.
>
> I think the biggest challenge in truly implementing IMC is the widest demographic targeting that I have encountered in any industry. Within football, you only exist within your own universe of fans, who are so diverse. How can you be consistent and tap into all these fans' feelings? How can you have continuity when there's nothing similar between the different groups of your fans?.

As it can be seen through the quotes, level 2 clubs appreciate the effects marketing communications can have on the clubs' brand and consequently focus their efforts on controlling the channels and integrating their messages. Nevertheless, they are not able to implement IMC to its full potential due to the challenges presented, which were identified by the interviewees as the main hurdles.

It could be argued that the main reason behind these clubs' delimitation in a rather early stage in IMC's implementation is that 'redefining the scope of marketing and communications', as level 2 entails (Kitchen & Schultz, 1999, p. 34), is a rather perplex and time consuming process. As it has been argued (Pettigrew, 2000/2001; Schultz & Schultz, 2004; Christensen, 2008b), it is this step that requires additional attention and determination on behalf of each organisation and its employees, in order for the potential hurdles to be overcome.

According to the studies on IMC's implementation, such as the ones conducted by Kitchen et al. (2004), Kitchen and Tao (2005) and Eagle et al. (2007), a large number of the companies in which the participants of the studies were employed or contracted to were also trapped in the second level IMC. This fact was noted by the researchers, who underlined the challenges involved in progressing from this step. However, Kliatchko and Schultz (2014) argued that the challenges associated with the limitation to this step can and will be overcome over time.

As the interviewees argued, the strategic nature of IMC is understood and appreciated; nevertheless, implementing IMC to a more advanced level would require significant and fundamental changes to the current practices. Since a discrepancy exists between the appreciation of IMC and its implementation in these clubs, the integration scenario that occurs is the *practitioners' strategy paradox*. As far as the question of intention behind it is concerned, according to the interviewees, it is the nature of the EPL and the challenges associated with it that have been obstructing IMC's strategic implementation. In other words, the external reasons that have been impeding IMC's implementation on a strategic level have been trapping the practitioners unintentionally in this stage.

In order to truly examine the question of intention behind the *practitioners' strategy paradox*, the full spectrum of the EPL clubs needs to be taken into consideration. A question can be then raised on whether this limitation to the second stage of IMC's implementation is in fact unintentional or not. As it was argued in the level 1b section above, all five level 3 and 4 clubs have managed to implement IMC to a more strategic level and thus overcome the challenges mentioned by the level 2 clubs' interviewees. It could therefore be claimed that the challenges presented might be impeding the progress, but do not in reality categorically halt it. The fact that these challenges can be overcome and IMC's implementation can progress to a more strategic level can make the author question the level 2 clubs' limitation to this early stage. It can consequently be argued that the reasons behind this limitation and, as a result, the *strategy paradox* are intentional and originate from the individuals' or the organisational attachment to the current marketing communication practices. Examining where this intentional limitation originates would require additional research on the particular cases discussed in this section.

The interviewees did not present the author with evidence to suggest that the current practices will change. Additionally, no indication was provided on attempts to face and handle the challenges discussed above. On the contrary, the tone of the interviewees suggested that since the hurdles to strategic integration are considered insuperable, there are no plans to change the current situation.

Perceptions in Level 3

A different situation than the one described in all levels 0, 1 and 2 was presented by the interviewees in level 3 clubs. The four level 3 clubs' interviewees were not only confident that they know what IMC entails but also that IMC is truly implemented in the clubs, as the following quote shows.

> I like to think that everything we do is integrated and I work very much holistically to make sure that the key messages and the brand is integrated to what we are trying to achieve as a business, because the level of the communications we have with our fans goes through everything we do. And I do believe we have some key important messages we want to communicate to our fans and fundamentally the brand underpins everything that we do.

According to the interviewees, these clubs have already redefined the scope of marketing communications and have managed to achieve an integrated approach in the way their marketing communications activities are ran. As the examination of their practices showed, the clubs have achieved a high level of integration which they are currently attempting to increase further. Their main focus, as the following quote will demonstrate, is capitalising on the investments they have made in information technology and the time and effort they have already been devoting to it.

> *Yes, we are on the journey to that (implementing IMC). A lot of that is based on our ability to use the CRM system, which we spent time and effort developing, and we're getting to that point where we can start understanding the full power of that. We have a holistic view of our customer, a single view of the customer, a holistic view of what we're sending to whom and when... Most of what we do is data, data acquisition on our fans, understanding that data and real deep analysis of this data, behaviours of our fans, the journey they take and how do we take actions against this analysis. We don't move a finger unless this analysis is done and we are able to understand what will and can happen.*

The level 3 clubs appear to grasp what IMC entails and the stages through which its implementation can be achieved. The strategic nature of IMC is also appreciated and remains the target for these clubs, which recognise that their implementation of IMC has not reached its full potential yet. According to the interviewees, implementing IMC on a strategic level is the end of the process they are currently in.

In other words, level 3 clubs are not trapped in this stage of IMC's implementation, but on the contrary are currently included in this level, while working towards reaching a higher level of integration. For these clubs, the '*application of information technology*' which is required in this level, is just a step before '*financial and strategic integration*' achieved in level 4 (Kitchen & Schultz, 1999, p. 34), to which the investments they have been making in time and effort will lead.

A point that is worth underling is that during the interviews with level 3 clubs, the word '*restructure*' was mentioned by all the interviewees. Initiated by either the higher management of the club or the individual in charge of marketing or marketing and communications, this restructure within the club was presented as either the focal point or the key turning moment in which the implementation of IMC begun or progressed significantly respectively.

> *We have managed to structure ourselves according to our own needs. We wanted to be innovative. For us, it is about the increasing importance of the direct and constant communication, dialogue with our fans. We felt that it made sense for us to then restructure in a way that allows for this dialogue to be facilitated.*

This restructure was presented by all level 3 clubs as a time-consuming process that took place over the period of more than a few seasons / years. The restructure was also supported, according to the interviewees, by a carefully designed plan which was drafted and implemented by the initiator of the process as presented above (higher management of the club, or director of marketing or marketing and communications). The result of this long and challenging process of restructuring was presented by the interviewees as a key element of the way in which marketing communications is managed as the following quote shows.

> It took us many years to get where we are now. I have to say that I have fought hard to get this structure going, to get everyone on board with the idea and actually materialise what I had in mind. But we are now integrated, our marketing and communications is integrated.

The restructuring process described above resembles the idea of organisational redesign that can allow for an IMC business wide process to be adopted, as Pettigrew (2000/2001), Schultz and Schultz (2004) and Christensen et al. (2008a) suggested. Unfortunately, the interviewees did not share additional information on this restructuring process, such as the reasons that triggered it and the response it had from the employees at the time, which does not allow for a more thorough insight to be provided. As it was argued by the interviewees, providing additional details on the process would require sharing sensitive information which they were reluctant to reveal. It is suggested that additional research on the process could enhance the understanding and potentially assist greatly in IMC's progress.

While the idea of restructuring described above underlines the importance of management and leadership behind integration from either the higher management or the department director, it also highlights an additional point. This restructuring is in fact the redefinition of the scope of marketing communications (level 2) that is required in order for IMC to be implemented in a more strategic level as Schultz and Schultz (1998) and Kitchen and Schultz (1999, 2001) have argued. Having gone through this stage and the various challenges it can be potentially associated with, these clubs can show that the overall challenges faced by clubs within the same industry can in reality be overcome. Additionally, two of these clubs had since been relegated in the second division of the sport (Championship), which consequently translates to a severely decreased income generated every season (Noll, 2002). Yet, unlike what was presented by level 2 clubs, their efforts and success in implementing a more structured and planned integration has not been affected, according to their views.

Moreover, as far as the nature of the EPL is concerned, a distinction has to be made. All four level 3 clubs underlined the peculiarities of the EPL as a differentiating factor from other sectors; however, this difference was not presented as a challenge or a hurdle to IMC. On the contrary, it was either acknowledged as a mere difference that does not affect IMC's implementation or as an enhancing factor to IMC's implementation and potential success:

> I would give my right arm to have the customer engagement and loyalty we have here when I was working in X (a very popular and successful commercial retailer company). We had to work so hard to get something that we get here for free. It doesn't make it easier, but it gives you a head start. IMC makes perfect sense in football.

Taking the above into consideration, it could be argued that these clubs appreciate the strategic potential of IMC's implementation, which they are also trying to achieve. They are currently unable to do so and are thus limited in an earlier integration stage unintentionally, due to the extensive and demanding process through which IMC's strategic implementation can be realised. In order for an investigation to be conducted on this unintentional limitation, additional research should be overtaken in these clubs, so that the progress to achieving strategic integration is monitored, and details on this extensive and demanding restructuring process are gained.

Based on the analysis conducted above, it could be argued that achieving strategic integration and thus progressing to the final integration scenario could take place once this transitional process is finished, overcoming the existing discrepancy between IMC's appreciation and implementation. This would, in turn, suggest that the *practitioners' strategy paradox* occurs unintentionally in level 3 clubs but for a limited, yet undefined, amount of time before *strategic integration* can be achieved.

Perceptions in Level 4

The one level 4 club presented the author with a similar image as level 3 clubs in terms of fully understanding and appreciating IMC. As such the strategic value of IMC was underlined and in fact presented as a widely respected value throughout the club. The interviewee suggested that IMC is viewed as a *'business priority'* and as such it stems from the overall company-wide strategy of the club, as it was discussed earlier in the study. The word 'strategy' was in fact used frequently during the interview when marketing communications practices were discussed. It can be argued that planning and strategizing is an integral part of this club that has in fact achieved *strategic integration*.

'Feedback' was another word that was mentioned numerous times throughout the interview, since it is one of the areas attention is drawn to.

> The CEO is very interested in what we do and especially the fan engagement area. We get feedback because he enjoys it and he gets it. But it doesn't only come from him. We are seeking for feedback in everything we do and we give feedback too. As a department, as a team, as an individual, you are evaluated and appraised constantly, which helps us achieve our goals and get better

Additional emphasis is also placed on measuring and assessing the results of these function-specific strategies, according to the interviewee. Processes and systems are in place to track any targets set annually, monthly and weekly, in order for an updated detailed view of the progress to be kept. KPIs and surveys are used regularly for these assessments to be made. As the interviewee underlined, smart, quantifiable, measurable and time sensitive results are a priority for the club, since they allow for the strategic implementation of IMC to be traced and measured as the following quote better illustrates:

> We can and we will track everything we do. We always want to see the results of our efforts. Ninety percent of the things we do can be measured using KPIs that result in hard figures that we can easily track. And then there are additional figures, like member satisfaction which we do still track through surveys. Overall, I don't think it's that big of a challenge for us to track them. We do have the processes and the systems to track them on an annual, monthly and weekly basis as well

As it can been seen, this emphasis on results and feedback is supported with relevant processes that allow for this constant evaluation to take place. The club-wide culture of the organisation, as the interviewee suggested, encourages further the idea of constant evaluation and feedback, since it allows the teams and their employees to track their performance while pinpointing the areas that might need additional attention in a timely manner. This constant feedback provided both by superiors and colleagues from other departments, as it was described by the interviewee, resembles Schultz and Schultz' (2004), Beverland and Luxton's (2005) and Kitchen's (2016) suggestions for an open and continuous flow of communication, recommendations and advice encouraged through vertical and horizontal interaction channels within an organisation.

> The key thing in terms of our department and any department here is that we're very functional, we work very closely with each other and it all tends to be joined. We achieve integration through working like we do. We use all our assets, all our channels, all our touch-points. I know that it wasn't always like that, but now it is.

As the interviewee argued, the club had gone through a carefully planned and cautiously executed restructuring process prior to them joining:

> I cannot give you any more details because I wasn't here at the time. What I do know, however, is that the moto used at that time was that "we're building a new big club". And they meant it. Everything was changed to match the plan and it worked. We are now working like a well-oiled machine because everything is built in an efficient and functioning way.

Since details on the restructure are missing, the role leadership and management played during the process cannot be assessed. Unlike the answers provided by clubs in levels 0, 1, 2 and 3, the level 4 club interviewee did not present the author with a disparity between the appreciation of IMC's strategic nature and its application. As it can be seen throughout the examination of marketing communications practices discussed in the previous sections of this chapter and the focus on collaboration and feedback presented in this section, IMC is implemented on a strategic level in club AA. IMC is appreciated as a company-wide business process and concept that guides and defines the level 4 club, which, according to this study, represents an exception to the practices examined throughout EPL clubs.

While examining practitioners' perceptions of IMC, a great disparity among the clubs was found in a number of areas, such as practitioners' knowledge and appreciation of IMC and its strategic potential. This careful examination of practitioners' perceptions allowed for the identification and presentation of the four integration scenarios that can be found in the EPL. Examining IMC's implementation in regard to practitioners' perceptions allowed for these scenarios to be pinpointed, while also investigating the conditions and the levels in which they can be studied. Bearing in mind that the academic literature available has identified only one integration scenario (*full strategic integration*), pointed towards the existence of a second (*practitioners' strategy paradox*), and hinted towards potential other scenarios, it could be argued that identifying the additional two scenarios (*unintentional implementation paradox* and *no integration*) has deepened our knowledge of IMC and added to the current understanding of its appreciation and implementation. A more extensive analysis of the football practitioners' perceptions and the four integration scenarios will be presented in the following chapter.

Conclusion

This chapter focused on the examination of football practitioners' perceptions of IMC. First, using the five IMC levels suggested in Chapter 2, the clubs examined were grouped in five categories, each one representing the level or stage of IMC in which the clubs belong to, based on their marketing practices. This categorisation then assisted in the analysis and presentation of practitioners' perceptions of IMC and its strategic potential, which allowed for the identification of patterns of integration, or integration scenarios, which will be discussed in the following chapter.

References

Beverland, M. & Luxton, S. (2005) 'The projection of authenticity: Managing integrated marketing communications through strategic decoupling', *Journal of Advertising*, 34 (4) 103–116.

Christensen, L. T., Firat, F. A. & Torp, S. (2008a) 'The organisation of integrated communications: Toward flexible integration', *European Journal of Marketing*, 42 (3/4) 423–452.

Christensen, L. T., Morsing, M. & Cheney, G. (2008b) *Corporate communications: Convention, complexity and critique*, London: Sage.

Dmitrijeva, K. & Batraga, A. (2012) 'Barriers to integrated marketing communications: The case of Latvia (small markets)', *8th International Strategic Management Conference, 21–23 June 2012, Barcelona, Spain*.

Duncan, T. R. & Everett S. E. (1993) 'Client Perceptions of Integrated Communications', *Journal of Advertising Research*, 32 (3) 30–39.

Eagle, L. & Kitchen, P. J. (2000) 'IMC, brand communications, and corporate cultures: Client / advertising agency co-ordination and cohesion', *European Journal of Marketing*, 34 (5/6) 667–686.

Eagle, L., Kitchen, P. J. & Bulmer, S. (2007) 'Insights into interpreting integrated marketing communications: A two-nation qualitative comparison', *European Journal of Marketing*, 41 (7/8) 956–970.

Ewing, M. T., de Bussy, N.M. & Caruana, A. (2000) 'Perceived agency politics and conflicts of interest as potential barriers to IMC orientation', *Journal of Marketing Communications*, 6 (1) 107–119.

Ferdous, A. S. (2008) 'Integrated internal marketing communication (IIMC)', *The Marketing Review*, 8 (3) 223–235.

Haire, M. (1950) 'Projective techniques in marketing research', *Journal of Marketing*, 14 (5) 649–656.

Han, D., Kim, I. & Schultz, D. E. (2004) 'Understanding the diffusion of integrated marketing communications', *Journal of Advertising Research*, 44 (1) 31–45.

Kitchen, P. J. (2016) Is IMC "Marketing oriented"? In L. Petruzzellis & R. S. Winer (Eds.) *Rediscovering the essentiality of marketing* (pp. 441–442), New York: Springer International Publishing.

Kitchen, P. J., Kim, I. & Schultz, D. E. (2008) 'Integrated marketing communication: Practice leads theory', *Journal of Advertising Research*, 48 (4) 531–546.

Kitchen, P. J. & Schultz, D. E. (1999) 'A multi-country comparison of the drive for IMC', *Journal of Advertising Research*, 39 (1) 21–38.

Kitchen, P. J. & Schultz, D. E. (2001) *Raising the corporate umbrella: Corporate communications in the twenty-first century*, Hampshire: Palgrave Macmillan.

Kitchen, P. J., Schultz, D. E., Kim, I., Han, D. & Li, T. (2004) 'Will agencies ever "get" (or understand) IMC?', *European Journal of Marketing*, 38 (11/12) 1417–1436.

Kitchen, P. J. & Tao, L. (2005) 'Perceptions of integrated marketing communications: A Chinese ad and PR agency perspective', *International Journal of Advertising*, 24 (1) 51–78.

Kitchen, P. J. & Tourky, M. (2015) *Integrated communications in the postmodern era*, Hampshire: Palgrave Macmillan.

Kliatchko, J. (2008) 'Revisiting the IMC construct: A revised definition and four pillars', *International Journal of Advertising*, 27 (1) 133–160.

Kliatchko, J. G. & Schultz, D. E. (2014) 'Twenty years of IMC: A study of CEO and CMO perspectives in the Asia-Pacific region', *International Journal of Advertising*, 33 (2) 373–390.

Manoli, A. E. (2020) 'Brand capabilities in English premier league clubs', *European Sport Management Quarterly*, 20 (1) 30–46.

Manoli, A. E. & Hodgkinson, I. R. (2019) 'The implementation of integrated marketing communication (IMC): Evidence from professional football clubs in England', *Journal of Strategic Marketing*, 28 (6) 542–563.

Manoli, A. E. & Hodgkinson, I. R. (2021) 'Exploring internal organisational communication dynamics in the professional football industry', *European Journal of Marketing*, 55 (11) 2894–2916.

Moriarty, S. E. (1994) 'PR and IMC: The Benefits of Integration', *Public Relations Quarterly*, 39 (3) 38–44.

Noll, R. G. (2002) 'The economics of promotion and relegation in sports leagues the case of English football', *Journal of Sports Economics*, 3 (2) 169–203.

Ots, M. & Nyilasy, G. (2015) 'Integrated marketing communications (IMC): Why does it fail?', *Journal of Advertising Research*, 55 (2) 132–145.

Ouwersloot, H. & Duncan, T. (2008) *Integrated marketing communications*, London: McGraw-Hill Education.

Pettigrew, L. S. (2000/2001) 'If IMC is so good, why isn't it being implemented?: Barriers to IMC adoption in corporate America', *Journal of Integrated Communications*, 11 (1) 29–37.

Porcu, L., del Barrio-García, S. & Kitchen, P. J. (2012) 'How Integrated Marketing Communications (IMC) works? A theoretical review and an analysis of its main drivers and effects/¿ Cómo funciona la Comunicación Integrada de Marketing (CIM)? Una revisión teórica y un análisis de sus antecedentes y efectos', *Comunicación y sociedad*, 25 (1) 313–348.

Rose, P. B. (1996) 'Practitioner opinions and interests regarding integrated marketing communications in selected Latin American countries', *Journal of Marketing Communications*, 2 (3) 125–139.

Schultz, D. E. & Kitchen, P. J. (2000) A response to 'Theoretical concept or management fashion?', *Journal of Advertising Research*, 40 (5) 17–21.

Schultz, D. E. & Schultz, H. F. (1998) 'Transitioning marketing communication into the twenty-first century', *Journal of Marketing Communications*, 4 (1) 9–26.

Schultz, D. E. & Schultz, H. F. (2004) *IMC: The next generation*, New York: McGraw-Hill.

Chapter 7

Integration Scenarios

Introduction

Having presented the implementation of IMC in EPL clubs, through the detailed examination of their marketing communications practices, and practitioners' perceptions of IMC and its potential, this chapter will present a synthesis of IMC's appreciation and application in the clubs examined. First, through a discussion of football practitioners' collective understanding of IMC as well as through an examination of whether football clubs want the implementation of IMC. And second, by introducing and offering a thorough analysis on the four integration scenarios encountered in the study.

Synthesis of Football Practitioners' Understanding of IMC

While examining football practitioners' perceptions of IMC, a number of extremely dissimilar opinions were expressed by the interviewees. In fact, based on their perceptions of IMC, a Venn diagram presenting the points of agreement and disagreement among them would find the area of agreement empty, since there is not a single element related to IMC that found all interviewees in accordance.

First, 12 of the interviewees (40%) had not even heard of the words '*integrated marketing communications*' before the interviews were conducted, according to their statements. Additionally, out of the remaining 18 interviewees (60%) who claim to understand IMC, the actual knowledge of five of them could be questioned, based on their reactions during the interviews. However, even within the interviewees who stated that they are aware of its strategic nature, IMC's potential to be implemented does not find them all in agreement, which according to Atkinson (2003) should be considered a common phenomenon.

The lack of support expressed on the current and potential IMC's implementation, combined with the misconceptions on brand and the disagreement on communications alignment, can underline that the '*one-voice*' idea and the synergy behind coherence and consistency do not find the practitioners' in accordance. On the contrary, as it was presented earlier in the study, clubs in the lower

DOI: 10.4324/9781003140238-7

IMC levels, especially in level 0, have argued against adopting a single *'one-voice'* and instead supported the idea of polyphony, which according to the interviewees, allows for the individual employees to express their own voices and enhance the relationship built with the fans. This view contradicts not only the research conducted by numerous academics such as Moriarty (1993, 1994), Stammerjohan et al. (2005), Lauska et al. (2014), Manoli (2020) and Manoli and Hodgkinson (2021) but also the opinion expressed by the clubs that belong in the higher IMC levels, that opt for more coherent and aligned communications.

Furthermore, based on the lack of knowledge of IMC, topics such as IMC's benefits and hurdles would automatically be considered areas of disagreement. Even within clubs that appreciate and implement IMC, these topics did not find the practitioners in accordance. For example, the cost-effectiveness of IMC that was brought up by one level 3 club contradicts the view expressed by a level 1 club, whose interviewee argued that it would be too resource intensive to be implemented:

> *It (IMC) is not a top strategic goal right now because the investment versus reward of it is not that easy to quantify.*

Moreover, a number of the hurdles mentioned, such as interdepartmental silos and poor communication, which were also identified by a number of scholars (Duncan & Everett, 1993; Moriarty, 1994; Eagle & Kitchen, 2000; Schultz, 2000, 2001; Dmitrijeva & Batraga, 2012), did not find all clubs in accordance. Level 3 and 4 clubs presented the author with a collaborative approach to interdepartmental communication and collaboration that does not hinder but enhance the implementation of IMC, as studies on IMC have also argued (Rouziès et al., 2005; Christensen et al., 2008a; Ferdous, 2008; Vernuccio & Ceccotti, 2015).

The existence and use of customer data management systems regarding integration was only discussed by the clubs belonging in higher IMC levels, while clubs in level 0 and 1 suggested that similar databases are not used that often. Systems are in fact in place in all clubs; however, the way in which they are used and appreciated differs significantly. As a result, the use of CRM systems in these clubs, as it was presented to the author, does not facilitate integration and, on the contrary, is believed to be the reason behind miscommunication and frictions between different departments' employees. This contradicts the suggestions made by Duncan (2002) and Schultz et al. (2013) who argued that CRM can be an indispensable tool for data-driven audience-centric communication.

In addition, the majority of the clubs (level 0, 1 and 2) focused their emphasis on communicating with their fans/customers, while only level 3 and 4 clubs underlined that their communications are also targeting their employees and other stakeholders. Thus, it can be argued that the multiple stakeholders of marketing communications presented by academics such as Schultz and Schultz (1998, 2004) and Kliatchko (2005, 2008) have not been appreciated in the EPL yet, with the outward communications of most clubs being primarily customer-focused

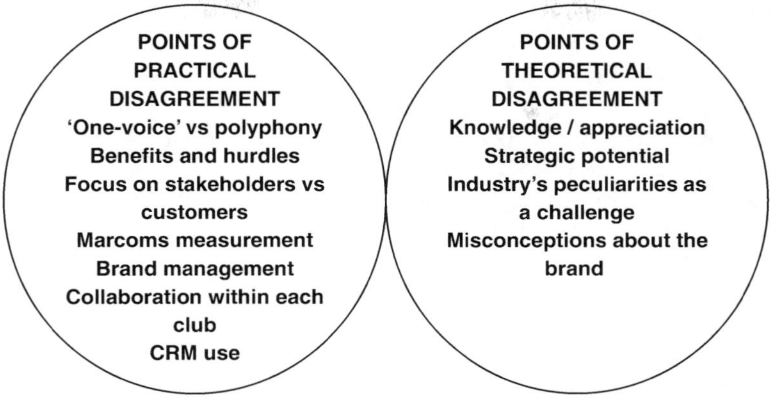

```
        POINTS OF                      POINTS OF
        PRACTICAL                     THEORETICAL
      DISAGREEMENT                   DISAGREEMENT
  'One-voice' vs polyphony        Knowledge / appreciation
    Benefits and hurdles              Strategic potential
  Focus on stakeholders vs       Industry's peculiarities as
         customers                       a challenge
    Marcoms measurement           Misconceptions about the
     Brand management                       brand
  Collaboration within each
            club
          CRM use
```

Figure 7.1 Football practitioners' perceptions of IMC.

(Manoli, 2016). Paradoxically, all clubs appear to appreciate that the stakeholder groups overlap, as it was suggested by Duncan and Moriarty (1998), since they all suggested that a number of each clubs' employees are also supporters of the club. Nevertheless, the way in which marketing communications is managed indicates that audience-centric communications has yet to be appreciated.

Figure 7.1 summarises the points of agreement and disagreement among football practitioners, with the points of practical disagreement presented on left circle, and the points of theoretical disagreement on the right one. Based on the broader scope provided through this study, it could be suggested that richer data on a particular client sector such as the EPL, can enhance our understanding of practitioners' perceptions of IMC, which, in turn, informs its implementation in practice.

Do Clubs Want IMC's Implementation?

Examining practitioners' perceptions while investigating the level of IMC's implementation in the clubs could raise an additional question as to whether and why clubs might want to integrate marketing communications in the first place. In other words, do clubs want to be positioned in the higher levels of IMC, and if yes, do they understand the benefits that this might bear? Based on a study by Luxton et al. (2015), which followed on the work of Naik and Raman (2003) and Reinold and Tropp (2012), having an IMC capability can directly influence both the campaign effectiveness and the market performance of a brand, irrespectively of the size of the organisation. Additionally, IMC can have an indirect effect on the brand's financial performance, if the IMC capabilities of a company are explored and utilised to their maximum. While examining data to support this argument would be rather challenging if not problematic in the case of football clubs, based on the direct and significant influence a club's playing success can have on a brand's performance, both on market and on financial terms (Richelieu & Pons, 2006), it could be argued that an alternative method can be used.

The study's participants' opinions on both their and other clubs' brand performance (expressed during the interviews) could be examined, which in relation to IMC's implementation, provides the author with enough evidence to allow for the following observations to be made.

First, as the quotes below illustrate, the positive effects of IMC are visible and can be appreciated, even by clubs that do not know and do not practice integration (level 0):

> We are not x or y (mentioning a level 3 and the level 4 club) and we know it. In fact, we know we are not going to be them any time soon, our brand is not that strong. We are not that strong in managing it either.

Or by clubs that practice integration unintentionally (level 1a):

> It is a long process to get there and it will take time. But for now, we cannot aspire to be x (level 4 club), because we know we cannot. But I am sure we can work towards becoming y or z (both level 3 clubs), even if we currently don't have the capabilities, we can still follow their lead and this is what I aspire to do.

As the quotes illustrate, there appears to be an appreciation of the performance of the brand of each club, irrespectively of the club's size / playing success.[1] According to the interviewees' statements, an appreciation for clubs that belong in higher levels of IMC was expressed, even though the author did not reveal or confirm the level of IMC in which each club mentioned belongs. As a result, and despite each club's choice to implement or not implement IMC, it can be argued that the effects IMC has on a club's brand can be noted and appreciated.

The reasons why clubs might choose not to implement IMC, however, vary. As it was argued earlier in the study, one of the reasons behind the level 0 practitioners' anchoring in their non-integration practices could be considered the lack of information or education on the topic, which has led to a number of misconceptions regarding the clubs' brand, its value and appreciation. According to Duncan and Everett (1993), Pettigrew (2000/2001) and Ots and Nyilasy (2015) these mistaken beliefs originating from a lack of understanding are considered to be a significant barrier in IMC's implementation.

Level 2 clubs appear to be rather critical on the practical aspects of implementing IMC strategically, resembling the arguments made by the critics of IMC, such as Spotts et al. (1998), Cornelissen and Lock (2000) and Cornelissen (2001, 2003), who argue that IMC might be impractical and difficult to achieve results in practice. Nevertheless, the way in which their appreciation of level 3 and 4 clubs is shown, points towards an opposite direction. This direction could be better linked to the arguments made by Naik and Raman (2003), Reid (2003) Reinold and Tropp (2012) and Luxton et al. (2015) who suggest that applying IMC and using the IMC capabilities to their maximum potential has a direct effect to a brand's market performance and brand communications campaigns.

It could be claimed that these contradicting views and rather limited aspirations to improve further could be traced back to the way in which the topic of IMC has been handled by the academic community. As numerous scholars such as Kitchen and Schultz (1999), Kliatchko (2005, 2008) and Schultz et al. (2013) have argued, the research available has been focused on defining and redefining IMC, and even arguing about its originality, instead of focusing on studying its application on client organisations and measuring the effects its strategic implementation can have.

A clearer view of why clubs should implement IMC was expressed by level 3 and 4 interviewees, who presented the author with their efforts or success in reaching strategic integration. Level 3 interviewees underlined that an understanding exists regarding the effort and time strategic integration requires, while highlighting that due to the peculiarities and playing success focus of football, these efforts can be particularly challenging.

> *Fundamentally, the brand underpins everything that we do. But we have to try harder than anyone else cause we don't have the glamour that they have (referring to the level 4 club that is more successful on the field).*

As the quote shows, while the interviewees underline the potential challenges they might face due to the nature of the EPL, their efforts are targeted towards strategic integration (level 4), since that is where their brand will be appreciated more. As the level 4 interviewee suggested:

> *I believe that we try to do that (implement IMC). We will never be perfect, we are not robots. However, we know that if we follow the processes and use our abilities accordingly we have a good consistent voice, which makes our brand strong and our campaigns followed and appreciated.*

Even though additional details were not offered as to why the clubs would aspire and work towards strategic integration, the strength of the brand appeared to be the common factor underpinning their efforts. Based on the analysis of their statements regarding both their and other clubs' brands, it could be argued that the effects integration has on a club's brand are noticed and appreciated, to the extent that enables other football practitioners to distinguish between the clubs that belong in level 3 and 4, without having any knowledge of the theory behind IMC. The views expressed by the practitioners do not seem to align with the critics of IMC (Spotts et al., 1998; Cornelissen & Lock, 2000; Cornelissen, 2001, 2003), but on the contrary resemble the opinion expressed by Schultz and Kitchen (2000b) that integration is unavoidable and thus implementing IMC is and should be the norm for any brand to survive. Level 3 and 4 clubs' appreciation for IMC is additionally underpinned by their understanding and respect for each club's brand, which is the reason behind their efforts to achieve and maintain strategic integration as it was argued by Eagle and Kitchen (2000) and Madhavaram et al. (2005, 2016).

Overall, observing this phenomenon of appreciating the effects of IMC regardless of the practitioners' knowledge of the theory behind it, can be linked to Schultz' (1996) view on the inevitability of IMC, which has also been supported by a number of other scholars over time (Kliatchko, 2002; Kitchen & Burgmann, 2010; Porcu et al., 2012; Kitchen & Tourky, 2015). As Schultz (1996) argued in his work, regardless of how IMC is called or defined, all audiences integrate the messages they receive in their minds and are therefore able to appreciate the effects IMC has, even without having any knowledge of what IMC is.

Any views expressed on other clubs' integration practices were not prompted by the author, who also refrained from mentioning or confirming any estimation on each club's IMC level. As a result, it could be argued that even though the views expressed are a subjective way to assess the appreciation of the effects of integration, the fact that the interviewees voiced their thoughts on the effectiveness of IMC's implementation (based on level 3 and 4 clubs' practices and their effects), without any particular encouragement from the author, could be considered a sign of an honest but subjective expert evaluation. According to Minichiello et al. (1995) this expert evaluation can be accepted as a rather subjective but still valid method, in order for the practitioners' appreciation of IMC effects to be supported.

Finally, taking the five IMC levels into consideration, as well as the practitioners' knowledge and perception on whether IMC is implemented, Figure 7.2 can be created. This figure presents the implementation of IMC, according to the extensive investigation of the findings and informed with the analysis of the practitioners' perceptions. As it can be seen in the figure, level 1 is split into two sub levels, so that the unintentional implementation can be underlined.

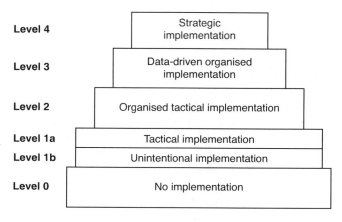

Figure 7.2 IMC's implementation in EPL clubs.

Figure 7.2 can be then considered to be the beginning of the answer to the research question of this study, while illustrating the extent to which IMC is implemented in the English Premier League.

Based on the lack of relevant research on the topic, and following the richer data on a particular client sector provided through this study, it could be argued that additional research on client sectors could enhance the understanding of IMC's appreciation by practitioners, which, in turn, informs its implementation in practice.

Integration Scenarios

Examining IMC's implementation in regard to the football practitioners' perceptions allowed for the identification of four integration scenarios that can be encountered in the English Premier League. These four scenarios present the full spectrum of integration states that can be identified within the industry sector studied, as they emerged from the study. It could thus be suggested that the four scenarios presented in this study provide a holistic view of the integration states an organisation might fall under, and therefore allow for a more detailed and rounded view of IMC's appreciation and implementation. The limited scope of the available research on IMC so far has allowed for only one scenario (*strategic integration*) to be examined, while suggesting that additional scenarios might exist.

As it was argued in the introduction of this chapter, and in line with the retroductive approach followed in this study, providing an account of these four scenarios, does not only allow for this holistic view to be achieved which enhances our understanding of IMC but also supports the current and potentially future practices that inform integration. The four integration scenarios are illustrated in Figure 7.3, and presented alongside the conditions under which they exist, which are the nature of IMC's implementation and the practitioners' perceptions of IMC. The scenarios will be presented below in more detail.

Full Strategic Integration

The first integration scenario encountered, *full strategic integration*, describes the state in which IMC is being appreciated fully by the practitioners, who in fact implement it strategically in their work. This state is the only scenario that has been described by academics such as Porcu et al. (2012) and Kitchen and Tourky (2015), since it is the only stage in which the full potential of IMC can be achieved. In other words, it is the only scenario in which IMC is viewed as a strategic business process and concept that can produce measurable results through the management of content, channels and stakeholders (Kliatchko, 2005, 2008; Ferdous, 2008; Fill, 2008; Gabler et al., 2014).

This scenario can be observed in level 4, which according to the organisations operating in the industry sector examined, accounts for one club out of the 30

120 Integration Scenarios

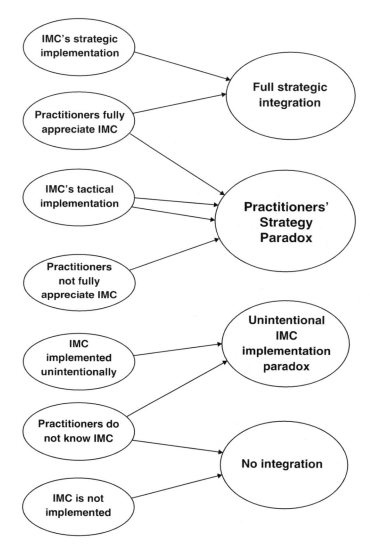

Figure 7.3 The four integration scenarios.

studied. It could thus be argued that the scenario that has attracted the most academic attention so far, captures the least popular state in the EPL. This could be traced back to the fact that the organisations studied in research so far represent the biggest and most successful companies within each country or sector, and could even suggest that literature so far has been presenting a rather optimistic, yet unrealistic representation of IMC's appreciation and implementation.

Nevertheless, and based on the brand performance recognition the level 4 club received by the other interviewees (as it was discussed above), it could be argued that the *full strategic integration* represents the state that many organisations aspire to achieve.

Practitioners' Strategy Paradox

The second scenario describes what was presented above as the *practitioners' strategy paradox*, a state in which a discrepancy exists between the practitioners' appreciation and implementation of IMC. As it was discussed, even though scholars such as Han et al. (2004), Kitchen et al. (2004), Kitchen and Tao (2005), Eagle et al. (2007) and Dmitrijeva and Batraga (2012) have noted that organisations stay anchored in early stages of IMC's implementation, their analysis has not focused on this phenomenon or examined the reasons why it occurs.

According to the findings of this study, organisations are being driven to this scenario when one of the following situations occurs. First, when practitioners' fully appreciate IMC but implement it on a tactical level and second, when practitioners do not appreciate IMC fully, regardless of their claims of truly understanding its potential, and are thus implementing IMC on an elementary level.

As a result, the *strategy paradox* can be observed in organisations where IMC's implementation does not match its appreciation by the practitioners, which occurs according to this study in all levels 1, 2 and 3. Even though the paradox can exist for different reasons regarding the practitioners' appreciation of IMC, the fact that integration is not implemented strategically makes this scenario the dominant scenario encountered in the sector. Consequently, 17 out of 30 clubs (all level 3 and 2 and five level 1 clubs) fall under this integration scenario, which suggests that the paradox can currently describe the prevailing integration state in the sector. Based on the high percentage of the companies in which the paradox represents their integration state, a question can be raised on the frequency of this scenario in other industry sectors, which can only be studied through additional research.

Examining the question of intention behind the paradox allowed for additional light to be shed on this scenario. As it is shown in Figure 7.3, the *strategy paradox* exists due to the practitioners remaining intentionally or unintentionally anchored to their practices. This anchoring occurs intentionally, due to the practitioners' preferences, or unintentionally, as a result of the state in which a company is (while attempting to progress to strategic integration), or of the vicious circle of integration (through the unaware clients driving integration). Even though agency practitioners' views were not studied, the vicious circle of integration is applicable in the EPL, based on the fact that agencies are not involved in marketing communications decision making, as the interviewees argued, while the clubs drive integration.

Based on the analysis of the findings, it could be suggested that level 3 clubs are currently 'trapped' in the scenario unintentionally, while in the process of achieving strategic integration. This 13.33% of the sector represents the clubs that aspire to progress to level 4 and are at that particular moment in time in a transitional stage, while waiting for the results of their restructuring process to materialise. This process resembles the redesign suggested by Pettigrew (2000/2001), Schultz and Schultz (2004) and Christensen et al. (2008a) who argue that it allows for any obstacles to be overcome and for new concepts and processes to be adopted. It could consequently be argued that level 3 clubs are trapped in the scenario unintentionally for a limited, yet undefined, amount of time, until they progress to *full strategic integration*.

The vicious circle of integration that leads to an unintentional anchoring in the paradox can be observed in clubs where the practitioners' understanding of IMC's potential is limited, regardless of their claims. While evaluating the practitioners' knowledge would require additional research, based on the way in which the interviewees answered the questions regarding IMC, it can be argued that level 1b clubs are restrained in the paradox unintentionally, due to the limited actual appreciation or understanding of IMC's potential, as Laurie and Mortimer (2011) argued in their work. Since these clubs represent 16.66% of the sector examined, the limited research available on clients and their implementation of IMC (by academics such as Rose, 1996; Schultz & Kitchen, 1997; Dmitrijeva & Batraga, 2012), combined with the need for additional evaluation of practitioners' true appreciation of IMC, underline the need for further research on the topic. Until this additional evaluation of practitioners' appreciation of IMC is conducted, it cannot be clear whether level 1b clubs are anchored in the *practitioners' strategy paradox* scenario unintentionally or intentionally.

The intentional limitation can be better observed in level 2 clubs that appear to be implementing IMC on a tactical level, even though the practitioners fully appreciate its potential. The interviewees in these clubs appeared to be sceptical regarding strategic integration, resembling the views presented by Spotts et al. (1998), Cornelissen and Lock (2000) and Cornelissen (2001, 2003), who argue that IMC might be impractical and difficult to achieve results in practice. At the same time, this 26.66% of the sector did not present evidence to suggest that changes will occur in current practices, indicating a lack of aspiration to reach strategic integration. Taking the restructuring process discussed by level 3 clubs into consideration, this could, in turn, suggest that progressing from level 2 to level 3 could in fact be the key turning point in achieving strategic integration. In other words, '*redefining the scope of marketing and communications*', as level 2 entails (Kitchen & Schultz, 1999, p. 34) could be the key that allows for the way to strategic integration to open. Therefore, additional emphasis should be placed in examining organisations that are intentionally limited in this scenario, in order for the individuals' or organisational attachment to the current marketing communications practices to be investigated.

Unintentional IMC Implementation Paradox

The third scenario identified is the one where another paradox can be studied, the *unintentional IMC implementation paradox*. This scenario occurs when practitioners do not know what IMC is, but integration is implemented in the organisation unintentionally. As the practitioners argued, this happens in an *organic*, *instinctive* or *unintentional* way, which can be better observed in level 1a clubs that represent 20% of the sector examined.

On the one hand, the *unintentional paradox* could be used to raise the question of IMC's originality, which was argued by academics such as Cornelissen and Lock (2000) and Cornelissen (2001, 2003), who claimed that integration was applied by practitioners before it attracted academics' attention. Or on the other hand, it could point towards the idea of inevitability of integration supported by Schultz (1993a, 1993b), Brown (1997), Schultz and Kitchen (2000) and Kliatchko and Schultz (2014), who argue that the originality debate is in fact irrelevant, since practitioners appreciate the need for enhanced strategic integration due to the increased pressure for coherency by the stakeholders and the multiplication of media. Based on the fact that the interviewees appeared positive that their practices could improve, suggesting that a more strategic integration could be achieved in the future, it could be argued that the *unintentional paradox* in reality points towards the inevitability of integration.

While evaluating the effectiveness of unintentional integration would require additional research, identifying that IMC can be implemented unintentionally could suggest that integration, even on a tactical level, is becoming increasingly popular in the sector examined. In fact, based on the practitioners' ability to implement tactical integration unintentionally, it could be argued that applying IMC might not be such a laborious and demanding process, as Schultz' (1992) suggested. However, progressing to a more strategic integration (such as the one encountered in level 2, 3 and 4) might require additional effort, which can be suggested based on the fact that the *unintentional paradox* scenario can be observed only in level 1 clubs.

An additional point that is worth studying is whether the fact that the football practitioners were informed of the existence and meaning of IMC through the interviews conducted for this study has changed their actions in a way that will make this *unintentional paradox* non-existent. If such a change can be detected, then it could be suggested that progressing to the next level of IMC is a matter of dissemination of information, education and potential training.

No Integration

The final scenario encountered is the one in which *no integration* occurs when the football practitioners do not know what IMC is and consequently do not implement it. This scenario contradicts some studies on IMC, such as the ones by Kliatchko and Schultz (2014) and Kitchen and Tourky (2015), which argue that integration is widely spread and implemented in all companies examined (which could be traced back to the fact that the organisations studied represent the biggest and most successful companies within each country or sector). It could therefore be argued that had this study not included a large number of clubs / companies operating within the EPL, as is common practice of IMC research, this scenario would have been possibly neglected.

The no integration scenario occurs in clubs in level 0. Neither the scenario nor the level have been acknowledged in the literature available with the exception of the Manoli and Hodgkinson's (2019) study, which one could argue tends to neglect the less developed IMC implementation cases and instead focuses more on the successful *best-case* scenarios. A more optimistic and rather unrealistic view of IMC's appreciation and implementation is then presented, which in the case of this study would suggest that 20% of the clubs / companies of the EPL / sector are ignored.

Based on the fact that the practitioners in level 0 appear to be appreciative of the brand performance effects of integration, their limitation to this scenario could be linked to the suggestion that the barriers of IMC (studied by academics such as Duncan & Everett, 1993; Moriarty, 1994; Eagle & Kitchen, 2000; Schultz, 2000, 2001; Dmitrijeva & Batraga, 2012) have not been overcome. Additionally and most importantly, it could suggest that misconceptions about the brand and its management (that contradict the work of scholars such as Keegan et al., 1992 and Keller, 2009, 2016) are still prevailing, as it was identified in this study.

Thus, it could be underlined that, as it was emphasised by Kliatchko (2005) and Schultz et al. (2013), the significant definitional issues regarding IMC have in fact hindered its implementation and obstructed scholars from focusing on IMC's practical issues. However, even when research focuses on IMC's implementation, an optimistic and rather myopic approach is adopted, which tends to neglect the organisations that do not practice integration. As a result, the existence of barriers and misconceptions is perpetuated, which hinders IMC's potential appreciation and implementation further. It is suggested that placing additional emphasis on the no integration scenario would allow for key information to be acquired regarding the potential to implement IMC in these clubs, which could therefore assist in the understanding and future of IMC.

Figure 7.4 presents the interplay between the four integration scenarios and the five IMC levels, as it was discussed in this section. This framework can be then considered to be the visual representation of the answer to the main research aim of this study, which was to gain insights to the way and extent to which IMC is appreciated and implemented in the EPL. It could be possibly suggested that this framework does not only present the integration landscape in the EPL, but it can in fact illustrate a detailed and rather holistic view of practitioners' perceptions and implementation of IMC in any industry, capturing not only the best possible scenarios but also the scenarios in which integration does not occur as successfully as previously described.

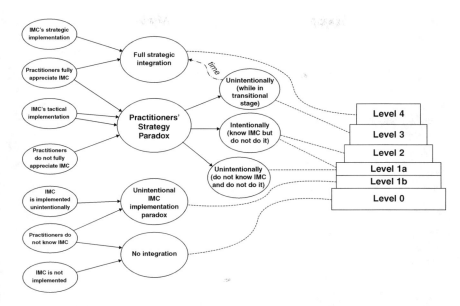

Figure 7.4 Interplay between the four integration scenarios and the five IMC levels.

Conclusion

As this chapter has demonstrated, examining a wider spectrum of client organisations allowed for a more detailed and wider view of practitioners' perceptions and implementation of IMC to be achieved. First, using the football practitioners' perceptions and their appreciation of its potential allowed for the discussion to explore the extent to which IMC is appreciated and can be implemented in the EPL. Second, introducing the four integration scenarios in relation to the conditions that lead to them and the levels in which they can be observed allows us to better encapsulate a wider and previously ignored spectrum of perceptions and implementation of IMC within the client organisations studied, potentially offering insights to similar views and applications in other client organisations.

Note

1 Some of the clubs mentioned have had considerably less playing success than the ones employing the interviewees.

References

Atkinson, C. (2003) 'Integration still a pipe dream for many', *Advertising Age*, 10 (1) 47.

Brown, J. (1997) 'Impossible dream or inevitable revolution? Investigating the concept of integrated marketing communications', *Journal of Communication Management*, 2 (2) 70–81.

Christensen, L. T., Firat, F. A. & Torp, S. (2008a) 'The organisation of integrated communications: Toward flexible integration', *European Journal of Marketing*, 42 (3/4) 423–452.

Cornelissen, J. P. (2001) 'Integrated marketing communications and the language of marketing development', *International Journal of Advertising*, 20 (4) 483–498.

Cornelissen, J. P. (2003) 'Change, continuity and progress: The concept of integrated marketing communications and marketing communications practice', *Journal of Strategic Marketing*, 11 (4) 217–234.

Cornelissen, J. P. & Lock, A. R. (2000) 'Theoretical concept or management fashion? Examining the significance of IMC', *Journal of Advertising Research*, 40 (5) 7–16.

Dmitrijeva, K. & Batraga, A. (2012) 'Barriers to integrated marketing communications: The case of Latvia (small markets)', *8th International Strategic Management Conference, 21–23 June 2012, Barcelona, Spain*.

Duncan, T. R. (2002) *IMC: Using advertising and promotion to build brands* (International Edition), New York: The McGraw-Hill.

Duncan, T. R. & Everett S. E. (1993) 'Client Perceptions of Integrated Communications', *Journal of Advertising Research*, 32 (3) 30–39.

Duncan, T. R. & Moriarty, S. E. (1998) 'A communication-based marketing model for managing relationships', *The Journal of Marketing*, 56 (2) 1–13.

Eagle, L. & Kitchen, P. J. (2000) 'IMC, brand communications, and corporate cultures: Client / advertising agency co-ordination and cohesion', *European Journal of Marketing*, 34 (5/6) 667–686.

Ferdous, A. S. (2008) 'Integrated internal marketing communication (IIMC)', *The Marketing Review*, 8 (3) 223–235.

Fill, C. (2009) *Marketing communications; Interactivity, communities and content*, Essex: Pearson Education.

Gabler, C., Agnihotri, R. & Moberg, C. (2014) 'Collaborative communication between sales and logistics and its impact on business process effectiveness: A theoretical approach', *Journal of Marketing Channels*, 21 (4) 242–253.

Han, D., Kim, I. & Schultz, D. E. (2004) 'Understanding the diffusion of integrated marketing communications', *Journal of Advertising Research*, 44 (1) 31–45.

Keegan, W., Moriarty, S. E. & Duncan, T. R. (1992) *Marketing, branding*, Hoboken, NJ: Prentice Hall.

Keller, K. L. (2009) 'Building strong brands in a modern marketing communications environment', *Journal of Marketing Communications*, 15 (2/3) 139–155.

Keller, K. L. (2016) 'Unlocking the power of integrated marketing communications: How integrated is your IMC program?', *Journal of Advertising*, 45(3) 286–301.

Kitchen, P. J. & Burgmann, I. (2010) *Integrated marketing communication*, Hoboken, NJ: John Wiley & Sons, Ltd.

Kitchen, P. J. & Schultz, D. E. (1999) 'A multi-country comparison of the drive for IMC', *Journal of Advertising Research*, 39 (1) 21–38.

Kitchen, P. J., Schultz, D. E., Kim, I., Han, D. & Li, T. (2004) 'Will agencies ever "get" (or understand) IMC?', *European Journal of Marketing*, 38 (11/12) 1417–1436.

Kitchen, P. J. & Tao, L. (2005) 'Perceptions of integrated marketing communications: A Chinese ad and PR agency perspective', *International Journal of Advertising*, 24 (1) 51–78.

Kitchen, P. J. & Tourky, M. (2015) *Integrated communications in the postmodern era*, Hampshire: Palgrave Macmillan.

Kliatchko, J. (2002) *Understanding integrated marketing communications*, Pasig City: Inkwell Publishing.

Kliatchko, J. (2005) 'Towards a new definition of integrated marketing communications (IMC)', *International Journal of Advertising*, 24 (1) 7–34.

Kliatchko, J. (2008) 'Revisiting the IMC construct: A revised definition and four pillars', *International Journal of Advertising*, 27 (1) 133–160.

Kliatchko, J. G. & Schultz, D. E. (2014) 'Twenty years of IMC: A study of CEO and CMO perspectives in the Asia-Pacific region', *International Journal of Advertising*, 33 (2) 373–390.

Laurie, S. & Mortimer, K. (2011) "IMC is dead. Long live IMC': Academics' versus practitioners' views', *Journal of Marketing Management*, 27 (13/14) 1464–1478.

Lauska, D., Laurie, S. & Mortimer, K. (2014) The management of corporate personality: An IMC perspective. In *Proceedings of the 47th Academy of Marketing Conference, AM2014: Marketing Dimensions: People, Places and Spaces*, Bournemouth: Academy of Marketing.

Luxton, S., Reid, M. & Mavondo, F. (2015) 'Integrated marketing communication capability and brand performance', *Journal of Advertising*, 44 (1) 37–46.

Madhavaram, S., Badrinarayanan, V. & Bicen, P. (2016) Integrated marketing communication (IMC): Conceptual and theoretical lacunae, foundational premises, and framework. In K. K. Kim (Ed.) *Celebrating America's pastimes: Baseball, hot dogs, apple pie and marketing?* (pp. 335–336), New York: Springer International Publishing.

Madhavaram, S., Badrinarayanan, V. & McDonald, R. (2005) 'Integrated marketing communication (IMC) and brand identity as critical components of brand equity strategy', *Journal of Advertising*, 34 (4) 69–80.

Manoli, A. E. (2017) Media relations in English football clubs. In J. J. Zhang & B. G. Pitts (Eds.) *Contemporary sport marketing: Global perspectives*, (pp. 120–138), London: Routledge.

Manoli, A. E. (2020) 'Brand capabilities in English premier League clubs', *European Sport Management Quarterly*, 20 (1) 30–46.

Manoli, A. E. & Hodgkinson, I. R. (2019) 'The implementation of integrated marketing communication (IMC): Evidence from professional football clubs in England', *Journal of Strategic Marketing*, 28 (6) 542–563.

Manoli, A. E. & Hodgkinson, I. R. (2021) 'Exploring internal organisational communication dynamics in the professional football industry', *European Journal of Marketing*, 55 (11) 2894–2916.

Minichiello, V., Aroni, R., Timewell, E. & Alexander, A. (1995) *In-depth interviewing* (2nd ed.), Melbourne: Longman.

Moriarty, S. E. (1993) The circle of synergy: Theoretical perspectives and an evolving IMC research agenda. In E. Thorson & J. Moore (Eds.) *Integrated communication: Synergy of persuasive voices*, (pp. 333–353), Mahwah, NJ: Lawrence Erlbaum Associates.

Moriarty, S. E. (1994) 'PR and IMC: The benefits of integration', *Public Relations Quarterly*, 39 (3) 38–44.

Naik, P. A. & Raman, K. (2003) 'Understanding the impact of synergy in multimedia communications', *Journal of Marketing Research*, 40 (4) 375–388.

Ots, M. & Nyilasy, G. (2015) 'Integrated marketing communications (IMC): Why does it fail?', *Journal of Advertising Research*, 55 (2) 132–145.

Pettigrew, L. S. (2000/2001) 'If IMC is so good, why isn't it being implemented?: Barriers to IMC adoption in corporate America', *Journal of Integrated Communications*, 11 (1) 29–37.

Porcu, L., del Barrio-García, S. & Kitchen, P. J. (2012) 'How integrated marketing communications (IMC) works? A theoretical review and an analysis of its main drivers and effects/¿ Cómo funciona la Comunicación Integrada de Marketing (CIM)? Una revisión teórica y un análisis de sus antecedentes y efectos', *Comunicación y sociedad*, 25 (1) 313–348.

Reid, M. (2003) 'IMC–performance relationship: Further insight and evidence from the Australian marketplace', *International Journal of Advertising*, 22 (2) 227–248.

Reinold, T. & Tropp, J. (2012) 'Integrated marketing communications: How can we measure its effectiveness?', *Journal of Marketing Communications*, 18 (2) 113–132.

Richelieu, A. & Pons, F. (2006) 'Toronto maple leafs vs football club Barcelona: How two legendary sports teams built their brand equity', *International Journal of Sports Marketing & Sponsorship*, 7 (3) 213–230.

Rose, P. B. (1996) 'Practitioner opinions and interests regarding integrated marketing communications in selected Latin American countries', *Journal of Marketing Communications*, 2 (3) 125–139.

Rouziès, D., Anderson, E., Kohli, A. K., Michaels, R. E., Weitz, B. A. & Zoltners, A. A. (2005) 'Sales and marketing integration: A proposed framework', *Journal of Personal Selling & Sales Management*, 25 (2) 113–122.

Schultz, D. E. (1992) 'Integrated marketing communications: The status of integrated marketing communications programs the US today', *Journal of Promotion Management*, 1 (1) 99–104.

Schultz, D. E. (1993a) 'Integrated marketing communications: Maybe definition is in the point of view', *Marketing News*, 18 January

Schultz, D. E. (1993b) 'We simply can't afford to go back to mass marketing', *Marketing News*, 15 February.

Schultz, D. E. (1996) 'IMC has become a global concept', *Marketing News*, 30 (5) 6.

Schultz, D. E. (2000) 'Structural flaws dash marcom plans', *Marketing News*, 34 (3) 14.

Schultz, D. E. (2001) 'Campaign approach shouldn't exist in IMC', *Marketing News*, 35 (5) 11–13.

Schultz, D. E. & Kitchen, P. J. (1997) 'Integrated marketing communications in US advertising agencies: An exploratory study', *Journal of Advertising Research*, 37 (5) 7–18.

Schultz, D. E. & Kitchen, P. J. (2000) 'A response to 'Theoretical concept or management fashion?'', *Journal of Advertising Research*, 40 (5) 17–21.

Schultz, D. E., Patti, C. H. & Kitchen, P. J. (2013) *The evolution of integrated marketing communications: The customer-driven marketplace*, London: Routledge.

Schultz, D. E. & Schultz, H. F. (1998) 'Transitioning marketing communication into the twenty-first century', *Journal of Marketing Communications*, 4 (1) 9–26.

Schultz, D. E. & Schultz, H. F. (2004) *IMC: The next generation*, New York: McGraw-Hill.

Spotts, H. E., Lambert, D. R. & Joyce, M. L. (1998) 'Marketing déjà vu: The discovery of integrated marketing communications', *Journal of Marketing Education*, 20 (3) 210–218.

Stammerjohan, C., Wood, C. M., Chang, Y. & Thorson, E. (2005) 'An empirical investigation of the interaction between publicity, advertising, and previous brand attitude and knowledge', *Journal of Advertising*, 34 (4) 55–67.

Vernuccio, M. & Ceccotti, F. (2015) 'Strategic and organisational challenges in the integrated marketing communication paradigm shift: A holistic vision', *European Management Journal*, 33 (6) 438–449.

Chapter 8

Conclusion

Introduction

This final chapter aims at providing an overview of the concluding thoughts derived from the research data generated, synthesised and analysed in the present book. This chapter therefore focuses on the contributions of this book to IMC knowledge and the theoretical, methodological and applied insights developed from the analysis of the systematic review findings and the exploratory research that followed. In addition, this chapter reflects on the main limitations associated with the book, not only in terms of methodological design but also in terms of findings. Finally, future research directions related to the research findings produced in this thesis are presented.

Research Contributions

Focusing this research on IMC, its implementation and practitioners' perception, answers a key gap in the IMC and wider marketing literature (Tafesse & Kitchen, 2015), by studying theory and practice through engaged scholarship (Van de Ven, 2007). Using the EPL as the platform for this research also allowed for benefits to be offered to the wider developing but rather under-studied area of sport marketing, which is expected to be better understood and potentially receive greater interest by scholars. This book makes a number of theoretical, methodological and applied contributions that will be presented below.

This engaged scholarship research focused on acquiring the perspectives and practices of practitioners in order for the complex issue of IMC, its appreciation and implementation to be better and more thoroughly understood. In line with the suggestions of Van de Ven and Johnson (2006), Van de Ven (2007) and Lukka (2014), conducting research that focuses on a theory's implementation and appreciation is an area in need of further attention from academics, since the knowledge translation and transfer gap appears to be widening. This research answered this call, by conducting *'informed basic research'* (Kelemen & Bansal, 2002; Van de Ven, 2007, p. 272) and thus focusing on practitioners' perceptions and implementation of IMC.

DOI: 10.4324/9781003140238-8

By investigating the translation and transfer of the theory in detail and thus delving in practitioners' perceptions and practices, a more accurate, realistic and holistic view of theory appreciation and practice was offered in this book. In fact, its findings demonstrate that theory's appreciation and implementation deviates from the rather myopic suggestion of full and successful integration (Kliatchko, 2008; Kliatchko & Schultz, 2014), and on the contrary uncovers the existence of oxymora in the way in which theory is translated and knowledge is being transferred in practice (*practitioners' strategy paradox* and *unintentional IMC implementation paradox*). The insights offered through this book have thus deepened our understanding of not only IMC within football, but overall of theory appreciation and implementation by key stakeholders.

In particular, this engaged scholarship research has shed light on the way in which marketing communications are perceived and implemented by practitioners, which has uncovered previously neglected aspects. First, the investigation on the existence or lack thereof of marketing strategies and respecting goals revealed a wide disparity among clubs, while highlighting aspects that marketing literature has missed (Jobber & Ellis-Chadwick, 2012; Kotler et al., 2015). Notably, this research underlined the existence of commercially focused marketing strategies that in reality undermine the role of marketing in organisations, raising an important question regarding the true relevance of marketing's current literature. While marketing is increasingly viewed and presented as a strategic managerial process (Morosan et al., 2014; Baker & Magnini, 2016), the findings suggest that there might still be elements that the marketing literature has missed, especially in regard to its strategic potential and appreciation.

Since recent studies on marketing argue its value as a managerial process (Homburg et al., 2015), the interdepartmental silos and misconceptions regarding formal internal communications highlighted in this book represent key challenges marketing is facing that have yet to be fully captured in the literature available. Additionally, the brand and brand management misconceptions uncovered enrich our understanding of marketing communications management, while demonstrating the wide knowledge gap between academia and practice. As a result, practitioners' appreciation and implementation of the aspects examined in this book; marketing strategy and targets, internal communications, marketing communications alignment and brand management, provide an indication that the current marketing literature falls short in truly uncovering marketing communications management. Unlike conceptual studies on the topic (e.g. Schultz & Patti, 2009; Porcu et al., 2012; Schultz et al., 2013), this research used the instrumental case studies of EPL clubs to identify and underline these issues that can potentially shape the future directions of marketing literature. They can also reinforce and clarify IMC's position within the marketing literature, while appreciating its potential as a base or a framework that can replace traditional marketing (Schultz et al., 2014; Kitchen, 2016) and guide marketing communications management.

Following the review of the state of the IMC literature, this book answered the call to deepen our understanding of IMC through the study of its appreciation and implementation, in an attempt to better clarify the existing confusion on what it represents (Schultz et al., 2013, 2016; Kitchen, 2016). Exploring IMC through marketing communications management provided an account of what it represents in practice, while elucidating its characteristics and its links with interdepartmental relations and structure within an organisation.

Cross-examining IMC with marketing communications management represents a key contribution of this book, which continues from the work of academics such as Reid (2002, 2003), Beverland and Luxton (2005), Tsai (2005) and Christensen et al. (2008a, 2008b). This cross-examination has a two-fold purpose that represents both a theoretical and an applied contribution of this research. In terms of its theoretical value, it deepens our understanding on what IMC and each of its levels represents, while demonstrating its complex and multi-facet application. It also acts as a detailed IMC categorisation tool, while demonstrating the course of progression through which an organisation can advance to strategic IMC. Based on the discussion and debate IMC has stirred in the academic community, demonstrating what IMC stands for through this cross-examination contributes towards the IMC literature, while simultaneously clarifying the position of IMC within the overall marketing literature.

Moreover, the findings of this thesis shed light on the under researched area of integration (the practice of implementing IMC – Schultz, 1992, p. 100), through the investigation of practitioners' perceptions and implementation of IMC in an industry sector of client organisations (EPL clubs). Examining integration in a wider sample of companies allowed for all four integration scenarios to be uncovered and examined in detail. As a result, it was demonstrated that *full strategic integration*, the main integration state captured by the literature available (e.g. by Kliatchko & Schultz, 2014; Kitchen & Tourky, 2015), in reality represents the 'best-case' scenario of integration, which is the rarest scenario encountered in this book.

Three additional integration scenarios were identified and examined in this thesis, in relation to the conditions under which they take place and the IMC levels where they can be observed. First, the *practitioners' strategy paradox* was presented as the discrepancy between the theoretical support of IMC's strategic nature and the lack of practical evidence of strategy in its implementation, while its analysis also introduced the question of intention behind it. Second, the *unintentional IMC implementation paradox*, the phenomenon in which IMC is implemented unintentionally, despite the practitioners' lack of knowledge of IMC, was also uncovered in this book. Third, the *no integration* scenario was identified, a state in which there is no knowledge and implementation of IMC. All three scenarios mentioned above were examined in this book in order to further enhance the understanding of IMC's appreciation and application, following the work of Manoli and Hodgkinson (2019). These four scenarios represent the full spectrum of integration states an organisation might fall under, and thus allow for a more comprehensive and rounded view of integration to be achieved.

The framework designed to encapsulate this analysis by presenting the four integration scenarios, the conditions under which they occur and their interplay with the five IMC levels can be considered the visual representation of the answer to the research question. In other words, the framework presented in this book captures the complexity of the full integration landscape, while illustrating the full extent of practitioners' perceptions and implementation of IMC in the sector studied. This framework could now act as a tool that can potentially capture the full spectrum of integration states in any industry sector, thus providing a comprehensive view of the integration landscape.

The use of the EPL clubs as the instrumental case studies of this research allowed for a number of contributions to be made to sport and football marketing literature. First, this book is, to the best of my knowledge, the only research that has ever focused to this extent on IMC's appreciation and implementation in sports. Even though attempts have been made to approach the topic by academics such as Kelly and Whiteman (2010), Kinney (2010, 2014), Micu and Pentina (2014), Watkins (2014), Manoli and Kenyon (2018) and Manoli and Hodgkinson (2019), IMC in sports can be still considered an *'unchartered territory'*. As a result, the insights provided through this research on IMC's implementation and perceptions within EPL can pave the way and guide further research on the topic, focusing not only within football but also in other sports.

While a number of the marketing communications practices examined in this book have attracted academics' interest in regard to sports (Beech & Chadwick, 2004; Couvelaere & Richelieu, 2005; Clavio & Walsh, 2014; McCarthy et al., 2014; Manoli & Hodgkinson, 2017, 2021; Manoli, 2020), this research underlines the overlap and connection between them (e.g. communications alignment and brand management), while stressing their link with strategic marketing communications management. Investigating all 30 clubs allowed for a range of management practices to be identified, while uncovering and stressing the existence and characteristics of both the successful and the unsuccessful ones.

In regard to the less successful practices encountered, this research identified the existence of misconceptions on brand value and management, suggesting that marketing communications in the EPL, one of the most commercially advanced sports league in the world (Fetchko et al., 2013; Deloitte, 2016), are still underdeveloped. Additionally, based on the lack of knowledge and appreciation for IMC and its potential (40% of the interviewees had not heard of IMC before), this research uncovered a significant knowledge translation and transfer gap which is currently affecting the efficiency and effectiveness of the marketing communications within the EPL.

Examining the underlying patterns that influence these practices and thus IMC's implementation also took place in this book, offering three noteworthy indications that have not been identified before. First, there is no analogy between integration and playing success of clubs, indicating that no analogy would be also found between integration and club size (since playing success can be considered an indication of size – Schmidt & Berri, 2001; Szymanski & Kesenne, 2004). Second, a direct analogy exists between the number of marketing employees of each club and the IMC level it belongs to, suggesting that not implementing IMC in level 0 could be considered a consequence or a causality of the majority of the clubs' decision to employ zero to one marketing staff. Third, an analogy can be detected between the organisational structure of a club and the extent to which IMC is implemented, since clubs in higher IMC levels do not place marketing under the commercial umbrella, but position it as a separate department. All three patterns identified underline for the need for further research on the topic.

From a methodological point of view, it was evident that there is much room for the employment of qualitative methodological designs following a retroductive approach, that have the capacity to provide deeper insight into the IMC practices. In fact, the study of the underlying patterns and mechanisms that is facilitated through the employment of retroduction, is an area in need for further research. Conducting engaged scholarship and employing retroduction could then lead the way in further investigations of theory's appreciation and implementation.

An additional methodological contribution of this book was to offer insights to a wider spectrum of companies within the selected industry sector, which had not been attempted before. This also allowed for emphasis to be placed on client organisations that have been understudied, since agencies have been the main platform of IMC research so far (e.g. Ebren et al., 2005; Kitchen & Tao, 2005; Eagle et al., 2007; Kitchen et al., 2008; Awad, 2009; Schultz et al., 2016), despite the widely accepted argument that clients drive integration (Caywood & Ewing, 1991; Eagle et al., 2007; Schultz et al., 2016). In this book, IMC's appreciation and implementation was studied within the diverse context of the EPL, answering this call. Therefore, a more holistic and comprehensive view on IMC's implementation and practitioners' perceptions was offered, which can enrich the way in which IMC, its appreciation and application is perceived and potentially assist in progressing towards strategic integration. Obtaining access to commercialised and popular professional sports organisations, such as the EPL clubs, is considered to be particularly challenging (Moore & Stokes, 2012; Manoli, 2014), which could be considered the reason behind the limited studies involving participants from them. This could further underline the methodological contribution of this book, which involved all EPL football clubs of the following consecutive seasons: 2010/2011, 2011/2012, 2012/2013, 2013/2014 and 2014/2015.

Examining IMC's implementation in these 30 clubs allowed for the already existing frameworks to be further developed, in order for the additional underrepresented organisations to be also incorporated. As a result, an extra IMC level was added to the ones developed by Schultz and Schultz (1998), level 0, which precedes level 1 and captures the organisations that do not implement IMC. By developing the five stages of IMC, this study responded to the need to expand IMC frameworks and models to not only correspond to organisations that are highly advanced, since at the same time less advanced integration-wise organisations and their related practices and settings have not provided a platform for IMC research. It is therefore argued that further research conducted on the full spectrum of other sectors could investigate IMC's implementation using the five levels introduced in this book, in order for a more comprehensive view to be acquired.

Additionally, introducing the interplay between the four integration scenarios and the five IMC levels framework in this book permits for a holistic view to IMC's implementation to be offered, capturing the links between practitioners' perceptions and IMC's application. This framework represents the answer to the research question of this research and is a tool that can be used to provide a holistic and comprehensive view of the integration landscape of a full industry sector.

From a practical perspective, the findings of this book are valuable in that they provide an account of all IMC implementation scenarios and corresponding marketing communications practices that can be encountered when examining a broader spectrum of companies within an industry sector. This account can be particularly helpful for both client and agency marketers, in order for their current approach to be fully understood and appreciated within the overall spectrum and potential of strategic integration.

The account of the practices and scenarios in relation to the corresponding levels allows for a two-fold contribution to be achieved. First, it can assist practitioners in identifying and appreciating their current integration practices in relation to IMC's implementation within the sector, while being able to conceptualise the full integration landscape. Second, it can reveal the course of progression through which an organisation can proceed from not practising integration to implementing IMC strategically. As a result, it can provide both valuable information on the current practices, and support and potential guidance to the current and future marketing communications practices that inform integration. It could consequently be argued that this account can act as a guide to facilitate IMC's implementation and assist in creating and developing the course of actions that can lead to strategic integration.

By identifying and discussing the appreciation a number of the interviewees expressed for the marketing communications practices of other companies within the sector, it can be argued that this book can enable the practitioners to appreciate the potential value of IMC, which can, in turn, influence their current and future practices. Notably, by recognising their current misconceptions on brand management and limiting the interdepartmental silos.

In particular, in regard to football marketers, the fact that this book inquired about practitioners' knowledge and appreciation of IMC triggered a discussion on its meaning and value with the interviewees. As a result, IMC was presented and explained to the interviewees that were not aware of it (which represent 40% of the participants of this research). Translating and disseminating this knowledge allowed for a direct applied contribution to be achieved, which aligns with the concept and practice of engaged scholarship. Even though this knowledge translation cannot guarantee the implementation of the theory in practice, it ensures that key stakeholders were informed about IMC, which could, in turn, prompt a discussion or a potential change in their future practices.

Discussing particular marketing communications practices and the way in which they were carried out, required the interviewees to reflect on their systems and methods, while often pinpointing areas in need for further attention. This reflection on issues such as brand misconceptions and interdepartmental silos might have triggered an internal dialogue within the clubs, which can potentially lead to improved practices. At the same time, identifying and discussing areas like brand misconceptions within football clubs in this book can draw additional scholarly attention in football and sport in general, encouraging academics to conduct further research on the matter.

It is worth mentioning that this research has already impacted on the practices of one club, the interviewee of which suggested that the first communications alignment meeting within the club took place following our interview, since the questions asked inspired them to intensify collaboration within the organisation. This dialogue regarding marketing communications practices that was triggered from the interviews conducted for this research could represent a significant applied contribution of this book, while suggesting that additional engaged scholarship on the topic can impact the future of the sport. Providing all the interviewees with a report of the findings of this research, including the range of the marketing communications practices encountered, could then intensify this dialogue and potentially influence and even improve their future practice. Through the report, the route to a more strategic marketing communications practice will be outlined in detail, facilitating and encouraging the clubs to further develop their efforts and thus progress to a higher IMC level.

Limitations

While it could be argued that this study's contributions are substantial, it is worth acknowledging that, as with any research, this research features a number of limitations.

Beginning with the review of the literature, even though the author's aim was to include as many studies relevant to IMC as possible, the review cannot be considered truly global. The studies were selected based on particular criteria (e.g. the language criterion – only studies published in English), which can justify why the majority of the research originates from the USA, the UK, Australia and New Zealand. Scholarly interest outside these areas might also be high, yet since their research is not published in English but in other languages, it was not considered for this book.

Additionally, focusing on a single sport / industry sector in one country (EPL), through the use of instrumental case studies, may raise concerns on any efforts to generalise the findings. However, given that the research was designed to improve understanding and knowledge about practitioners' perceptions and implementation of IMC, it is argued that the research was following what Yin (2009, p. 38) calls *'analytic generalisation'*. As Yin suggests, analytic generalisation entails detecting any patterns expected in the data, based on the relevant theory, and as a result allowing the case study to contribute to theory testing and development. Therefore, the author does not aim to generalise the findings of this sector to the wider population, but instead to identify and underline the detailed and suggestive insights that can be transferred in other settings with similar characteristics to the particular case study. It is suggested that additional research on different sports and non-sport sectors and in different countries could further enrich the existing knowledge on IMC's appreciation and implementation.

Moreover, it should be acknowledged that qualitative research is often criticised for not meeting particular validity and reliability criteria. The author might not have met the established positivistic measures of reliability and validity; however, a number of alternative and more appropriate strategies of trustworthiness and credibility were employed in order for the accuracy of the findings and the credibility of the investigation to be ensured. These included member checking, peer debriefing and external audit, sporadic triangulation, intra and inter-coder agreement, rich and thick description of the methodological process and the findings, and adherence to a comprehensive case study protocol.

Furthermore, based on the author's professional association with the football industry, researcher's bias, a possible limitation of this research had to be addressed. While the author believes that as with any qualitative research, bias cannot be avoided, a number of appropriate strategies (Orlick & Partington, 1988) were employed in order for this bias to be mitigated. These involved the adoption and adherence to a coherent and consistent interview protocol, the careful design of the interview questions in order for the author's input to the interviews to be minimised, respondent validation through which all interview transcripts were checked by the respective interviewees, involvement of four interviewees in the data analysis process, inter-coder agreement, peer debriefing and external audit. At the same time, it is worth acknowledging that the author's involvement with this particular sector provides her with valuable pre-understanding (Strauss & Corbin, 1990) and should be considered a positive bias that in reality increases the validity of the research (Merriam, 1998; Kilminster, 2004). Also, as it was made clear through the interviews, had the author not been considered an *insider* to the industry, conducting such a research would not have been possible.

Finally, the author acknowledges that the self-reported retrospective data collected through the interviews might be influenced by a number of factors, such as respondent bias, bad articulation or poor memory recall, in line with Stenbacka (2001) view that the fallibility of any particular method or data needs to be acknowledged. Nevertheless, since interviewing was selected as the most efficient and valid way to acquire information for EPL clubs (Creswell, 2013), efforts were made to avoid these factors by allowing for participant involvement and member checking of the transcribed interviews and data analysis, as well as triangulating the data when possible.

Future Research Directions

While examining the findings of this research, it could be suggested that a number of issues can be identified that exceed the purpose of this research. These issues could potentially act as a platform for further research in the field of IMC, its appreciation and application. Beginning with the review of the literature that was the basis of this research, the findings underlined the need to conduct additional engaged scholarship studies to examine practitioners' perception and implementation of IMC in different contexts. As it was argued earlier in this book, additional research is needed on the way in which IMC is applied by client organisations, with more focus placed on less successful and smaller companies, in both developed and developing English and non-English speaking countries.

In spite of the fact that the empirical research conducted in this book focused on a less researched context, the EPL, and attempted to acquire data on marketing communications practices and integration approaches that are met in this specific context, the need for additional research is apparent, focusing on both similar and less similar contexts. It would be interesting, for example, to identify whether the integration scenarios that emerged in this research – ranging from strategic to no integration – apply to England-based companies only, or to equally developed contexts in general. Examining the marketing communications practices and perceptions identified, as well as studying the two paradoxes introduced in this book, in any other context could also enable the development of concrete and comprehensive arguments about IMC's appreciation and implementation. Moreover, the literature review underlined the need for additional qualitative investigation and for longitudinal research studies, that could potentially have a significant contribution in capturing the principles and progress of IMC's implementation.

Regardless of the fact that the empirical research in this book was guided by the issues raised in the literature review, in an attempt to investigate the rather under-studied areas linked with IMC, the need for additional research on the topic is evident, in order for further light to be shed on the examination of integration approaches and the respective marketing communications practices. Additional research would allow for the mechanisms and structures impacting and shaping integration to be investigated, since such attempts have been limited in the literature. Further exploration topics could include the investigation of potential links between integration and organisational structure and culture, number of marketing communications employees, and leadership and coordination within an organisation. Acquiring thorough information on organisational characteristics and employees' knowledge and perceptions of IMC would also allow for the two paradoxes that emerged through this research to be investigated, while further exploring and potentially answering the question of intention behind the *practitioners' strategy paradox*.

Another issue that has been underlined in this book is the need for further research examining integration in client organisations. Although IMC has been repeatedly and extensively studied from the perspective of the agency organisation, more research is required in order for the integration efforts, approaches and practices of client organisations to be explored. This additional research could also shed light on the challenges they are faced with in their attempt to implement IMC, bearing in mind that, as it has been identified, clients are in fact driving integration. Less successful client marketers' perceptions of IMC and its implementation are rather absent in the literature, regardless of their value and importance in deepening and enriching our understanding of the integration phenomenon. In reality, according to the literature available, the clients' views and response is considered as rather complementary to the far more developed work investigating the agencies' views and approaches. Examining the client organisation's marketing communications practices and the respective integration approaches is the other neglected side of the coin which, if explored to the same degree, would provide a substantially fuller picture of the IMC appreciation and implementation activity. Among their practices, a noteworthy mention is the investigation of online communications and the way in which it enables or hinders IMC's implementation.

Moreover, different industry sectors should be considered in further research that could as well include a number of different sectors within the wider sport industry. As it was discussed while reviewing the existing literature, football is a sport that has been densely explored in sport marketing literature, even though few attempts have been made to link the studies with IMC (Hopwood in Beech & Chadwick, 2007; Batchelor & Formentin, 2008; Kinney, 2014). IMC's appreciation and implementation in a wider sporting context or in different country context could be investigated in future research, that could be influenced by dissimilar sporting cultures and different country contexts, where significant variations and differentiations in the practices might be encountered. Equally, in the wider context of industry sectors, IMC's implementation should be studied in organisations operating in similar or less similar sectors, which are based in less developed and non-English speaking countries.

A further research direction could be towards cross-examining IMC's appreciation and implementation in different sectors within each country, or within similar sectors based in different countries. In this way, the marketing communications practices encountered and the integration scenarios identified could be compared, allowing for a more thorough understanding of their relevance and applicability. Cross-examining IMC's appreciation and implementation could allow for key under-researched issues that were encountered in this research to be further explored, such as the potential relation between leadership, organisational structure or number of marketing employees with integration.

Finally, an additional possible matter for exploration within the same context / industry sector (EPL) could be a qualitative methodological design comparing customers' / supporters' perceptions based on the IMC levels and integration scenarios identified in this book. Such a project could build on the findings of this book and deepen the understanding and appreciation of IMC's implementation on the specific context, while building on the literature that supports integration and its strategic potential.

Concluding Remarks

Exploring the question of *how IMC is perceived and implemented in English Premier League clubs* in this book illustrated that IMC's appreciation and application extends beyond what academia has captured so far. The critical realist approach of this engagement scholarship research allowed for the answer to the question to provide a more accurate, realistic and holistic view of theory appreciation and practice. As a result, the findings of this book captured diverse scenarios of integration, while uncovering previously neglected oxymora in the way in which theory is translated and knowledge is being transferred in practice (*practitioners' strategy paradox, unintentional IMC implementation paradox*), which has deepened our understanding of not only IMC within football, but overall of theory appreciation and implementation by key stakeholders.

IMC's examination through marketing communications management and practitioners' perceptions in this research has offered clarifications on what IMC stands for, a topic that has stirred abundant debate in academia so far. Apart from developing an existing framework in order for a wider range of companies to be studied, this research identified that within EPL clubs, integration can be taking place strategically, operationally, or not at all, in the form of the following four scenarios; *full strategic integration, practitioners' strategy paradox, unintentional IMC implementation paradox* and *no integration*. Each integration scenario can be linked to a different level of IMC's implementation which corresponds to diverse marketing communications management. This book identified and acknowledged this range of integration scenarios, as well as their link with the marketing communications practices of an organisation and its employees' appreciation of IMC. In response to the limited viewpoint presented by the literature available, this book provided a detailed and holistic account of IMC's perceptions and implementation in the EPL, which is also illustrated in the interplay between the four integration scenarios and the five IMC levels framework introduced. This framework provides a comprehensive view of the integration landscape by capturing the full extent of IMC's appreciation and implementation, and linking it with the corresponding marketing communications practices, the employees' perceptions of IMC and the related scenario of integration.

This book has shown that there is still ample room for research on IMC's appreciation and application, through the study of practitioners' perception and implementation of the theory, particularly in broader samples and full industry sectors. Selecting the EPL clubs as the instrumental case studies of this research underlined this need, as well as the need for further research on marketing communications management in football in particular and sport in general. Through the investigation of marketing strategies and goals, and internal and external marketing communication management, it was highlighted that within EPL clubs a wide disparity of practices and views can be encountered, a number of which remain 'unchartered territories', stressing further the demand for scholarly interest.

Conclusively, it is suggested that studies on marketing in general and IMC in particular must become better equipped to understand the broader application of the theories and models suggested, by focusing on a broader spectrum of practitioners and examining them from a realistic and not an optimistic viewpoint. Future engaged scholarship studies could be then assisted by the use of the five IMC stages framework, the marketing communications practices in IMC levels table, and the interplay between the four integration scenarios and the five IMC levels framework that were introduced in this book.

References

Awad, T. A. (2009) IMC – An Egyptian advertising agency perspective. In P. D. Jawahar (Ed.) *Contemporary issues in management research*, (pp. 71–91), New Delhi: Excel Books.

Baker, M. & Magnini, V. P. (2016) 'The evolution of services marketing, hospitality marketing and building the constituency model for hospitality marketing', *International Journal of Contemporary Hospitality Management*, 28 (8) 758–778.

Batchelor, B. & Formentin, M. (2008) 'Re-branding the NHL: Building the league through the "My NHL" integrated marketing campaign', *Public Relations Review*, 34 (2) 156–160.

Beech, J. & Chadwick, S. (2004) *The business of sport management*, Harlow: Pearson Education.

Beech, J. & Chadwick, S. (2007) *The marketing of sport*, Harlow: Pearson Education.

Beverland, M. & Luxton, S. (2005) 'The projection of authenticity: Managing integrated marketing communications through strategic decoupling', *Journal of Advertising*, 34 (4) 103–116.

Caywood, C. & Ewing, R. (1991) 'Integrated marketing communications: A new master's degree concept', *Public Relations Review*, 17 (3) 237–244.

Christensen, L. T., Firat, F. A. & Torp, S. (2008a) 'The organisation of integrated communications: Toward flexible integration', *European Journal of Marketing*, 42 (3/4) 423–452.

Christensen, L. T., Morsing, M. & Cheney, G. (2008b) *Corporate communications: Convention, complexity and critique*, London: Sage.

Clavio, G. & Walsh, P. (2014) 'Dimensions of social media utilization among college sport fans', *Communication & Sport*, 2 (3) 261–281.

Couvelaere, V. & Richelieu, A. (2005) 'Brand strategy in professional sports: The case of French soccer teams', *European Sport Management Quarterly*, 5 (1) 23–46.

Creswell, J. W. (2013) *Qualitative inquiry and research design: Choosing among five approaches* (3rd ed.), London: Sage Publications.

Deloitte (2016) *Annual review of football finance*, Manchester: Deloitte.

Eagle, L., Kitchen, P. J. & Bulmer, S. (2007) 'Insights into interpreting integrated marketing communications: A two-nation qualitative comparison', *European Journal of Marketing*, 41 (7/8) 956–970.

Ebren, F., Kitchen, P. J., Aksoy, S. & Kaynak, E. (2005) 'Probing integrated marketing communications (IMC) in Turkey', *Journal of Promotion Management*, 11 (1) 127–151.

Fetchko, M., Roy, D. & Clow, K. E. (2012) *Sports marketing*, Boston, MA: Pearson.

Homburg, C., Vomberg, A., Enke, M. & Grimm, P. H. (2015) 'The loss of the marketing department's influence: Is it really happening? And why worry?', *Journal of the Academy of Marketing Science*, 43 (1) 1–13.

Jobber, D. & Ellis-Chadwick, F. (2012) *Principles and practice of marketing* (7th ed.), New York: McGraw-Hill.

Kelemen, M. & Bansal, P. (2002) 'The conventions of management research and their relevance to management practice', *British Journal of Management*, 13 (2) 97–108.

Kelly, L. & Whiteman, C. (2010) 'Sports sponsorship as an integrated marketing communications tool: An Australian sponsor's perspective', *Journal of Sponsorship*, 4 (1) 26–37.

Kilminster, R. (2004) From distance to detachment: Knowledge and self knowledge in elias's theory of invovlement and detatchment. In S. Loyal & S. Quilley (Eds.), *The sociology of norbert elias* (pp. 25–41), Cambridge: Cambridge University Press.

Kinney, L. (2010) 'An IMC strategy for introducing game-day jersey sponsorships to American sports leagues', *International Journal of Integrated Marketing Communications*, 2 (2) 44–53.

Kinney, L. (2014) 'IMC or ET?', *International Journal of Integrated Marketing Communications*, 6 (1) 52–62.

Kitchen, P. J. (2016) Is IMC "marketing oriented"? In L. Petruzzellis & R. S. Winer (Eds.) *Rediscovering the essentiality of marketing* (pp. 441–442), New York: Springer International Publishing.

Kitchen, P. J., Kim, I. & Schultz, D. E. (2008) 'Integrated marketing communication: Practice leads theory', *Journal of Advertising Research*, 48 (4) 531–546.

Kitchen, P. J. & Tao, L. (2005) 'Perceptions of integrated marketing communications: A Chinese ad and PR agency perspective', *International Journal of Advertising*, 24 (1) 51–78.

Kitchen, P. J. & Tourky, M. (2015) *Integrated communications in the postmodern era*, Hampshire: Palgrave Macmillan.

Kliatchko, J. (2008) 'Revisiting the IMC construct: A revised definition and four pillars', *International Journal of Advertising*, 27 (1) 133–160.

Kliatchko, J. G. & Schultz, D. E. (2014) 'Twenty years of IMC: A study of CEO and CMO perspectives in the Asia-Pacific region', *International Journal of Advertising*, 33 (2) 373–390.

Kotler, P., Burton, S., Deans, K., Brown, L. & Armstrong, G. (2015) *Marketing*, Sydney: Pearson Higher Education.

Lukka, K. (2014) 'Engaged scholarship requires close collaboration', *Controlling & Management Review*, 58 (4) 57–72.

Manoli, A. E. (2014) 'The football industry through traditional management analysis', *Scandinavian Sport Studies Forum*, 5 (1) 93–109.

Manoli, A. E. (2020) 'Brand capabilities in English premier league clubs', *European Sport Management Quarterly*, 20 (1) 30–46.

Manoli, A. E. & Hodgkinson, I. R. (2017) 'Marketing outsourcing in the English premier league: The right holder/agency interface', *European Sport Management Quarterly*, 17 (4) 436–456.

Manoli, A. E. & Hodgkinson, I. R. (2019) 'The implementation of integrated marketing communication (IMC): Evidence from professional football clubs in England', *Journal of Strategic Marketing*, 28 (6) 542–563.

Manoli, A. E. & Hodgkinson, I. R. (2021) 'Exploring internal organisational communication dynamics in the professional football industry', *European Journal of Marketing*, 55 (11) 2894–2916

Manoli, A. E. & Kenyon, J. A. (2018) Football and marketing. In S. M. Chadwick, P. Widdop, D. Parnell & C. Anagnostopoulos (Eds.) *Routledge handbook of football business and management*, (pp. 88–100), Oxon: Routledge.

McCarthy, J., Rowley, J., Jane Ashworth, C. & Pioch, E. (2014) 'Managing brand presence through social media: The case of UK football clubs', *Internet Research*, 24 (2) 181–204.

Merriam, S. B. (1998) *Qualitative research and case study applications in education* (2nd ed.), San Francisco, CA: Jossey-Bass.

Micu, A. C. & Pentina, I. (2014) 'Integrating advertising and news about the brand in the online environment: Are all products the same?', *Journal of Marketing Communications*, 20 (3) 159–175.

Moore, N. & Stokes, P. (2012) 'Elite interviewing and the role of sector context: An organizational case from the football industry', *Qualitative Market Research: An International Journal*, 15 (4) 438–464.

Morosan, C., T. Bowen, J. & Atwood, M. (2014) 'The evolution of marketing research', *International Journal of Contemporary Hospitality Management*, 26 (5) 706–726.

Orlick, T. & Partington, J. (1988) 'Mental links to excellence', *The Sport Psychologist*, 2 (2) 105–130.

Porcu, L., del Barrio-García, S. & Kitchen, P. J. (2012) 'How integrated marketing communications (IMC) works? A theoretical review and an analysis of its main drivers and effects/¿Cómo funciona la Comunicación Integrada de Marketing (CIM)? Una revisión teórica y un análisis de sus antecedentes y efectos', *Comunicación y sociedad*, 25 (1) 313–348.

Reid, M. (2002) 'Building strong brands through the management of integrated marketing communications', *International Journal of Wine Marketing*, 14 (3) 37–52.

Reid, M. (2003) 'IMC–performance relationship: Further insight and evidence from the Australian marketplace', *International Journal of Advertising*, 22 (2) 227–248.

Schmidt, M. & Berri, D. (2001) 'Competitive balance and attendance: The case of major league baseball', *Journal of Sports Economics*, 2 (1) 145–167.

Schultz, D. E. (1992) 'Integrated marketing communications: The status of integrated marketing communications programs the US today', *Journal of Promotion Management*, 1 (1) 99–104.

Schultz, D. E., Chu, G. & Zhao, B. (2016) 'IMC in an emerging economy: The Chinese perspective', *International Journal of Advertising*, 35 (2) 200–215.

Schultz, D. E., Kim, I. & Kang, K. (2014) Integrated marketing communication research. In H. Cheng (Ed.) *The handbook of international advertising research* (pp. 455–483), London: Wiley Blackwell.

Schultz, D. E. & Patti, C. H. (2009) 'The evolution of IMC: IMC in a customer driven marketplace', *Journal of Marketing Communications*, 15 (2–3) 75–84.

Schultz, D. E., Patti, C. H. & Kitchen, P. J. (2013) *The evolution of integrated marketing communications: The customer-driven marketplace*, London: Routledge.

Schultz, D. E. & Schultz, H. F. (1998) 'Transitioning marketing communication into the twenty-first century', *Journal of Marketing Communications*, 4 (1) 9–26.

Stenbacka, C. (2001) 'Qualitative research requires quality concepts of its own', *Management Decision*, 39 (7) 551–555.

Strauss, A. & Corbin, J. (1998) *Basics of qualitative research* (2nd ed.), Thousand Oaks, CA: Sage.

Szymanski, S. & Kesenne, S. (2004) 'Competitive balance and gate revenue sharing in team sports', *Journal of Industrial Economics*, 52 (1) 165–177.

Tafesse, W. & Kitchen, P. J. (2015) 'IMC–an integrative review', *International Journal of Advertising*, 36 (2) 210–226.

Tsai, S. P. (2005) 'Integrated marketing as management of holistic consumer experience', *Business Horizons*, 48 (5) 431–441.

Van de Ven, A. H. (2007) *Engaged scholarship: A guide for organizational and social research*, Oxford: Oxford University Press.

Van de Ven, A. H. & Johnson, P. E. (2006) 'Knowledge for theory and practice'. *Academy of Management Review*, 31 (4) 802–821.

Watkins, B. (2014) 'An integrated approach to sports branding: Examining the influence of social media on brand outcomes', *International Journal of Integrated Marketing Communications*, 6 (2) 30–40.

Yin, R. K. (2009) *Case study research: Design and method* (4th ed.), Thousand Oaks, CA: Sage.

Index

Note: *Italic* page numbers refer to figures and page numbers followed by "n" denote endnotes.

agency marketers 19, 45, 47, 134
Aiyeku, J. F. 54
analytic generalisation 136
Armstrong, G. 4
Atkinson, C. 26, 28, 113
Awad, T. A. 27, 28

Baker, M. 4
Balboni, B. 50
Barnes, J. 6
Batchelor, B. 54
Batraga, A. 29, 45, 96
Batra, R. 49
Beard, F. 25
Beverland, M. 27, 53, 109
Black, J. S. 7
Bowen, D. E. 6
Boyle, R. 9
brand control 84, 89
brand equity, defined as 29n7
brand guidelines 84–89, 91
brand management 84–91, 130
brand misconceptions 26, 135
brand police 84, 86
brand training 89
brand value 21, 24
Brault, S. 7
Broderick, A. 25, 64
Brown, J. 123
Bruner, J. S. 6
Brunswik, E. 6, 11n2
Burgmann, I. 86
Burmann, C. 86
Burns, J. M. 6
Burton, R. 54
business priority 108
Butterworth, D. S. 7

centralisation 52; of communication responsibilities 27, 53; *vs.* decentralisation 81
Chadwick, S. 10
Christensen, L. T. 46, 50, 72, 107, 122
client marketers 19, 45, 47, 134
clubs: classification in IMC levels 95–98; outwards communications 98; restructure of 106–107; strengthening marketing communications of 101
club-wide culture, of organisation 109
club-wide integration 103
collaborative communication 68, 70; leadership role in 71
collaborative cross-functional communication 51
commercial social media 78
communication: company-wide 24; coordinated marketing 24; external 78–79; formal *vs.* informal 68–72
communications alignment 79; differences in utilising Integration Czar 81–82; Integration Czar 79–81
communications non-alignment 82–84
company-wide communication 24
company-wide implementation, of IMC 67
control issues 27–28
coordinated marketing communications 24
coordination issues 27–28
Cornelissen, J. P. 28, 52, 122

cost-effectiveness 37, 114
COVID-19 pandemic 23
cross-disciplinary skills 47
cross-examination 96, 131, 138
cross-functional communication 68, 69; patterns 97; *vs*. silos 68
cross-functioning collaboration 74
cross industry analysis, of marketing managers 53
customer data management systems 114
customer relationship management (CRM) system 49, 78

Davis, B. 54
Davis, J. H. 7
Dean, J. W. 6
decentralisation: centralisation *vs*. 81; of communication responsibilities 27, 53
decision-making process 52
Dewhirst, T. 54
direct analogy 66, 133
Dmitrijeva, K. 29, 45, 96
Dos Santos, M. A. 54
Duncan, T. 64
Duncan, T. R. 21–23, 25, 74, 114–116

Eagle, L. 27, 28, 42–44, 46, 52, 104, 118
Ellis-Chadwick, F. 2
engaged scholarship 4, 5, 8, 29, 53
engaged scholarship research 129, 130
English Premier League (EPL) 1, 2, 4, 8, 9, 129
English Premier League (EPL) clubs: IMC's implementation in 118, *118*; instrumental case studies of 130, 132, 135
Esposito, A. 28, 29
Everett, S. E. 22, 23, 25, 116
Ewing, M. T. 24, 26–27
external communications 78–79

Farrelly, F. J. 54
Ferdous, A. S. 70
Fetchko, M. 9
football, IMC in 53–54
football practitioners: clubs, IMC's implementation 115–119, *118*; of IMC, synthesis of 113–115
formal interdepartmental meetings 71, 72
formal internal communications 130

formal *vs*. informal communication 68–72
Formentin, M. 54
full strategic integration 43, 47, 48, 101, 119–121, 131
function-specific strategies 108–109

Gabrielli, V. 50
Gambetti, R. C. 25, 29
George, J. M. 6
Gould, S. J. 36
Griffin, T. 52
Gurau, C. 53

Han, D. 26, 28, 29, 39, 45, 96
Hart, S. 4
Haynes, R. 9
Henry, J. 6
Hill, M. 7
Hochberg, J. 6
Hodgkinson, I. R. 19, 41, 43, 54, 74, 99, 101, 131

IMC-focused literature 17, 20, 28
IMC-focused publications 39
IMC Process Model 21
implementation uncertainty 7
industry sector (EPL) 96, 97
informal *vs*. formal communication 68–72
informed basic research 129
integrated marketing communications (IMC) 1–3, 54, 95, 98, 113; benefits of 26; clubs, implementation in 133; cost-effectiveness of 114; definition of 20–23; implementation of 8, 38–42, 108; intentionally due to reluctance 46–48, *48*; key debates of 26–29; key issues of 24–26; levels of 39, *39*, 41; and marketing communications management 49–53; potential success 108; practitioners' perceptions of 36–38; practitioners' strategy paradox 42–44; results-oriented aspect of 37; in sports/football 53–54; state of literature 17–20; strategic nature of 104, 106; strategic planning process 4; theoretical appreciation 20; unintentionally due to lack of knowledge 45; unintentionally while on transitional stage 46
integration: club-wide 103; full strategic 131; scenarios and IMC levels, interplay

… Index 147

between 48, *48*; structured and planned 107
Integration Czar 27, 52, 79–81; differences in utilising 81–82
integration scenario 99, 110, 119, *120*, 131, 132, 134, 137–139; full strategic integration 119–121; no integration 123–124, *125*; practitioners' strategy paradox 121–122; unintentional IMC implementation paradox 123
interaction, vertical and horizontal 109
interdepartmental formal meetings 70
interdepartmental relationships 68–70, 97, 131
interdepartmental silos 72–75, 130, 135

Jackson, S. K. 7
Jenkinson, A. 64
Jobber, D. 2
Johnson, P. E. 5, 129

Keegan, W. 20, 21
Kelemen, M. 71
Keller, K. L. 4, 27, 49, 74
Kelly, L. 54
Kerr, G. F. 29
Key Performance Indicators (KPIs) 97
Kinney, L. 54
Kitchen, P. J. 3, 4, 8, 25, 27–29, 37–41, 43–46, 52, 64, 82, 86, 87, 96, 97, 100, 101, 104, 107, 109, 117, 118, 123, 125
Kliatchko, J. G. 21, 22, 27, 29, 39–41, 49, 51, 89, 96–97, 100, 104, 117, 123–125
Kotler, P. 20

Latham, Gary 10n1
Laurie, S. 23, 122
Lauska, D. 49, 67
Lawlerl, Ed 10n1
leadership: and management 91, 107, 109; organisational culture and 70; role in collaborative communication 71
leadership issues 27–28
Lock, A. R. 122
long-term strategic cross-discipline approach 47
'look, sound and feel' integration 22, 25
Low, G. S. 52, 53
lucrative partnership agreement 80
Lukka, K. 129

Luxton, S. 26, 27, 53, 109, 115, 117

Madhavaram, S. 29, 52, 86, 118
management research, implementation in 7
Manoli, A. E. 19, 41, 43, 54, 74, 99, 101, 131
marketing communication culture 53
marketing communications 25–26, 28, 39, 67, 104, 130; scope of 106; tactical coordination of 101
marketing communications management 49–53, 131, 139
marketing communications practices 10, 95–98, 132, 134, 135, 137, 138, 140; examination of 110
marketing communication strategy 50
marketing goals 64–68
marketing strategy 61–64
marketing targets 64, 65, 67, 68
marketing team 63, 65, 66, 73, 74, 78, 84–87
McArthur, D. 52
McGregor, D. 6
measurement issues 27
media, multiplication of 25
Melewar, T. C. 84, 88
Micu, A. C. 54
Minichiello, V. 118
Mischen, P. A. 7
Mohr, J.J. 52
Moore, J. 4
Moriarty, S. E. 22, 24, 47, 50, 74, 115
Mortimer, K. 23, 122
multiple stakeholders 24

Naik, P. A. 26, 115, 116
National Basketball Association (NBA) 54
National Hockey League (NHL), re-branding process of 54
no integration 123–124, *125*, 131
non-strategic level 46, 55
Nyilasy, G. 116

one-to-one communication 79, 81, 86, 90
one-voice concept 22, 25, 78–79, 82, 113, 114
on-line marketing 23
online media 25
orchestrating 51–52
organisational and structural issues 27
Ots, M. 116

outward communication 79, 80, 84, 85, 91, 98, 114
Ouwersloot, H. 64

Papasolomou-Doukakis, I. 71
Patti, C. H. 24, 29
Pentina, I. 54
perception 6–7; in level 0 98–99; in level 1 99; in level 2 103–105; in level 3 105–108; in level 4 108–110; in level 1a 100–101; in level 1b 101–103
permission-based marketing 24
Pettigrew, A. M. 5, 18
Pettigrew, L. S. 46, 107, 116, 122
Phelps, J. E. 52, 81
philosophical, IMC 44, 46
Pickton, D. 25, 64
Plessis, E. du 26
Porcu, L. 3, 8, 21, 22, 29, 70, 82, 89
Porter, L. W. 7
practitioners' perceptions, of IMC 36–38
practitioners' strategy paradox 42–44, 100–103, 105, 108, 121–122, 131, 137
Punt, A. E. 7

qualitative methodological designs 133
Quester, P. G. 54

Raman, K. 26, 115, 116
Reid, M. 26, 49–51, 67, 116
Reinold, T. 26, 115, 116–117
restructuring process 106–107
return on investment (ROI) 97; measurement techniques 21
Roderick, M. 10
Rosenberg, A. A. 7
Rose, P. B. 40, 96

Schultz, D. E. 3, 4, 8, 20–22, 24–25, 27, 29, 37–41, 43, 45, 46, 50, 52, 79, 80, 82, 87, 89, 96–97, 100, 101, 104, 107, 109, 114, 117, 118, 122–125, 133
Schultz, H. F. 21, 22, 27, 41, 43, 46, 89, 97, 107, 109, 122, 133
Seric, M. 52
Shimp, T. A. 3

silos: cross-functional communication vs. 68; interdepartmental 72–75
Smith, P. R. 22, 25
Smolianov, P. 54
social media 79, 86–87; brand's representation on 90
sponsorship 10, 54
sport industry, IMC in 53–54
sports branding 54
Spotts, H. E. 122
Stake, R. E. 11n3
standardised questionnaires 18
Steers, R. M. 7
Stenbacka, C. 136
strategic brand business process 45
strategic integration 22, 117; see also integration scenario
strategic marketing communications 61, 62
superficial, IMC 44, 46

tactical integration 100, 102, 103, 123
Tao, L. 104
task-oriented activities 49
Taylor, J. 22, 25
theory appreciation 6
Thorson, E. 4
Tourky, M. 64, 82, 100, 125
traditional management processes 8
transitional stage 46
Tropp, J. 26, 115, 116–117
Tsai, S. P. 26, 68, 84
two-way communication platform 74

unchartered territory 20, 132, 139
unintentional IMC implementation paradox 100, 101, 123, 131

Van de Ven, A. H. 4–5, 18, 129

Walker, C. 88
Walker, D. 6
Watkins, B. 54
Webster, F. E. 3
Whiteman, C. 54

Yin, R. K. 135–136

Zeplin, S. 86